TOPICAL COMMENT

TOPICAL COMMENT

ESSAYS IN
DYNAMIC ECONOMICS
APPLIED

BY

ROY HARROD

LONDON
MACMILLAN & CO LTD
NEW YORK · ST MARTIN'S PRESS
1961

MACMILLAN AND COMPANY LIMITED
London Bombay Calcutta Madras Melbourne

THE MACMILLAN COMPANY OF CANADA LIMITED
Toronto

ST MARTIN'S PRESS INC
New York

PRINTED IN GREAT BRITAIN

PREFACE

I HAVE chosen a few articles from among the many that I have written on contemporary events during the last nine years for presentation in this volume. My aim has been to provide the reader with a sort of conspectus of the successive phases of our economic development in the period. Only certain aspects are dealt with; but they are the aspects of central importance for the formation of public policy. I believe that if those responsible for economic policy lack a thorough understanding of what has been going forward in recent years, they will be unlikely to succeed in the tasks that lie before them.

I am grateful for the leave to publish these papers, given by the Committee for Economic Development, New York (No. 1), the International Monetary Fund (No. 2), *The Financial Times* (Nos. 3, 6, 8, 13, 15, 17, 19, 20, 24, 28, 29, 33, 35), *The Banker's Magazine* (Nos. 4, 5, 7, 19, 23), Dr. Erhard (No. 5), the *Director* (Nos. 9, 10, 18, 21, 27, 30), the *Economic Journal* (No. 11), the Institute of Municipal Treasurers and Accountants (No. 16), a firm of stock-brokers to whom I submitted monthly memoranda for private circulation (Nos. 22, 23, 25) and the *Westminster Bank Review* (No. 31).

I have ventured, on the kindly suggestion of Professor Tress, to add, at the end of this volume, a list of my writings (subject to certain exceptions, see p. 251) in the period from 1951 to 1959. The idea was that this list might be useful to a research-worker who was concentrating on some particular aspect or part of the period in question. It must be admitted that there is some repetition in this great mass of writing; but I believe that it will all stand up to scholarly scrutiny; and, once one begins such a compilation, it is difficult to resist the stamp-collector's urge to be inclusive. Furthermore, if one were to try and select, one might lay oneself open to the suspicion of having deliberately omitted references to articles containing predictions that one would rather have forgotten, or indeed might even succumb to the temptation to do so ! I cannot be sure that the list comprehends all that I have written during the period ; but I have included everything that I have been able to trace in my far-from-tidy files.

January 1960

CONTENTS

CHAPTER I

INTRODUCTORY

The sub-title of this book might be thought pretentious ; it is intended to be provocative. There is, of course, no settled corpus of doctrines that can be called 'dynamic economics'. Thus it might be held that dynamic theory is as yet by no means ripe for 'application' to practical affairs. I have felt myself, on the contrary, ever since the last war, that valuable lessons might be learnt by viewing passing events in the light of a dynamic theory, however rudimentary it might be. The followers of Adam Smith did not wait a hundred years, namely until the static parts of his system were perfected by Alfred Marshall and his continental contemporaries, before applying his thought to current affairs.

It is possible that the attempt to understand passing events in terms of an elementary dynamics may bring to light, more clearly than attempts at elaborate model building, the crucial importance, hitherto unsuspected, of certain factors. It was, for instance, by repeatedly reviewing the progress of events against a background of dynamic theory, that I became convinced that the volume of orders on investment account plays a more important part in the contemporary trade cycle pattern than the volume of investment itself. Another finding was that variations of output per person employed have at least a parity of importance — and indeed a greater importance for prompt and appropriate policy reactions — by comparison with variations in the level of employment.

One can hardly be an economist, even in this age of specialization, without seeking to have some understanding of current economic events. Within the period in which my own attempts have fallen, there have been two revolutions, each seeming greatly to enrich one's capacity for understanding. The first, of course, was the Keynesian revolution. That was an indispensable precursor. The second, not less important according to my judgement, has been the substitution of a dynamic theoretical system in place of a static one.

The latter has involved invariably making one's assessment of a current situation subject to a certain mental self-discipline.

This discipline comprises at least two precepts. One is that current events should be reviewed against some pre-supposed 'normal' rates of increase. These 'normal' rates are analogous to the 'normal' or 'natural' prices of static economics. Of course the presupposed norms must be provisional only and subject to frequent revision. Secondly, one must establish, again provisionally only and subject to revision, what the current phase of the trade cycle is ; thus no situation should be judged without reference to what has been happening in the three or four preceding years, and policy recommendation should be related to a projection over some time ahead.

From time to time I have found myself, during this period, in rather sharp disagreement, as regards both diagnosis and recommendation, with esteemed economic colleagues. On many occasions I have been convinced that the difference was due to their not having been truly converted to the dynamic approach. For instance, in 1951, when we had an external deficit, I held that we should not strive for the time being to increase the *volume* of our exports. On this I was regarded as a wicked paradox-monger and was conscious of losing credit in consequence. If one took the cross-section view appropriate to statics, an external deficit seemed to point to the need for an increase of exports. But these had recently been given an abnormal boost by the devaluation of sterling ; this seemed to be a departure from balanced growth and it was increasing domestic inflationary pressure in a harmful manner. No attention was paid to my seemingly perverse recommendation. But sometimes Nature ('the natural laws of political economy') takes charge and brings about what is required, despite policy. And so it happened after 1951 ; for the volume of our exports did indeed fall thereafter and did not surpass its 1951 level until 1955.[1] Differences from esteemed colleagues in the matter of

---

[1] On the topic of the British trade balance I made a number of predictions in 1951 in *The Pound Sterling* (International Finance Division ; Princeton), quoted also in my *Policy Against Inflation*, 1958, p. 140.

diagnosis and recommendation in 1957 may be similarly explained. On the one hand one might regard the rise in retail prices, then occurring, in isolation — through blinkers I would say — and accordingly deem some 'anti-inflationary' measures expedient. If one regarded the development in 1957 as part of a process through time, a different interpretation was indicated.

It should be added, however, that the conversion of colleagues to a 'dynamic approach' is proceeding apace. In the field of applied economics we now have the newly launched *Economic Review* ; I agree with Professor Tress [1] that the diagnosis and prescription of that excellent publication are still a little too short-term. It is true that a longer view introduces more uncertainties and is to that extent more dubious ; but this is often *outweighed by the fact* that the longer view makes it possible to make a greater use of dynamic economics in an assessment, and to correct the inadequacy of statics.

It is in this broad and general sense that the topical writings here presented may be regarded as being, and were at the time of writing intended to be, illustrations of 'dynamic economics applied'.

I have a second purpose in offering these articles. That is to provide an economic history of certain general aspects of the recent period. I recall hearing the first Earl of Birkenhead unkindly describe history as a 'bogus' subject to a company of learned persons, including some historians. 'If he, in his position of vantage as Cabinet Minister, was unable to discover what was happening at the time, or why something was happening, how could some scribe, writing a hundred years hence, hope to discover the truth ?' At the time I thought that this was a little too sceptical ; but I no longer think so. History must involve selection, generalization, and interpretation, since a compilation of all atomic facts would rapidly outgrow the space on this planet available to accommodate it. How are the selection, generalization, and interpretation involved in the record of current history achieved ? By learned scholars ? Not usually. Events move quickly and the contemporary record is compiled quickly. There are some who give a quick interpretation, to the best of their ability, simply because it is their duty to do so — responsible Ministers or leader writers.

[1] *Economica*, August 1959, pp. 206-211.

They may rely on more profound scholars to make the necessary amendments in due course. But it often happens that the scholars have other preoccupations. The initial interpretations pass into circulation and become accepted in a wider circle as facts of history. I have had the feeling, during recent years, of seeing contemporary history wrongly written under my very eyes. And, while it will be the duty, and even pleasure, of future historians to go over the ground and to re-interpret, it may not be altogether easy for them to do so. Where an incorrect interpretation is given, without serious challenge, by dozens of contemporary authorities, they will have to have great perspicuity to detect the error.

Accordingly, one of my motives in collecting these essays is to provide future economic historians of recent events with an alternative version, that they will be unable conscientiously to ignore. I fear that this is an audacious claim. The only credential that I can offer is that, during these years, I have concentrated my attention on a highly selected number of aspects — on those, however, which are most important from a general point of view — and that I have, by prolonged and arduous brooding over the relevant figures, tried to understand them in the light of dynamic theory.

In these pages the reader will find what amounts to an economic history of certain aspects of our affairs since 1950. If he pays careful attention to the *dates* of the articles, he will find that a not unsubstantial part of this 'history' was written *before* the events. The dates do not indeed do me justice as a predictor, as the articles were naturally written before they appeared, and some, such as that in the *Economic Journal* (March 1956), several months before they appeared. In this collection of articles the narrative proceeds backwards and forwards, dealing with the successive phases of a moving economy ; to the extent that a broad dynamic diagnosis of a current situation is correct, then some prognostication ought to follow from it, although subject to the usual uncertainties. The existence of a predictive element in these narratives may incline historians to look favourably on the interpretations which they contain. I would put the matter in this way. If one has predicted certain events as likely to flow from certain causes, and these events have happened, and if one attributes them to the same causes *ex post* as one did *ex ante*, and if one is then confronted with an alternative theory of the causation of the events, one is surely entitled to ask the proponent of the alternative theory of causation, if *he* predicted the events on the strength of the causes that he alleges. If he did not do so, is there not a presumption in favour of the theory of causation on the basis of which the events were predicted, as against the alternative *ex post* theory, perhaps equally plausible *a priori*, which did not, however, enable its proponent to predict the events ?

Reviewers of my *Policy Against Inflation* have taken me to task for having 'bees in my bonnet', for example about our errors in not funding the 'sterling balances' after the war and in allowing an excessive and premature devaluation of sterling in 1949. Although I am unrepentant, these matters are not prominent in the present volume.

On the other hand, I see now that I am in danger of being accused of a new 'bee', namely concerning the events of 1957. I shall feel it a duty to continue to expatiate upon them. A minor, but respectable, reason is an academic regard for historic truth. In my opinion there is danger of a false interpretation remaining permanently on the record. These matters are touched on at the appropriate place in the text of this book.

My major reason for continuing to dwell on these events is that we shall surely have another 1957, and that it is important that we should react differently next time. I regard the phenomena of 1957 as characteristic of the early phase of a recession ; except in the unlikely event of our succeeding in ironing out the trade cycle completely, we shall in due course have another such 'early phase'. It is true that 1957 had certain peculiar features not likely to be repeated. There were certain consequences of the Suez crisis. More important, 1957 came at the tail-end of an eighteen-year period of almost continuous price inflation, which had left its imprint on the minds of those responsible for wage demands and of those responsible for fixing 'administered prices'. If those conditions do not obtain next time, that may help towards the formulation of a better policy. All the same, it is important that the phenomena of early recession should be recognized immediately, when next they occur, and that the question of what the Bank of England should do and what our general economic policy ought to be in that phase should be coolly and objectively discussed in advance.

And then there is another quite different aspect of 1957, which may also be repeated, although not necessarily simultaneously with the early phase of a recession. There is no guarantee that sterling will not one day again come under pressure in consequence of persistent rumours that some other important currency is likely to be valued upwards. Seven per cent should not be our routine reaction to such an eventuality.

CHAPTER II

THE LONGER FUTURE

This short essay was written before the publication, although doubtless not before the writing, of Professor Kenneth Galbraith's important and notable work, *The Affluent Society*. It was contributed, on the invitation of the Committee for Economic Development, to a symposium on the most important economic problem for the United States in the next twenty years.[1]

1

The Possibility of Economic Satiety
Use of Economic Growth for Improving the
Quality of Education and Leisure

DURING the next twenty years we expect the income of the United States to grow largely. During the seven years from 1948 to 1955, the gross national product per person in employment, reckoned at constant prices, grew at the average rate of 3·3 per cent a year. In the twenty-year period from 1935 to 1955, it grew at the average annual rate of 2·7 per cent; this period included, in the early part of it, years of unemployment, when advance was less rapid.

Since, currently, technological progress is by no means lacking in momentum, it does not seem unduly optimistic to forecast a continuing increase of 3 per cent a year or of 80 per cent in twenty years. This would yield an average income of about 11,500 dollars per person employed.

Faced with such a figure, one is bound to raise the question whether an approach to a satiation point may not come into prospect in this period. It is sometimes argued that the needs, or desires, of men are unlimited, and that there is, accordingly,

---

[1] *Problems of United States Economic Development*, Vol. I, Committee for Economic Development, New York, January 1958.

no satiation point.   In support of this it may be noted that
many persons, both in the United States and other countries,
both recently and for many centuries, have enjoyed and depended for their way of life on incomes far in excess of 11,500
dollars a year.   It is inferred that there is no reason why the
main mass of the population should not also find satisfaction
and enjoyment in incomes of similar size.

Such an argument is fallacious.   The maximum level of
income, if any, that can give satisfaction to a minority, *i.e.* its
satiation point, is necessarily far above the satiation point of
the majority.   There are two types of satisfaction available to
a minority that could never, in any circumstances whatever, be
made available to the majority of people : one is expenditure
on direct personal services, and the other is expenditure on
objects or amenities that contain what may be called a substantial 'rent' element, namely objects or amenities scarce
either intrinsically or through the imprimatur of fashion, or
objects requiring for their fabrication human qualities that are
scarce for either reason.

1. A large proportion of the expenditure of the rich has
always consisted, but more markedly in former times than
recently, in the direct employment of servants and retainers of
various kinds — for cooking, cleaning, gardening, housekeeping,
driving carriages or automobiles, care of children, tutoring,
etc.   Some objects that seem purely material, such as great
mansions to live in, private parks and gardens, stables full of
horses, yachts, are worthless unless a considerable amount of
personal services can be attached to them for their upkeep.
A person whose income is elevated well above the average can
enjoy all these things.   But when it is a question of a general
rise in the incomes of the majority, then no rise, however great,
can achieve them.   There is an unbridgeable gulf between the
nature of what may be called oligarchic wealth and democratic
wealth.   The first principle of democratic wealth is that it is
impossible for one man, however high the democratic standard
of living has been raised, to engage in any one year the services
of more than one man-year of the labour of others.   This puts
a severe limitation upon the range of possible satisfactions
achievable through a democratic increase of income.

2. The other limitation arises from scarcity, natural or

artificial. A young man may have the ambition that, when he grows rich, he will live in the choicest part of New York, have good seats at all the best plays and operas, go to the most select night clubs, buy fine old masterpieces or patronize the best living artists. And he may get all these things, if he grows rich oligarchically. But democratic wealth can never achieve them. If an unequal distribution prevails, the richer people will price these rare things beyond the pocket of the average man. Or, if really equal shares prevailed, one would have to arrange a rationing system for every man to go to the very best night club in turn, but it would only be once in a lifetime, and he can do that under the existing system, however poor he is, if he really wishes to.

This problem is solved, in part at least, in various ways, by modern science. For instance, by radio and television, it reproduces original performances and brings them into every home. But this very process of reproduction cheapens these amenities, and one no longer has to be rich, either democratically or oligarchically, to acquire them. Reproductions of fine works of art get ever more perfect. Precious stones are imitated. Centuries ago printing brought the greatest treasure of all — books — within the means of every man. Thus more things are successively rendered available to the citizen of moderate income, and of other things the majority would not be available to the average man, however high his income rose.

The democratic standard of living can be raised only by more material things, capable of mass production, being made available. It cannot be raised either in respect of direct personal services or in respect of the enjoyment of objects or amenities intrinsically scarce, or rendered so by the imprimatur of fashion.

Is it so clear that within these limits the standard of living of the average American citizen could be doubled or quadrupled? It may be argued that the tout or advertiser will always be able to think up some new gadget to whet the consumer's appetite. But is this a solution of the problem? Is it not rather a danger to be guarded against? Was this man's destiny, that, when he had reached the highest phase of material civilization yet known, he should be at the mercy of the salesman showing him how to spend the money burning his pocket on some tomfool idea?

It may be that the economic struggle, which we have been accustomed to regard as the central feature of the human situation, may in the long run of history prove to have been a transitional episode. In the early stages man's needs were limited by his ignorance, and his life was brutish and short. Then prospects began to open up, and he has had a hard fight to bring the relevant material equipment within the range of all. In most parts of the world this process is only in an early phase, and Americans will, in the next twenty years, undoubtedly think and do more about that aspect. None the less it must remain for them relatively a side issue ; it cannot be the central theme of their own way of life. And so it may be that, the economic problem being so largely solved, there will re-emerge for the Americans in these next twenty years the question, no less — what is the purpose of man's existence on this globe ?

What stands out at once is that we should contemplate more 'leisure', in the sense of a reduction in the proportion of time devoted to economic activity. But this is only a negative prescription. How fill in the leisure ? One may think of culture, which, unlike material wealth, is indeed limitless in its range. But one should not build too much on that prospect. It may well be that there is a certain genetical stability in the composition of the population, so that the joys of philosophy, poetry, music, and the visual arts can be a consuming passion only for a minority of the population. For the rest they can be an occasional pleasure or source of illumination, but not the central theme.

If one looks back on history, as likely to provide a key to this problem, one encounters a disquieting feature. The occupation that has taken precedence even over the economic struggle itself has been war. While we now rightly think of avoidable war as immoral, it is relevant that war fulfilled man's urge to have a serious purpose in life, and called forth certain qualities, in which he has always taken pride. When the main mass became deeply involved in the economic struggle, there was a long period in which, for the class enjoying highest social esteem, war remained the primary occupation, with blood sports tagging along as a second-best alternative or hobby. There may be danger in the passing away of the economic phase in human history. Give a man leisure, and he will be up to some mischief. He will not rest content with fun and games.

Hard on the heels of the idea of more 'leisure' comes that of more education. Man has to be educated, if he is to make good use of leisure.

But, important as education is, there is danger in going too fast, lest standards slip. If the education of the vast mass of people is to be raised, enough educators have to be found and themselves educated to a higher level than before ; there is a maximum possible rate of expansion, as in the case of a force of pilots in war-time.

In the field of science and technology this problem has been in the foreground for some time ; but in education for leisure the arts side must be stressed, and there the problem, though less evident, is no less real. Just as in science itself, the empirical test gives a decisive criterion of truth, so in education for science there are fairly clear-cut criteria for what has to be achieved to turn a lad into an efficient scientist. On the arts side there are no such clear criteria in respect either of the finished product or of the educational requirements, and a slipping down of standards may accordingly be undetected.

Unfortunately, the economic situation is strongly unfavourable to education. For education, at least on the arts side, is by far the foremost example of a direct personal service, where mass production aids can contribute nothing whatever. I would suggest as a minimum requirement for an arts education that every boy should, during the course of his school career, have been in contact with at least one teacher who seemed to give him a fleeting and provisional notion of the 'purpose of man's existence on this globe'. No doubt he will reject that teacher's view in due course, but, in doing so, he will be stirred to replace it by a better one ; and, once his mind is moving on that plane, he will have no problem in finding a fruitful use of leisure.

As material output rises, the incomes of industrial executives at all the various levels rise correspondingly ; if the salaries of educators are not also stepped up in line, we cannot expect to attract the same proportion, still less a rising proportion, of our very best citizens into the educational profession. A sense of vocation may, and happily does, go some way to make up for lack of adequate remuneration. But it would be misplaced idealism to rely on a sense of vocation only. I believe that the authorities, whether at state or federal level, have not yet begun to figure out the bill that will have to be met for personnel, if a large and rising proportion of the highest quality citizens are to be attracted into the teaching profession on the arts side, at schools no less than at universities.

I would therefore conclude that the most important economic problem to be faced by the United States in the next twenty years is how to secure the channelling of a sufficient supply of top quality resources into the educational field, especially on the arts side, so as to equip citizens with the mental resources required to make fruitful use of the more leisured way of life that lies ahead. And now we see that 'leisure' is not quite the right word. Rather it is a question of filling, in an active and purposeful way, the gap in a man's span of years that will no longer have to be devoted to economic activity.

CHAPTER III

POST-WAR MALADJUSTMENTS

After joining the Research staff of the International Monetary Fund in mid-1952, I was invited to engage upon a specific task, namely to attempt to discover what were the basic causes of the trade imbalance, and particularly of the dollar shortage, from which the world seemed still to be suffering.

I approached this task with a considerable sense of responsibility, and strove to clear my mind of all preconceptions.

It seemed that, before embarking on the question why an imbalance persisted, it would be good to know what the precise nature of the imbalance was. The value of world trade at that time, expressed in dollars, was about three times as great as it had been in the years 1936 to 1938. It struck me that, if one multiplied the main relevant 1936–38 figures, for regions, for countries, and for commodities, by 3, and compared these calculated totals with the actual current values of the items in question, one would get a clear picture of the changes that had taken place. This I proceeded to do. The work involved a considerable amount of research in relation to some of the relevant items.

When the first stage of the work was achieved, I had an enormous surprise. By far the biggest change, quite dwarfing almost everything else, consisted in the reduced value of newly mined gold flowing each year into the Treasuries of the world. I had indeed in previous writings (*e.g.* in *The Pound Sterling*) made some reference to the importance of the effect of the Americans not having raised the dollar price of gold in line with the dollar prices of commodities. But I had had no idea that the effect was so vast. Indeed it would hardly be an exaggeration to say that my findings suggested that the reduced commodity value of gold accessions was the main component of the persistent international imbalance. One had been hearing so much of the effect of U.S. productive dynamism, of inflations in other countries, of shifts in agricultural production, of accelerated investment, as causes of the trouble ; but these almost faded into insignificance, when one reduced the matter to quantitative terms, by comparison with the effect of the unchanged dollar price of gold.

If I was surprised, it is fair to say that my colleagues were shocked. The prejudices of Americans on this subject are well known. But I think I may add that my findings did not harmonize with the ideology of the International Monetary Fund itself. That body, after all, very properly conceived its duty to be to provide the world with a brave new monetary system ; the idea that anything to do with old-fashioned gold was still exerting an influence of major importance in our affairs jarred. I hastened to point out that I was not saying anything about what ought to be ; I had been asked to ascertain the nature of the existing imbalance, and, as a matter of hard incontestable fact, I was now obliged to report that by far the biggest feature of the imbalance was that accounted for by the changed commodity value of gold (*i.e.* its unchanged dollar value).

Despite the strong mental resistance of those concerned, my report was submitted and discussed (for two days) by the Executive Directors of the International Monetary Fund. Enlightenment was further shown by its publication in the I.M.F. Staff Papers (April 1953).

This paper follows and I have appended a short note on gold.

I call attention, however, to the fact that the paper, after its opening passages, is not mainly concerned with the gold question, but provides a thorough examination of many other aspects of the changed pattern of trade in the post-war years.

On the assumption that the whole gold question was taboo — as indeed it has so far continued to be — the findings of the report were extremely depressing. The analysis suggested that, whatever was done, it would take a very long time indeed to re-establish the equilibrium of trade. I was deeply discouraged by my own findings.

I would add, however, that the discussion of future prospects in the report is subject to two important limitations.

1. It was based on the assumption that in the future there would be no U.S. aid. I subjected myself to this limitation as

as matter of principle. It seemed to be wrong to argue about what ought to be done, on the basis that the Americans would extend their unprecedented generosity over a further term of years. In fact they have done so, not quite on the scale of the 'forties, but on a sufficient scale. Had I felt free to assume this, the whole problem would have looked entirely different. I could have written a thoroughly cheerful report, recommending an early return to convertibility.

2. The report states that 'The question of an expansion of U.S. capital abroad has not been considered'. This was my other self-imposed limitation. The reasons for it were two. (i) Any such expansion seemed too problematic and precarious to be relied on. (ii) I believed that such an expansion, if it occurred, would not be a long-run solution of the trade imbalance. This went counter to beliefs prevalent at the time, which I regarded as mistaken and possibly dangerous. An expansion of overseas investment may solve a problem of imbalance over a short period ; but one has to remember that the service charges (if the investment is by way of loan) or the profits (on the direct investment of capital) mount up over a term of years, and in due course overtop the sums going out by way of investment. Misleading lessons are sometimes drawn from the high rate of British overseas investment before 1914. The point there was that the steeply rising curve of British imports sufficed to provide means for foreigners to remit to Britain the service charges or profits on the British investments. It was not because Britain tended to have an *export* surplus that her large overseas investments secured an equilibrium, but, on the contrary, because she was tending to an *import* surplus.

In fact the U.S. export of capital did not expand rapidly in the years after this report was written ; it began to do so only in 1956. The combination of the continuance of U.S. aid, with the rather large expansion of capital exported in 1956 and afterwards, has produced a serious reverse imbalance, namely a U.S. deficit.

The consequence of this is that the grave problems presented in the report have not had to be faced. It was there shown how difficult it would be to get a shift in the pattern of trade adequate to secure a balance, subject to the two limitations aforementioned. But no such shift has been necessary.

I believe that the present U.S. deficit (December 1959) will prove somewhat obdurate in the period immediately ahead. It is possible that aid will be somewhat curtailed, as a remedial measure. Whether the present scale of U.S. capital export will continue we do not know. If it does, we shall have to face the time when the returns on that export will overtop the amount of capital exported. Thus, in a longer period, the United States could easily shift back into overall surplus. Some of the problems discussed in this memorandum may become relevant again; it is presented as providing a background to the history of the post-war period.

2

Imbalance of International Payments [1]

THE terms of reference of this report were to ascertain the causes of the imbalance of international payments from which the world has recently been suffering. Since 'causes' include policy decisions, which may be criticized from various points of view, it has been thought better in this first approach to limit the enquiry to ascertaining the changes that have in fact occurred in the pattern of international payments. In most of the report this has been narrowed to the differences between the pattern as it existed in the period 1950–mid 1952, or in 1950–51, and the pattern of 1936–38.

It must not be taken to be implied that none of the changes revealed would have taken place if World War II had not occurred. Nor is it implied that any of the changes that have taken place are undesirable. Furthermore, the report must not be taken necessarily to imply any pointers for future policy. For instance, if it appears that a particular factor has been responsible for a big dislocation, it does not follow that a remedy should be found by operating on that factor ; the best remedy may lie in introducing offsetting forces by operating on other factors. The relevance of the report for policy consists only in the contribution it may make to a better under-

---

[1] *International Monetary Fund Staff Papers*, April 1953. I have omitted the section on the reorientation of commodity trade, and the statistical appendices, in order to economize space. For these see *op. cit.*

standing of the quantitative importance of the various forces that have been at work.

It will be observed that gold plays rather a large part in the analysis of the changes in pattern that have occurred. The author of this report came to his work with no preconception of this matter. Indeed, it was only half-way through his work that the full significance of the changed position of gold was borne in upon him ; from this point forward there was no choice but to place emphasis on gold, since there was no other way of describing the larger changes of pattern that have taken place.

The report is necessarily confined to major items of change. It could also be used as a framework for consideration of the smaller items and of policy development.

GOLD

In any investigation into the causes of an imbalance of payments, it is proper to give first consideration to gold, which has for centuries been the principal medium of international settlement.

Under the forces of supply and demand, gold came to have a certain value in relation to goods, which enabled it to function smoothly as a medium of reserve and settlement. This value varied somewhat from time to time under the influence of new discoveries or the exhaustion of existing sources. If gold was becoming more abundant and reserves accumulating, the authorities felt able to have an easy credit policy ; this would tend to make prices move upward and the goods value of an ounce of gold downward. Conversely, if on the whole reserves were tight, a deflationary policy would prevail, prices would tend downward, and the goods value of an ounce of gold upward. Thus the goods value of an ounce of gold, and thereby the goods value of the world's monetary gold stock, tended to be adjusted upward or downward so as to enable that monetary stock to do the work required of it. This work was to provide sufficient reserves, by and large, to enable the authorities to feel that they had enough to cover normal expected fluctuations in their balances. Individual countries might always get into trouble, but if the majority of countries felt short, then the deflationary process got to work and adjusted the situation.

After World War I the gold situation aroused anxiety. It was feared that the annual supply of newly mined gold would be so low as to entail protracted deflation. The acute deflation which followed the spring of 1920 had caused serious unemployment and financial troubles, and the authorities were anxious that a strongly downward trend of prices should not continue indefinitely. Professor Cassel, a leading authority at that time, estimated on the basis of a historical survey that the monetary gold stocks ought to rise at the rate of 3 per cent per annum compound interest to maintain stable prices. Actually, in the period from 1924 to 1929 they grew at the rate of $2\frac{1}{4}$ per cent per annum ; at the same time the volume of world trade increased at 5·7 per cent (average), while its aggregate value increased at only 3·9 per cent.[1] The gold shortage did cause embarrassment ; for instance, in 1927 the Federal Reserve System deliberately eased credit in the United States in order to promote a moderate outflow of gold to help other nations. (Its action was subsequently criticized as inappropriate to the domestic situation.) Whether the world gold shortage was in part responsible for the world slump of 1929 remains an unsettled question.

The events of 1929–33, in all other respects disastrous, had one good by-product. The devaluation of the dollar, the pound, and other currencies in terms of gold, the great fall of prices even in terms of the devalued currencies, and the unhappy shrinkage in world trade greatly increased world liquidity. In 1924 the monetary gold supply constituted 32 per cent of the annual value of the world's export trade ; in 1933 it constituted about 100 per cent ;[2] gold held outside the United States alone constituted 60 per cent of the annual value of world trade, including that of the United States.[3] Furthermore, the stocks of gold in central banks and treasuries increased at the rate of 6·3 per cent compound interest between 1st January 1933 and 31st December 1938. The increment of gold supply alone was enough to finance 6·3 per cent of world trade.

Unhappily, this easement was largely neutralized by an

[1] League of Nations, *Review of World Trade, 1938* (Geneva, 1939), p. 60.
[2] This figure and all that follow exclude gold in the U.S.S.R.
[3] League of Nations, *op. cit.*, and Board of Governors of Federal Reserve System, *Banking and Monetary Statistics* (Washington, 1943).

enormous flow of capital to the United States, partly in quest of the high yields then obtainable on U.S. stocks and partly driven across the Atlantic by growing political tension in Europe. This flow of capital had to be financed by gold, and reserves outside the United States were depleted. In 1951 the world's gold outside the United States would suffice to carry only 17 per cent of the world's annual export trade. Between the end of 1945 and the end of 1951 the world's monetary gold stock grew at the rate of only 1·1 per cent per annum.

There were three causes of this great change, of which the first mentioned was also one cause of the other two. (1) By 1950–51, the value of the dollar in terms of goods entering international trade had fallen to about four-ninths of its 1937–38 value ; [1] but the dollar price of gold remained the same. Consequently, the goods value of an ounce of gold had fallen to about four-ninths. (2) By 1950–51 the volume of world trade had risen by about one-third ; [2] but gold production outside the United States and the U.S.S.R. had fallen from U.S.$928 million to U.S.$762 million. (By contrast, between 1936 and 1940 the production of gold *rose* by one-third.) (3) An amount of gold equal to more than half the gold output in the period 1946–51 ($2,667 million out of $4,790 million) has gone into private hoards.

In the past, gold shortage has tended to cause deflation. It has had no such effect recently. In the five years after World War II there were strong basic forces making for inflation, *e.g.*, the need for reconstruction. Monetary considerations would not have been strong enough to outweigh these forces, any more than they are during war itself. Furthermore, opinion has moved strongly against extreme deflation as an appropriate remedy. It is widely held that deflation should not and, indeed, could not be pushed to the point of causing substantial wage reductions or massive unemployment. And finally, in relation to the gold supply deflation would be of no value in securing an adjustment unless adopted by the United States. The amount of gold that the various nations consider from time to time that they need to hold as a reserve against fluctuation depends on the gold value, which in this period has meant the

---

[1] United Nations, *Monthly Bulletin of Statistics*, August 1952, p. xvii.
[2] *Ibid.*

dollar value, of their foreign trade. If the amount of gold available is fixed, gold can be brought into a better relation to the requirements for it only by a reduction in the gold value of trade. If the dollar price of gold is fixed, a reduction in the gold value of trade will occur only if the dollar value of trade is reduced ; that is, if the goods value of the dollar is appreciated. This would mean deflation in the United States itself. Deflations elsewhere would serve only to alter the values of local currencies. To reduce the dollar value of world trade to anything like its pre-war level would require a large reduction of U.S. wages. This may be ruled out as not only quite impracticable, but also undesirable. Consequently, it may be affirmed that a readjustment of the value of gold stocks and accessions to requirements for them will not take place by the traditional route of deflation.

But the matter does not rest there. Ruling out one mode of adjustment does not solve the problem. Each nation, finding itself short of reserves, bethinks itself of an alternative remedy, and finds it in direct import restriction. But while the evils of deflation were grave and there is no case for returning to it, it did at least solve the problem of inadequate reserves ; by reducing the value of trade as expressed in gold it restored liquidity. Import restriction, on the other hand, although it may temporarily ease the problem of a particular nation and indeed be necessary for it, has no tendency to solve the general problem. In this connection it is entirely beggar-my-neighbour. The total amount of gold being fixed and annual accessions of trifling quantity, what one nation gains by way of replenishment to its reserve, some other loses. It might be argued that if all the nations other than the United States were to push their restrictions so far as to induce an outward flow of gold from the United States, that would be a genuine easement. But to restore their reserves to their pre-war relation to trade, they would have to get all the gold out of Fort Knox, and long before that happened the United States would feel herself short. The plain fact of the matter is that, at the present valuation of gold in terms of goods, not all the gold in the world (including that in Fort Knox) is sufficient to provide nations with adequate reserves.

The dollar imbalance is such a prominent evil, and attracts

so much attention, that this more fundamental cause of trouble is likely to be overlooked. Many restrictions are due to the dollar shortage, but by no means all. It may safely be said that when the dollar imbalance is remedied the other evil will remain, unless a specific cure is found, and will continue to give rise to restrictionism.

Suggestions have been made in the past for supplementing an insufficient supply of gold by some gold substitute. One such was the bancor proposed in the British Treasury plan (1943). This plan for bancor contains the following proposal : 'Subsequently, after the elapse of the transitional period, quotas should be revised annually in accordance with the running average of each country's actual volume of trade in the three preceding years, rising to a five-year average when figures for five post-war years are available'. Another proposal was that of the Genoa Conference (1922), that central banks should hold the gold convertible currencies of other nations in lieu of gold. The dollar would be a thoroughly acceptable currency for this purpose, but in present conditions it is as hard to obtain as the gold in Fort Knox. It was partly in consequence of the views propounded at Genoa that sterling came to be widely held as an alternative reserve ; the holding of sterling has been adventitiously increased in consequence of the British methods of financing trade during World War II. Although sterling held outside the sterling area is not gold convertible, it has been playing a useful part as a means of international settlement in lieu of gold. The Bank of England report for 1951 states that £463 million was transferred during the course of the year to finance trade, both parties to which were outside the sterling and dollar countries ; this may be as much as about 6 per cent of the total of such trade. EPU units of account also represent an attempt to fill the lacuna caused by the lack of an adequate gold supply.

While these *ad hoc* expedients may serve a useful purpose for the time being, there is no doubt that in due course it will be desirable to devise a radical cure for the gold shortage.

The changed relation of the value of newly-mined gold to the value of world trade has also played a part of first-rate importance in relation to the dollar imbalance, which will be discussed in the next section.

THE DOLLAR

Of all the particular imbalances in the international payments pattern, that between the dollar and other currencies is the greatest. Unfortunately, it is extremely difficult to measure the amount of imbalance existing. Over and above the realized deficit, the continued existence of which has been made possible only through the provision of generous aid by the United States, there is, so to speak, a latent deficit consisting of the value of all the goods and services which the citizens of various countries would wish to buy from the United States at their existing prices, if only they were not prevented by discriminatory import restrictions from doing so. There is, however, an offsetting factor. It is probable that the aid so generously provided by the United States has led to the purchase of a certain number of goods from the United States, which would not have been purchased in the ordinary course of commerce even in the absence of import restrictions. This aid, in one form or another, grant or credit, has amounted to about $5 billion per annum since the war. Even if only one-fifth of this was spent on dollar goods that would not have been purchased in the absence of such aid, this would make an important difference to the size of the realized deficit. We are thus in ignorance of two important quantities, namely, the value of the dollar goods that would have been purchased had there been no discriminatory restrictions, and the value of the dollar goods that were purchased owing to aid granted but that would not have been purchased in the ordinary course of commerce. Ignorance of these two important quantities should lead to a suspension of judgement. It means that we cannot know in advance what measures would be adequate to rectify the situation and must proceed somewhat cautiously by trial and error.

There is a difficulty also in regard to the visible deficit. This was exceedingly heavy in the years from 1945 to 1949. In 1950 there was a spectacular improvement, followed by a relapse, but not to the previous position. The year 1950 was favourable to the rest of the world, partly because the United States was building inventories after the recession of 1949 and partly because the outbreak of the Korean war led to heavy U.S. purchasing abroad. This same purchasing and other events connected with the Korean war set off inflationary tendencies, which were inadequately controlled in certain countries, and led to heavy purchasing from the United States in 1951. It may be held that these conflicting tendencies to some extent offset one another, and that the average of the two

TABLE 1

U.S. BALANCE OF PAYMENTS *

(In millions of U.S. dollars)

Year	Visible Trade Balance (1)	Balance on Goods and Services (2)	Net Outflow of Private Long-term Capital (3)	Balance (Col. 2 + Col. 3) (4)
1948	5,524	6,021		
1949	5,271	5,849		
1950	764	1,237		
1951	2,356	3,232		
1952 (first half, annual rate)	2,962	3,370		
1950 — first half of 1952 (annual average)	1,840	2,462	− 851	1,611

* In this table and in all subsequent presentations, items flowing under military aid are excluded. The amounts shown under military aid have recently been running close to the 'special category' items which the U.S. Department of Commerce does not show by country of destination for security reasons. (In Table 3, below, special category items, instead of military aid items, are excluded, to obtain comparability with other figures in that table.) It may be assumed that, as long as world conditions remain as they are, these exports will be financed by special methods. It would be misleading to include them in an assessment of the economic disequilibrium. They averaged $1,225 million a year in the two and a half years, 1950–first half of 1952.
    Private donations are included in the balance on goods and services. Although not the payment for a service, it seems sensible to include them, since for several decades they have shown little change from year to year. This is a reversion to the older practice of the Department of Commerce, which used to include them in the current account.
    'Exports', as defined by the Department of Commerce, include the value of gold transferred from U.S. mines to Fort Knox. Although this appears to be an intrusive item, it has not been thought necessary to exclude it.

years may be taken as a fair indication of the dimensions of our problem. The earlier years were affected by the fact that the productive capacity of the rest of the world had not recovered from the dislocations of war and that inflationary pressures were much stronger than they have been more recently. Thus we may have some measure of confidence that there will not

C

be a relapse into the bad deficits prior to 1950, but at the same time we can only accept the figures for 1950 to mid-1952 *with caution.*

These figures suggest that, as a rough approximation, the imbalance may be thought of as a problem of $2 billion (see Table 1, columns 2 and 4). Such a figure has little meaning considered by itself. It is therefore desirable to consider the U.S. trade figures against the background of U.S. and world production indices. U.S. production has soared greatly by

TABLE 2

INDICES OF INDUSTRIAL PRODUCTION AND U.S. EXPORTS AND IMPORTS, 1948–51
(1937–38 = 100)

	1948	1949	1950	1951
U.S. industrial production *	190	175	198	219
World industrial production, excluding U.S. and U.S.S.R.	96·1	107·7	122·2	135·6
Volume of U.S. exports	200	204	169 †	207 †
Volume of U.S. imports	124	124	149	146
'Level' of U.S. imports ‡	144	145	196	212

* Since agricultural exports are important, the following combined index (1937–38 = 100) of U.S. industrial and agricultural production is of interest :

Year	Index	Year	Index
1948	170	1950	171
1949	162	1951	189

This is an arithmetic average of (1) an index weighting industry and agriculture according to the numbers employed in 1936–38 and (2) an index weighting industry and agriculture according to the numbers employed in 1950–51.

The increase in agricultural production in the outside world appears to have been about 15 per cent.

† Excluding 'special category' items.
‡ For description of this item, see text.

comparison with the rest of the world (Table 2). While the increase in U.S. productivity is a notable example to the world, it is important not to let exaggerated ideas of the rate of increase suggest that it must lead to recurrent crises of imbalance and the need for successive drastic devaluations. The increase of total U.S. production between 1937–38 and 1951 has been due in greater part to the increase of numbers employed than to the increase of output per man ; the former is not likely to be repeated and the latter should be capable of being looked after by upward adjustments of U.S. wages from time to time.

The figures in Table 2 are volume figures, except for the last line, entitled the 'level' of U.S. imports. A very important feature in the whole situation has been the deterioration in the U.S. terms of trade. This has caused her surplus on trade account to be considerably less than it would otherwise have been. The 'level' of imports is designed to show this; to obtain it, the volume of imports has been multiplied by a coefficient representing the quantity of U.S. exports required to buy one unit of imports (1937–38 = 1). Tables 2 and 3 show that, contrary to general belief, the value of U.S. imports had by 1950–51 risen fractionally more than the value of her exports.

TABLE 3

U.S. BALANCE OF TRADE, BY REGIONS*

Regions	Exports 1950–51 Annual Average	Imports 1950–51 Annual Average	Balance of Trade		Balance of Trade as Per Cent of Exports †	
			1936–38 Annual Average	1950–51 Annual Average		
	(1936–38 = 100)		(*million dollars*)		1936–38	1950–51
World	403	422	480	1,624	16·7	14·1
Canada	498	609	108	174	23·5	7·6
Latin America	601	574	− 28	− 18	− 5·1	− 0·5
Non-America	304	285	400	1,468	20·4	24·6
All OEEC countries	293	260	520	1,723	46·1	52·1
United Kingdom	142	231	326	306	65·1	43·1

* See Table 1, footnote.
† The minus figures indicate a negative trade balance.

The volume of her exports expanded more than the volume of her imports, but her worsened terms of trade offset this.

It will be noticed that the volume of U.S. exports expanded roughly in line with her production, while the volume of imports accorded more with world production. At first sight it would seem that each area had sent forth exports in proportion to its ability to produce generally. Yet the United States was able to buy all she needed, while the rest of the world had to restrict purchases. Such views have to be seriously modified when we proceed to the broad regional pattern. Volume figures by regions are not available. It has already been stated that between 1937–38 and 1950–51 world trade expanded by about one-third in volume, while the dollar prices of world-traded goods rose about $2\frac{1}{4}$ times, so that the dollar value of world trade rose approximately 3 times.

While global U.S. trade expanded more than in proportion to world trade (and world production), this was due entirely to a great growth of trade within the Western Hemisphere, which seems to have drawn closer together in this period. Despite all the aid given, U.S. exports to non-America (including, of course, the goods sent gratis [1]) did not expand more in value than world exports generally.

It is next necessary, for understanding, to compare the U.S. post-war balance with those in earlier periods. As shown in Table 4, the visible surplus of exports in the 1950–52 period

TABLE 4

U.S. BALANCE OF PAYMENTS ON GOODS
AND SERVICES

Period	Trade Balance	Balance on Goods and Services	Trade Balance as Per Cent of Exports	Balance on Goods and Services as Per Cent of Exports
	(million dollars)			
1924–29 .	819	769	16·2	15·2
1933–38	338	267	13·0	10·2
1936–38	480	378	16·7	13·5
1950–first half of 1952	1,840	2,462	14·7	19·6

is similar percentagewise to the surplus in earlier periods. There was, however, a sizeable change on the side of 'services', which were on balance negative in the pre-war period and subsequently positive (Table 5). Transportation constitutes the largest item of change ; U.S. receipts on transportation account were, however, particularly great in 1951, and it is thought that this figure will not be repeated.

Why a surplus which was not, percentagewise, so much greater than those accruing in earlier periods has caused so much more embarrassment, clearly calls for explanation. It is true that, expressed in dollars, the surplus was very much larger, but so are all other magnitudes in the pattern of world trade.

[1] Except 'special category' items.

During the 'twenties the surplus was wholly covered by the investment of U.S. capital abroad. This would seem to have been a healthy pattern for a rich and expanding country. It is true that some of the investments then made were ill-advised, but this was not surprising, considering that the United States was making her first experiments in foreign investment on a large scale. It was confidently expected that she would in due course develop sounder methods. Unfortunately, since that time conditions in the outside world have sadly deteriorated.

TABLE 5

CHANGE IN U.S. BALANCE OF PAYMENTS ON SERVICES

	Balance on Services as Per Cent of Exports *		Difference (Col. 2 minus Col. 1)
	1936–38 (1)	1950–51 (2)	(3)
Transportation	− 2·7	+ 2·8	+ 5·5
Travel	− 6·1	− 2·7	+ 3·4
Interest, etc.	+ 10·4	+ 12·1	+ 1·7
Private donations	− 5·4	− 3·7	+ 1·7
Other	+ 0·6	− 2·9	− 3·5
All services	− 3·2	+ 5·6	+ 8·8

* The minus figures indicate a negative services balance, and the plus figures, a positive balance.

The balance might alternatively be considered as a percentage of imports or of the mean of exports and imports. In this case, the alternative methods would yield approximately the same figures, since exports rose to 403 per cent of the 1936–38 average, and imports to 422. See Table 3.

The world slump, political insecurity, World War II, even greater political insecurity thereafter, have not offered an attractive field for foreign investment.

In the 'thirties the U.S. surplus was paid for by a flow of gold to that country. It is important to emphasize that not merely was the surplus paid for in gold, but it was paid for in gold four times over. The average annual surplus from 1933 through 1938 was $267 million; the average annual flow of gold to the United States during the same period was $1,140 million. This was due to a flow of capital to the United States, which, while justified and reasonable from the point of view of the individuals responsible for it, may be regarded as 'perverse' from the point of view of a balanced world. This large flow of gold imposed a strain on other countries and caused their reserves in total to fall, on the average, by $151 million per annum. Had they had to pay in gold for only the actual U.S. surplus on goods and services, they could have done this and still had their own collective reserves rise at the comfortable rate of 3·4 per cent per annum compound interest. They could clearly have paid for a considerably larger U.S. surplus and still remained reasonably comfortable.

It is desirable to consider what the pattern of international payments would have been in 1950–52 had the large change between the value of new gold accessions and the gold value of world trade not occurred. Since the accessions in the late 'thirties included some gold from hoards, it is fairer to take production figures for these years, in order to make a comparison. In 1936–38 gold production outside the United States and the U.S.S.R. was $892·3 million (annual average). Suppose that this had increased by 1950–51, in line with world production and trade generally, by one-third, viz., to $1,189·7 million. That this is not a fanciful hypothesis is indicated by the fact that by 1940 production had already increased to $1,094 million, and that important new gold discoveries have since been made. From this total subtract 5 per cent, which is the Bank for International Settlements' estimate of absorption by the industrial arts.[1] The remainder is $1,130·2 million. Finally, assume that the dollar price was raised 2¼ times, viz., in line with the rise in the dollar prices of goods entering international trade.[2] This would give an annual value of $2,549·9 million for new gold production outside the United States and the U.S.S.R. available for monetary use.[3] This may be compared with the actual annual U.S. surplus on goods and services account, from 1950 through the first half of 1952, of $2,462 million. It appears that, if new gold supplies had borne their

---

[1] *Seventh Annual Report*, p. 41, and *Eighth Annual Report*, p. 43 (Basle, 1937 and 1938).

[2] It is fair to add that the unit value of U.S. exports had not quite doubled. This disparity between the unit value of U.S. exports and the unit value (dollars) of world exports reflects the worsening of the U.S. terms of trade which has already been noted and brought into the reckoning.

[3] If the price of gold were only doubled, this figure would be $2,260·4 million.

pre-war relation to the value of world trade, the rest of the world would have been able to pay for its deficit in 1950–52 without aid ; [1] but the position would have been unsatisfactory and indeed somewhat strained, as the rest of the world would not have been able to add to its reserves. But if the outflow from the United States of private long-term capital of $851 million per annum is brought into the reckoning, the rest of the world could, as well as paying its deficit with the United States out of its own resources, have added to its gold reserves and/or reduced restrictions on dollar imports.

It should be emphasized that the foregoing paragraph implies no value judgement. It is a mere historical accident that, for some time, the United States has produced a smaller proportion, and the rest of the world a larger proportion, of the medium which has for centuries been used as money. There is no moral obligation upon the United States to add more than she wishes to her gold reserves. We are concerned solely with the fact that there has been a change of great magnitude involving a disturbance in the pre-war pattern and the need for adjustment. Other disturbances have also occurred, of which the worsening in the U.S. terms of trade has already been cited. There have been various shifts in the supply and demand for various particular categories of goods — such as grain and industrial equipment. It may safely be said that none of the shifts in individual categories of commodity trade are of comparable order of importance to the change in the gold situation. Its effects therefore should be observed carefully. The rest of the world will have to find acceptable goods to send to the United States in lieu of gold, or, alternatively, to buy correspondingly less from the United States.

It could be argued that the United States, by increasing her importation of other commodities (or the prices she has paid for them), has in fact made good the loss to the world resulting from the diminished flow of gold to her. But it has already been noted that this increase lay wholly in her imports from the Western Hemisphere. The dollar value of U.S. imports from non-America increased slightly less than in proportion to the growth of world production and trade. Thus non-America has not had an increased flow of dollars (other

[1] Apart from military aid items.

than by aid) which could fill the gap in the means of settling with the United States created by the great shrinkage of gold. The possibility of non-America capturing some of the additional U.S. dollars made available to Canada and Latin America by increased U.S. importation is discussed below.

Both before and since World War II, the deficit of the OEEC countries in trade with the United States was greater than that of the whole world including OEEC Europe (see Table 3). This was partly offset by contra items on services account (Table 6). It follows that if, owing to the shrinkage,

TABLE 6

U.S. BALANCE OF PAYMENTS ON GOODS AND
SERVICES, BY REGIONS, 1950–51

Regions	Trade Balance *	Services Balance	Balances as Percentages of U.S. Exports to Area †		
	(*million dollars*)		Trade *	Services	Goods and Services
All OEEC countries	+ 1,775	− 441	51·6	− 12·8	38·8
Canada	+ 222	+ 364	9·5	15·5	25·0
Latin America	− 83	+ 718	− 2·7	22·2	19·6
Rest of world	− 341	+ 150	− 10·9	4·8	− 6·1

* Excluding military aid.
† The minus figures indicate a negative balance.

to a trifling quantity, of the supply of newly-mined gold available as money, the rest of the world will have to learn to live in balance with the United States (instead of having a running deficit of the order of 15 per cent), the main burden of adjustment must fall on OEEC Europe. Before the war OEEC Europe, by having surpluses with gold-producing countries or by obtaining gold in multilateral exchange, was able to pay her heavy direct deficit to the United States in gold. This was a natural pattern, since Europe has a number of requirements she can best meet in the United States, while her manufactured products are more suitable for sale in third-party markets. This makes the adjustment now required more difficult. If the deficit of the world with the United States had been fairly evenly distributed among the various regions, being about 15 per cent everywhere, no doubt its elimination would have presented a difficult problem, especially at a time when the world has become much more dependent on certain U.S. supplies and desirous of others ; but it is much more difficult for a particular region (Europe) to eliminate a deficit as large as about 40 per cent. One has to cut more deeply into the established pattern of interchange.

It should be noted that the U.K. development differs somewhat from that of Europe as a whole. The rather poor showing of her exports to the United States in 1950–51 (see Table 3) was due partly to a real loss of *entrepôt* exports and partly to a mere statistical change by which the U.S. Department of Commerce, from whose returns all these figures are derived, altered its method of classification ; in 1936, and to some extent also in 1937 and 1938, it showed as coming from the United Kingdom goods whose actual origin was elsewhere, while in 1950–51 they are shown by their countries of origin. This means that the true U.K. deficit on visible trade account in respect of her own products was, in 1936–38, substantially greater than 65·1 per cent, and that makes her present problem of adjustment correspondingly more difficult.

The very small rise in the value of U.K. imports from the United States, which represents a large curtailment in the volume of those imports, was due to austerity and import restriction. As her initial percentagewise bilateral deficit with the United States was larger than that of continental Europe, it was needful for her to make more strenuous efforts to move towards bilateral balance.

When services are taken into account the distribution of the U.S. surplus is seen to be modified somewhat. Information is lacking for a regional sub-division of the pre-war services balance. Data are, however, available for the OEEC countries in 1937. The subsequent reduction of Europe's favourable balance on services account expressed as a percentage is seen to have some importance as an aggravating factor.

Table 6 indicates that Canada and the Latin American group of countries as a whole, as well as Europe, have had dollar imbalances of substantial proportions, after 'services' have been brought into the reckoning. However, the greater part of the outflow of U.S. private capital (see Table 1, col. 3) went to

Canada and Latin America. The flow to regions beyond the
Western Hemisphere was not of sizeable amount. The movement of capital is too variable for a tabulation covering only
two years to be meaningful. It may be noted that the flow of
private capital from the United States to Canada in 1950–51
was equal to 23 per cent of U.S. exports to Canada and so
almost completely offset the U.S. surplus (25 per cent) on goods
and services account. Thus, whether Canada proves to have a
chronic imbalance against the U.S. dollar will depend on her
power to attract a regular flow of capital of this order of
magnitude.

The capital flowing to the Latin American group of countries
as a whole was smaller in these years, and there was a sizeable
overall deficit. The problems, however, of this group are
markedly different from that of the European group. It has
been seen (Table 3) that in 1950–51 the dollar earnings on
trade account of the Latin American group were 574 per cent
of the 1936–38 average, while those of the European group were
only 260 per cent. Moreover, the Latin American group had a
much better bilateral balance than Europe had with the United
States before the war. While it may be natural and proper for
the Latin American countries to have greatly increased requirements for imports from the United States on account of their
capital and general expansion, a moderate curtailment of imports which have risen (in dollar value) nearly six times should
not be excessively difficult. It may well be that the true recipe
for the imbalance of the Latin American group as a whole lies
in the curbing of inflationary tendencies in certain of its members. For the most part, the European problem is of quite a
different nature.

Before proceeding to a more detailed scrutiny of the imbalance revealed in Tables 1-7, it may be well to make an
observation on the effect of inflation upon external balances.
If the aggregate purchasing power released within a nation
exceeds its supply potential, not only will there be a tendency
for internal prices to rise, or — to the extent that these are
subjected to control — for waiting lists and bottlenecks to
develop, but also there may be a tendency towards excess spending on external account. The external deficit is then a symptom
of aggregate internal over-spending. There is no doubt that

internal inflations, which were widespread after the war, tended
to cause external deficits ; to the extent that these inflations
were stronger in countries outside the United States than in
the United States, there is a ready explanation of the deficit of
the rest of the world with the United States.   It is probable
that in the late 'forties, when the aggregate world deficit with
the United States was running between \$5 billion and \$10
billion, inflations in other countries could be reckoned as the
principal cause of the imbalance.

TABLE 7

U.S. BALANCE OF PAYMENTS ON GOODS AND SERVICES WITH OEEC COUNTRIES AND REST OF WORLD

	Trade Balance	Services Balance	Balances as Percentages of U.S. Exports to Area *		
	(million dollars)		Trade	Services	Goods and Services
OEEC countries					
1937	+ 505	− 228	40·1	− 18·1	22·0
1950–51	+ 1,775†	− 441	51·6	− 12·8	38·8
Rest of world					
1937	+ 79	+ 243	3·9	12·0	15·9
1950–51	− 202	+ 1,232	− 2·3	14·3	12·0

* The minus figures indicate a negative balance.
† Excluding military aid.

In the 'fifties, inflations in most parts of the world have
abated considerably, although the events following the Korean
outbreak caused some revival of them in certain countries.   It
may be that some part of the dollar imbalance that has remained
has been due to local inflations ; continuing vigilance is
certainly necessary.   But it cannot be argued that because there
is external imbalance there *must* be internal inflation, except
by some fanciful definition of inflation, which would involve
arguing in a circle.   Without in the least derogating from the
importance of inflation as a persistent cause of imbalance in the
post-war years, it may be advisable now to concentrate attention
on a quite different cause that has operated to create a major
European dollar imbalance, namely, the shrinkage in the value

of newly-mined gold — to which the shrinkage of invisible income from the United States must be added as a minor cause. Even if Europe had not suffered from any internal inflations, she would still have been under the necessity of finding a new method for paying for some 35 per cent of her normal imports from the United States — or, alternatively, of dispensing with all or part of them. It is clear that such a change-over cannot be effected without great strain and dislocation. The need for making it has no connection with internal inflations and will continue to exist when they have been completely removed. It may be regarded as the hard core of the dollar problem. And it is probable that it constitutes the main part of the dollar problem as it now presents itself.

EUROPE'S DOLLAR PROBLEM

There are three ways in which Europe can redress her U.S. dollar position : namely, (1) an increase of exports of goods and services to the United States; (2) a decrease of imports of goods and services from the United States; and (3) a capture of dollars in third-party markets, in lieu of the gold formerly won there. In a world of fully multilateral trading relations, the third method would be expected to make the largest contribution. The third-party markets can provide U.S. dollars to Europe either through a rise of their sales to the United States or through the substitution of European exports for U.S. exports to those markets. Each of these must be considered in turn.

Europe has made considerable and, to some extent, successful efforts to expand direct sales to the United States. It is in the sphere of finished manufactures principally that one could hope for an expansion of exports by an organized 'export drive' or currency devaluation, other categories of goods depending more on the level of U.S. production and national income. The achievement of OEEC countries in 1950–51 is shown by the data in Table 8. Although these index numbers are subject to a margin of error, it can hardly be great enough to invalidate the broad relations displayed. The quantum figure is clearly satisfactory ; an 87 per cent expansion may be reckoned as large. But the total value figure is less satisfactory ; the OEEC countries kept their dollar prices down in these years. (It is interesting to compare the unit value index of 171 with the unit value index — 189 — of U.S. exports of finished manufactures in the same period.[1]) The total dollar proceeds of these European sales to the United States rose less than those of other countries because the prices of European goods rose less. The Belgian data in Table 8, however, show a somewhat different pattern.

Table 8 may be interpreted in one of two ways, each of which has an unsatisfactory moral. On the one hand, it may

TABLE 8

INDICES OF EXPORTS OF FINISHED MANUFACTURES
TO THE UNITED STATES, 1950–51 AVERAGE *

(1936-38 = 100)

Exporting Group	Quantum	Unit Value	Total Value of Sales
World	140	253	355
All OEEC countries	187	171	321
United Kingdom	165	191	319
Belgium	144	275	394

* These figures exclude such items as wood pulp, newsprint, and sacking. Each figure is the arithmetic average of the two figures for 1950 and 1951.

Source : Federal Reserve Bank of New York, *Pattern of United States Import Trade since 1923 ; Some New Index Series and their Application* (New York, 1952).

be that the OEEC group has made a mistake in policy in charging such low prices (a process which the devaluations of 1949 assisted), and would have gained more in total dollar receipts if it had sustained its selling prices at a higher level. This, if true, would be unsatisfactory, as all efforts in Europe are now addressed to paring down export prices by higher efficiency of output, and it will be unfortunate if these efforts merely lead to a loss of total dollar receipts. On the other hand, it may be that the OEEC group has been quite right in keeping prices down, and that it would have lost its markets in the United States rapidly, had it failed to do so. But this is also unsatisfactory. For what it must mean, taken in relation to Table 8,

[1] Based on data from *The Midyear Economic Report to the President, July 1952* (Washington, 1952).

is that the kind of manufactures which the OEEC countries are able to furnish to the United States, and which may consist largely of articles that differ from other U.S. imports of finished manufactures, find less easy access or sale in the United States than the manufactures drawn from other countries. Further consideration of this point would require an analysis article by article.

Total OEEC exports to the United States have risen less since 1936–38 (160 per cent) than exports of finished manufactures (221 per cent). Exports of crude foodstuffs fell 23·2 per cent in volume, materials rose only 19·3 per cent, manufactured foodstuffs fell 11 per cent, while beverages rose 55 per cent.

It is in place here to consider the more general question of the expansibility of U.S. imports. The Federal Reserve Bank of New York has made an analysis of the elasticity of demand for imports in the United States.[1] While its methods and conclusions will no doubt be criticized from various points of view, its broad conclusion will probably be accepted ; namely, that all categories other than finished manufactures depend more on the level of production and national income in the United States than on their relative prices. On the other hand, for finished manufactures the report finds responsiveness to price. Thus, while the rest of the world may expect an upward trend of total U.S. imports — and the findings of the President's Materials Policy Commission[2] suggest an acceleration in the more remote future — it is only in the sphere of finished manufactures that it would be possible to obtain a quick expansion by such methods as price competition.

The Reserve Bank study gives various figures for the 'price elasticity' of U.S. demand for finished manufactures from the OEEC countries, of which 2·5 may be chosen as representative. It may well be that this is too optimistic since it depends on observations in the depression years ; no such responsiveness was found in the 'twenties. If the figure of 2·5 is applied to OEEC exports of finished manufactures to the United States in 1950–51 ($641 million per annum), and if a reduction of 30 per

[1] *The Pattern of United States Import Trade since 1923 ; Some New Index Series and their Application* (New York, 1952).
[2] *Resources for Freedom :* Vol. I, *Foundations for Growth and Security* (Washington, 1952).

cent in the average of prices charged is assumed, the value of
U.S. imports of these goods from Europe would rise by only
$144 million.[1] This increase, based on two extremely optimistic
assumptions, would still not make an important contribution to
closing the European dollar gap. It is probably not legitimate
to apply the Reserve Bank's elasticity coefficient to U.S. imports
of manufactures from *all* quarters ($1,195 million per annum).
Even if this could be done, it would still yield an increase in
U.S. imports of only $269 million.

Although these calculations are highly precarious in detail,
the broad inference is safe ; namely, that the contribution
to closing the $2 billion gap that can be achieved by foreign
exporters' stimulating sales to the U.S. market by price
concessions, including devaluations, is small.

It does not follow that these figures show the limit of the
possibility of increased sales to the U.S. market. If sales could
be increased by methods other than price concessions, or by
methods in which price concessions played only a minor role —
e.g., by more diligent study of the needs of the U.S. market, the
offer of more prompt delivery, and better servicing — larger
increases of proceeds might be possible.

Finally, a word should be said about the U.S. tariff. Given
the elasticity of demand, a larger rectification of the balance
could be gained by a given percentage average reduction of the
tariff than by an equal percentage devaluation by all other
countries. Assuming once again the Reserve Bank's coefficient
of 2·5, an average tariff cut of 10 per cent of the value of finished
manufactures would increase U.S. imports of those manufactures by double the amount that would result from an
effective devaluation of 10 per cent by all other countries.

The upshot of these considerations is that the $2 billion gap
is not likely to be greatly reduced *in the near future* by an increase
of U.S. imports. Over a longer term, prospects are more hope-
ful, owing to the prospective rise of U.S. production and gross
national income. Consequently, if the dollar gap is to be closed
in the near future, it will mean a large curtailment of U.S.

---

[1] Let 1 stand for unit values before the price concession and 0·7 for unit
values after the 30 per cent concession ; if demand elasticity is 2·5, the volume
of sales will rise from 1 to 1·75. The sales proceeds in the new situation will
be 1·75 × 0·7, or 1·225 times the previous proceeds, an increase of 22·5 per
cent.

exports. For Europe this will mean either a curtailment of direct imports from the United States or a displacement of U.S. exports by equivalent European commodities, as a result of keen competition in third-party markets.

The figures for European imports (Table 9) show, on the whole, that continental Europe has used aid for what it was intended. The great increases since 1938 in imports of electrical and industrial machinery and chemicals are examples. These figures suggest that when programmes of industrial expansion

TABLE 9

EUROPEAN IMPORTS FROM THE UNITED STATES,
1950–51 AVERAGE

	Total Value (million dollars)	Indices (1938=100)			
		United Kingdom	OEEC countries, excluding U.K.	France, Germany, Italy, Belgium, Luxembourg	All OEEC countries
Food	756·1	116	452	600	281
Machinery and vehicles	620·5	123	437	600	333
Electrical and industrial machinery	395·5	143	981	1,144	541
Cotton	567·0	243	587	560	469
Tobacco	231·1	103	552	723	174
Chemicals	173·4	277	529	470	633
Coal	143·6	— *	— *	— *	— *
Petroleum	127·0	116	59	104	75
Textile manufactures	97·7	107	640	490	440
Iron and steel mill products	89·7	69	321	262	235
Vegetable oils and oilseeds, inedible	84·6	— *	— *	— *	— *

* Pre-war imports were negligible.

fostered by U.S. aid come to an end, the European deficit will fall substantially. On the other hand, the notable increases in imports of agricultural products by continental Europe were due to a shift in the balance of world supplies, which will be discussed later. Coal imports should end.

The much stricter curtailment of imports practised by the United Kingdom in contrast to continental Europe is shown clearly by Table 9. It is worth observing that, if the OEEC group as a whole had followed the U.K. policy and not allowed its pre-war dollar imports to rise by more than 42 per cent, its dollar imports in 1950–51 would have been $1,704 million per annum less than they were in fact, and there would have been no realized dollar deficit on account of the OEEC group. This is not intended to imply that the continental countries ought to have done this.

The question of the 'latent' dollar deficit has been raised earlier (see p. 22). On the one side, there are the goods that would be imported from the United States in the absence of restrictions ; on the other, there are those imports from the United States which have been stimulated by U.S. aid and would not have flowed under ordinary commercial motives. The figures suggest that the United Kingdom has a 'latent' deficit. With continental Europe it may be the other way round. Imports of machinery, etc., may have been stimulated beyond normal by the European Recovery Programme ; the large increase in the imports of textile manufactures into continental Europe, although not quantitatively very important, may be taken as a pointer. It is hard to believe that, if the authorities were denying their citizens many urgently needed dollar goods by import restrictions, they would have allowed so large an increase of dollar textile manufactures.

While restriction is the method available for quick action to curtail U.S. imports, an alternative method at longer term is to stimulate the production in third-party countries of commodities now imported from the United States. If Europe is to become dollar solvent in the near future, she will either have to curtail greatly her direct dollar imports, by comparison with 1950–51, or capture dollars by displacing U.S. exports from third-party markets. It has already been indicated that it is not likely that additional dollars will be available in sufficient quantities by an increase of third-party sales to the United States, although this may be the ultimate solution over a longish term of years. Consequently, if sufficient dollars are to be captured in third-party markets at an early date, it must be principally by a displacement of U.S. exports. It is important to emphasize this point, because the achievement of equilibrium is sometimes represented in a rather different light. Mr. A. Maffry, for instance, writes in an authoritative article [1] with reference to the advantages of the restoration of international

[1] *Lloyds Bank Review*, October 1952.

equilibrium, including the dismantling of restrictions and the convertibility of currencies, 'for the United States it would mean lifting the burden of various forms of assistance to foreign countries and giving much greater freedom to American exporters in seeking foreign markets'. The former point is, of course, correct. But the latter suggests that there would be an easement and a possibility of expansion for U.S. exporters. The reverse is the case unless equilibrium is achieved wholly by an increase of U.S. imports. It is quite true that when equilibrium was achieved, there would be no need for restrictions and inconvertibilities. But the essence of the equilibrium is that Europe should have balanced her accounts, and that means — apart again from a sufficient increase of U.S. imports — that, by whatever method of price competition, sales pushing, or market study, Europeans should have established themselves securely in a large part of the markets that the United States now enjoys. The United States would be debarred from these markets just as much after the equilibrium was established as now. The difference would be that, instead of being debarred by legal restriction, she would be debarred by prices that were so low or sales campaigns that were so aggressive that she would be unable to compete against them. The legal restriction of imports is merely a hit-and-miss way of moving towards that pattern of trade which believers in economic freedom wish to see eventually sustained by keen competition.

A question sometimes raised is, why there has not already been a more decided movement towards a new equilibrium pattern. Seven years is represented as being a long period, and Europe has had much assistance. In this connection it is important to remember that OEEC Europe has had a double problem, the dollar problem and the problem of her overall balance of payments. Of the first mentioned the most important ingredient is the changed position of gold, though significant contributions have also been made by the decline of invisible receipts and abnormal importations into continental Europe of U.S. machinery, chemicals, and cotton. The problem of her overall balance has different causes and is of larger dimensions. There has been considerable misunderstanding about the relation between the dollar imbalance and the overall imbalance.

The dollar problem presents itself as the more urgent, since immediate gold or dollar payments are required. The most quickly working method of coping with it is the direct restriction of dollar imports ; an export drive to the dollar area may also yield fairly quick results, and this has been vigorously pursued. A more slowly-working method of curtailing dollar imports is the stimulation of alternative sources of supply. These methods tend towards securing a bilateral balance ; but the most satisfactory method — which should in the long run, and when a true equilibrium in the international pattern of payments is achieved, yield the best result — is the capture of dollars in third-party markets. This third, most fundamental, and most beneficial method can be brought into play only *after* the problem of the overall balance has been thoroughly cured. For as long as the third-party countries are in surplus with Europe, they can pay the European countries in their own coin. (Exception must be made for certain special areas which do in fact yield dollars.) Thus the dollar problem of Europe is closely tied up with her overall balance of payments problem.

The overall balance of payments problem has arisen from the fact that Europe has had to increase her exports greatly in order to pay for the same imports that she was getting previously. This has been due to the loss of income on invisible account, most notably investment income, and the deterioration in her terms of trade.

In Table 10 an attempt is made to set out in quantitative terms the increased burden on certain European countries due to these two causes. It is fair to add that other European countries do not appear to have had large losses of investment income from abroad, so that the increased burdens upon them have not been so great as those borne by the countries cited. In this table, the values of invisible items accruing in 1948 and in 1950–51 have been reduced to allow for the rise in the prices of imports since 1938. The values of the different items, as thus established, have been subtracted from the values of the corresponding items in 1938 and the differences expressed as percentages of the exports of the different countries in 1938. This table thus answers the question, what expansion of its exports, from those in 1938, each country would have to make to replace precisely the loss of buying power of its invisible earnings ; in other words, by what amount each country would have to increase its exports so as to be able to buy that quantum of imports which the invisible items, present in 1938 but since lost, were then able to buy. Further, a figure is added showing by what percentage exports would have to be expanded to allow

TABLE 10

ESTIMATES OF INCREASES IN EXPORTS ESSENTIAL TO OFFSET LOSS OF INCOME ON INVISIBLE ACCOUNT, SELECTED COUNTRIES*

	United Kingdom		France †	Netherlands	
	1948	1950–51	1950–51	1948	1950–51
Gain (+) or loss (−) on account of invisible services expressed as a percentage of exports in 1938					
Transportation	+ 0·9	+ 2·1	− 7·3	+ 3·1	+ 4·7
Investment income	− 26·7	− 26·0	− 24·5	− 19·5	− 19·3
Government	− 3·6	− 3·0	..	− 3·7	− 1·8
Foreign travel⎫	− 1·2	+ 1·0	− 8·7	..	..
Other ⎭		+ 2·5	+ 0·8	..	..
Total	− 30·6	− 23·4	− 39·7	− 20·1	− 16·4
Quantum of exports required to buy 1 unit of imports (1938 = 100)					
	117·0	134·3	120	104·4	120·2
Percentage increase of exports required					
To make good loss of invisibles	35·3	31·4	47·6	20·9	19·7
To make good reduced buying power of visible exports	17	34·3	20	4·4	20·2
To offset two adverse factors together	52·3	65·7‡	67·6	25·3	39·9

* For description of the data, see text.
† The figures relate to trade and services between metropolitan France and the non-franc area.
‡ For the worse year, 1951, this figure is 85·6.

for the worsened terms of trade. It should be emphasized that the final figures make no allowance for any increased requirements for imports ; they merely state what the expansion of exports would have to be in order to buy precisely the same quantum of imports that was bought before. Thus, no allowance is made for the need to expand exports in order to obtain imports for a larger population or for higher productivity.

Furthermore, there is no implication in the table that trade balanced in 1938 ; the table only shows what increase of exports was required to make good the specific losses listed, not what increase of exports might be required to the extent that trade was out of balance in 1938.

This deterioration has involved very heavy burdens indeed. It has not been easy for countries, already great exporters and also burdened with internal tasks of post-war reconstruction, to expand exports by 50 or 60 per cent before even beginning to pay for such extra imports as might be needed, including those very necessary imports which have constituted the raw materials of the extra exports.

The causes of the deterioration in the terms of trade cannot be fully explored here. For the United Kingdom, the prices of imported food rose only 15 per cent against the prices of all her exports, but the prices of imported materials doubled against her export prices. This has probably been due to the large increase in manufacturing activity in a number of countries impinging upon supplies of raw materials that are insufficiently elastic. Note must be made of the great increase in the manu-facturing activity of the United States, entailing a correspond-ing increase in the demand for materials ; the production of the United States is so high that a doubling of it makes a large impression on world requirements for materials. The first effect of this has been a severe deterioration in the United States' own terms of trade, which has already been noted as being a factor of easement of major importance tending to reduce the world's dollar imbalance. But while this easement has allowed many countries to import more dollar goods than would otherwise have been possible, it has not extended its beneficial effect in this respect to Europe, but has, on the con-trary, increased Europe's difficulties. For Europe shares with the United States the role of being an importer of these materials ; the upsurge of production in the United States has had the effect of worsening Europe's terms of trade and thus adding to the problems that beset her.

To return to the question of 'seven long years'. By 1948 the United Kingdom had reconstructed her industry and raised her exports 38 per cent above their 1938 level ; by this means and a restriction of imports she achieved an overall balance, her dollar deficit being offset by an over-balance with other regions. This was not a sufficient recovery, since it was needful for the United Kingdom to have an overall over-balance, both to make overseas investments and to reduce her ex-war indebtedness. A special difficulty has confronted the United Kingdom throughout the period in the task of earning dollars in third-party markets; namely, the existence of large ex-war sterling balances which could be used by these third parties to pay for British surpluses. It was indeed needful to reduce these balances, but the rate at which they have been paid off has been governed by the fortuitous accrual of trade surpluses with particular countries rather than by any predetermined plan. In fact, sterling balances outside the sterling area were reduced from £1,306 million at the end of 1947 to £842 million at mid-1952. The recovery of continental Europe, and especially of Germany, had not proceeded so far by 1948, but she was on the upward grade and was to be greatly assisted by ERP.

Unhappily, after 1948 another evil befell. The terms of trade once more moved heavily against the OEEC countries (see Table 10). The worst year was 1951. In that year British terms of trade (prices of imports in terms of exports) had risen 16·8 per cent above the 1948 level. Since British imports were $9,792 million, f.o.b., the extra amount of exports required of Britain as a consequence of the worsening in the terms of trade was equal to $1,640 million. Britain had to export over $1·6 billion worth of goods to the world at large merely to balance and offset the extra claims upon her for goods consequent on the worsening in her terms of trade. This event removed her, to the extent of $1·6 billion, from that crucial point at which she would begin to earn dollars in multilateral exchange. According to a publication of the OEEC,[1] the European terms of trade (export prices of imports) rose 10 per cent between 1948 and 1951. The imports of Europe as a whole (including the United Kingdom) in 1951 were $33,673 million, c.i.f. Reducing to f.o.b. and applying 10 per cent it appears that Europe as a whole would have to send out $3,031 million extra goods merely to offset the worsening in her terms of trade.[2] She

[1] *Statistical Bulletins: Foreign Trade*, June 1952.
[2] Ten per cent is the average loss of buying power of all European exports. In the sphere of intra-European trade, the worsened terms of trade

would have to find additional markets for all these exports before she could begin to earn dollars in multilateral exchange.

There has been controversy, which cannot be settled here, concerning how far this further worsening, superimposed upon the worsening that had already occurred by 1948, was due to occur in any case, how far it was due to the devaluation of currencies in 1949, and how far to the Korean outbreak. Reference to the simultaneous deterioration in the U.S. terms of trade is not decisive, since her imports are more price-sensitive than those of Europe and were naturally more affected by her own post-Korea stockpiling. Whatever may have been the cause, the fact remains that a new heavy task was imposed on Europe [1] which had to be carried through prior to her beginning to earn dollars in quantity in multilateral exchange. Three years is by no means a long period to assign for its achievement.

A burden of this magnitude is much heavier for European countries, which have to devote a large proportion of resources to export, than for such a country as the United States, whose exports, although large, bear a much smaller proportion to national income. Reference may be made to the British case by way of example. By 1950–51 the volume of her exports had risen 80 per cent above the 1937–38 volume. This alone does not truly represent the magnitude of the strain. Food, drink, and tobacco have not shown a great increase, and coal, for special reasons that are well known, has lagged ; her manufactured exports have been more than double their pre-war level. This figure has to be taken in relation to the fact that even in 1937–38 an abnormally large proportion of her resources were devoted to exports. An analysis of the employment of British manufacturing capacity in 1948 [2] shows that 25·5 per cent of such employment was devoted to exports and only 37·5

of some countries exactly cancel the improved terms of others. If p was the fraction of European trade going outside Europe, the deterioration in the terms of trade of Europe with non-Europe must have been $\frac{10}{p}$ per cent.

Whether one applies the fraction $\frac{10}{p}$ per cent to European exports going outside Europe, or, as in the text, the fraction 10 per cent to *all* European exports one gets the same answer.

[1] In what follows, Europe is used for OEEC Europe.

[2] Central Statistical Office, *National Income and Expenditure, 1946-51* (London, 1952).

per cent to the provision of all the numerous consumers' goods that her population of 50 million people required. Since 1948 the volume of her exports has increased more than in proportion to total production while consumption has barely risen; by a rough calculation it appears that in 1950–51 the proportion of manufacturing capacity devoted to exports was about 27·5 per cent, and that devoted to home consumption was about 32·5 per cent.

It is desirable to add a rider concerning devaluation, not so much by way of historical retrospect as of warning concerning the future, and not so much by way of analysis of what happened as of what might have been expected to happen. Devaluation may be accepted when it is an *ex post* recognition that internal costs and prices have got out of line with those abroad; using it experimentally to improve an adverse balance is a much more doubtful matter. Devaluation is both inappropriate and dangerous when a country is suffering from internal inflationary pressure — inappropriate, because the correct remedy is to remove the pressure, a process which may itself suffice to correct the external imbalance, and dangerous because it adds fuel to the flames of internal inflation. In the old days devaluation was regarded as a form of currency debauchery; this was a healthy view of it. Devaluation is more likely to improve the balance of trade when applied to a small country only; much less likely when applied to a large region. Most important of all, devaluation is less likely to improve the balance of a country whose demand for imports is inelastic. The European demand for imports was inelastic in 1949, both because imports consisted largely of food, materials, and specialized capital goods, and because the demand for unnecessary imports had already been pruned away by administrative restrictions. It was hoped that the devaluations would make it easier for European producers to offer competitive prices *vis-à-vis* U.S. producers. This was only a minor aspect of its probable effect. The major effect for a group of countries whose demand for imports was very inelastic was likely to be to turn the terms of trade against them. But this very process would postpone the day when they would begin to be able to capture dollars in third-party markets. There was no force in devaluation tending to make dollar prices in world markets fall;

and they did not fall. The dollar prices of some European imports fell temporarily because they were protected by contracts. But the intended effect of devaluation was to make the dollar prices of European manufactures fall. If it did not produce this effect, owing to a quick marking up of internal costs, it would be rendered nugatory and had better not have taken place. The combined effect of stable dollar prices for imports from *all* sources — not from dollar sources only — and lower dollar prices for exports to all sources would be to create a large gap before an overall balance could be achieved. The maximum stimulus that devaluation could give to European exports to the U.S. market would, in any case, be only in terms of $100–200 million. The obstacle which devaluation was likely to plant in the way of Europe's earning dollars in third-party markets was of the order of $2–3 billion. This point is of central importance in the problem that still lies ahead of Europe. It was also hoped that devaluation would tend to encourage the production of raw materials and foodstuffs in non-dollar regions ; this was likely to be a long-run effect. If the hope is eventually realized, this will be of advantage.

In regard to what Europe has been able to achieve in a seven-year period, the burden of post-Korea rearmament must be mentioned. This directly limits her power to expand certain acceptable types of exports. These tasks taken together suggest that, despite the lapse of seven years, further patience would not be misplaced.

If Europe had to achieve dollar solvency without further curtailing dollar imports, it seems that she would have to displace U.S. exports to third-party markets by her own, to the value of between $1 billion and $1½ billion. This would have to be primarily by the export of semi-finished or finished manufactures. In 1951 the value of U.S. exports of these categories to all countries other than the OEEC countries lay between $7 billion and $7½ billion. In the same year the OEEC exports of these categories outside the United States and the OEEC countries themselves were also between $7 billion and $7½ billion. Thus it seems that, in order to capture sufficient dollars in third-party markets, the OEEC countries would have to capture the proceeds of about one-sixth of all these U.S. exports. In order to do this by price competition, they would have to displace considerably more than one-sixth of the U.S. exports, for the third-party countries could pay for part of the increased European exports in European currencies, owing to their lower unit prices, and would have to pay dollars only for the remainder. (See below.) Furthermore, there are no doubt many lines in which displacement is not truly feasible, so that a still larger proportionate displacement would have to occur in the lines in which European competition was practicable.

In recent years there has been a gulf between the thought of some writers concerned with international equilibrium and those concerned with the theory and practice of the home market. The international experts have tended to assume 'perfect competition', while home market experts have explained that 'imperfect competition' is all-pervasive in the field of manufactures. By the doctrines of imperfect competition a price concession, even if large, is not likely to capture the whole of a rival's market but only the fringe of it; the capture of a large part of it may be possible only as the end-result of a long process. Students of industrial organization have reached similar conclusions. When the conditions for an expansion of sales, and particularly for an encroachment on rivals' markets, are studied, it is taken as quite axiomatic that a combination of methods has to be employed simultaneously. Long and careful market research may be needed; also a well-thought-out campaign of aggressive salesmanship; also means of giving desired customers assurance of the continuity of supply; a concession on price is merely one item, and sometimes a less important item, in the whole campaign. It would also be treated as axiomatic that, in most cases, for a firm to expect to make an encroachment by a price concession alone, without having brought to bear all other considered methods of sales pushing, would involve it in a mere loss of money. Transferring this from the internal to the international sphere, it means that the attempt of a nation to improve its balance by price concessions alone is likely to worsen its balance. Yet a sudden devaluation — and devaluations in practice have to be fairly sudden — or the depreciation of a currency owing to some new force operating in a 'free market' are analogous to price concessions offered alone and without the necessary ancillary measures.

It is convenient to give a hypothetical example of the limitations of price concessions in themselves. Suppose that European and U.S. producers share, half and half, the third-party markets for a finished manufacture, and that Europe desires to capture the dollars representing 16 per cent of the U.S. sales. If this could be done by a small price concession — combined with a careful selling campaign — the result would be satisfactory. A large concession is likely to be needed to obtain a quick result — let us suppose 20 per cent. If a 20 per cent price concession captures as much as 45 per cent — a formidable onslaught — of the American market, the desired result would be achieved ; the third-party market would be able to pay for the first extra 25 per cent of the European article out of the European currency released by the 20 per cent price concession itself ; only for the next 20 per cent would it have to surrender U.S. dollars. (Since the European price is down by one-fifth, this 20 per cent of U.S. sales would bring in 16 per cent of the U.S. dollars previously used to buy the exports from the United States.) But if the 20 per cent price concession only displaced one quarter of the U.S. sales, Europe would have won no dollars at all. This illustrates that it may be impossible in the literal sense of the word to capture a large quantity of dollars by displacing U.S. exports by large price concessions — such as might be facilitated by sizeable devaluations.

A wise man may think it unlikely that Europe will in fact displace so large a proportion of U.S. exports to third-party markets in the near future, whatever method be adopted. There is no reason to despair of the eventual establishment of a multilateral pattern. This is more likely to be achieved gradually. If Europe makes strenuous and unremitting efforts to capture third-party markets, she may displace some dollar exports in the near future, but is more likely, at best, to succeed in capturing a lion's share of the new dollars that become available later owing to the secular rise of U.S. imports. But this can bring home enough dollars only over a rather long period. Until this is achieved, Europe, if she is to maintain solvency, will need to have discriminatory restrictions on dollar imports, save to the extent that alternative sources of supply of commodities now obtained from the United States become available.

The foregoing argument has suggested that it would not be

easy for Europe to capture sufficient dollars in third-party markets even if the rest of the world were in dollar balance. But it is not. A number of non-European countries have some way to go before they achieve their own dollar balance. For those countries a more plentiful supply of imports from Europe might be welcome because they would be substitutes for dollar expenditure and would enable those countries to get into better dollar balance ; but they would not at that stage be requited by dollars for Europe. Some of the countries in question are in overall imbalance. This position would have to be corrected before Europe could hope to earn dollars by a vigorous export drive to them.

It is important to emphasize that, in the fairly near future, the alternative to rather stringent discriminatory import restriction in Europe is a displacement of U.S. goods of large value from markets elsewhere. This form of statement may suggest methods of international co-operation. Planners may argue that the matter is a simple one : the United States has only to agree to withdraw from certain overseas markets that Europe could supply. Such a solution would no doubt be impractical and unacceptable ; it would violate the principle of competition and give no guarantee that the United States and Europe respectively supplied the goods which each was economically best fitted to produce. On the other hand, the ideal of competition may be pushed too far, as though it were an end in itself. International trade should not be regarded in terms of a football game, in which each side is exhorted to do its utmost to outwit the other. If it were a principle of high U.S. policy that it is better that the reduction of U.S. exports should be carried out on a rather wide front, rather than solely in Europe, help might be given in small ways.

Similar considerations arise in connection with the Point Four policy of the United States. This is conceived in statesmanlike terms to raise standards of production in underdeveloped countries. It could also be made to subserve, quite in accordance with its general aim, a better balance of international payments. It may often happen that a given project could be achieved more economically by European than by American equipment ; it may be in the best interests of an under-developed country that a project should be carried out in the most economical, rather than in the most perfect, way. American consultants would naturally tend to supply know-how implying American methods, both from normal and proper patriotic motives and, possibly, from ignorance of alternative methods. It would therefore be a way in which the United States could greatly assist recovery, if she authorized a liberal employment of European consultants and technicians on such schemes. This argument applies *a fortiori* to development projects sponsored by international agencies.

There is also a moral on the plane of international monetary and commercial policy. On the supposition that the disturbance to the previous economic pattern caused by World War II is too great for an adjustment to be achieved readily under conditions of completely free trade, and that the dollar must temporarily be regarded as a currency in short supply, we may ask what kind of discriminatory restrictions best accord with the international ideal. It should be emphasized that we are concerned only with discriminations during such a transitional period as may be deemed of reasonable length for securing the necessary changes in the structural pattern of production and trade. It might well be argued that, ideally, if the currency of one particular country is in short supply, discriminations against its use should be adopted universally, so as to impose roughly equal sacrifice on each country. At the opposite extreme is what is apt to happen in practice, namely, a tendency toward a bilateral balance of each country with the United States. Those countries whose natural pattern of trade is to be in strong deficit with the dollar are driven to impose violent discriminatory restrictions, while those tending rather to balance or to surplus impose no restrictions. This is all wrong. Ideally, the restrictions should exert equal pressure all round, those countries tending to surplus conserving the dollars won and handing them over to the strong deficit countries, so as to enable them to reduce the violence of their restrictions. That would conform to the principle of multilateralism and give the best distribution among the different nations of the quantum of dollar goods that the world as a whole is able to buy. What has here been described as the 'ideal' pattern of restrictions, if restrictions cannot be avoided, is no doubt quite impossible in practice. It should not, however, be too much to expect that international policy might be used to mitigate the tendency to bilateralism somewhat, by encouraging nations which have mild discriminatory restrictions to retain them, as long as there are other nations which through no fault of their own are having to impose more severe ones.[1]

SUMMARY AND CONCLUSION

The figures for the period 1950–mid 1952 suggest that the world's dollar imbalance may be thought of in round terms as having been a $2 billion per annum problem. If this period is compared with 1936–38, it is found that the value of U.S. imports (excluding gold) had risen as much as that of U.S. exports, including in the latter those sent out gratis other than 'military aid' proper. The volume of U.S. exports rose more than the volume of U.S. imports, but this was offset by the worsened terms of trade for the United States. U.S. trade rose in dollar value about a third more than world trade ; this was due entirely to more active trade between the United States and the rest of the Western Hemisphere ; U.S. trade with non-America (including gratis exports as above) did not rise more than world trade generally.

The U.S. surplus on trade account in the period 1950–mid 1952, considered as a percentage of her exports, was of the same order of magnitude as that in the periods 1933–38 and 1924–29. But a moderate deficit on 'services' account had changed to a moderate surplus, transportation being the largest factor of change. In the 'twenties the surplus on goods and services together was covered by overseas investment by the United States ; in the 'thirties it was covered by the payment of gold to the United States ; in the 'fifties it has been covered by 'aid'. Actually, the gold shipped to the United States in 1933–38 was four times the value of the U.S. surplus, owing to capital movement. The rest of the world could have paid the bare surplus of the United States in this period in newly-mined gold and at the same time added comfortably to its reserves.

If the pattern of trade in the period 1950–mid 1952 is compared with that in the 'thirties, the greatest single item of

---

[1] In the original paper a discussion of particular commodities occurs at this point.

difference is seen to be the shrinkage in the goods value of newly-mined gold available for central banks and treasuries. This was due to the fixity of its dollar price, to reduced output, and to the disappearance into private hoards of amounts equal to more than half the new putput.

The first section of this report (pages 17–21) argues, against an historical background, that the great decrease in liquidity for purposes of international settlement, which is due to the changed relation of the value of gold stocks and accessions to the value of world trade, has caused and is likely to cause a chronic tendency to import restrictionism. If the value of newly-mined gold becoming available for money outside the United States and the U.S.S.R. had borne the same relation to the value of world trade as it did in the 'thirties, the rest of the world could have paid for the whole realized surplus of the United States on goods and services account in 1950–mid 1952 without loss of reserves and without aid (other than military items).

This is not to be taken to imply that it is desirable for the United States to continue to import any given value of gold. As things are, the rest of the world has either to find acceptable goods to ship to the United States in lieu of the gold previously shipped, in order to pay for some 15 to 20 per cent of U.S. exports, or, to the extent that it fails, to reduce its imports from the United States by that amount.

Both in 1936–38 and in 1950–mid 1952, the deficit of OEEC Europe with the United States in bilateral trade was greater than that of the whole world including OEEC Europe. In the former period, the OEEC deficit was somewhat reduced by invisible items ; in the latter period, less so. Thus the main part of the readjustment required by the gold change has to be made by OEEC Europe. This concentration of the need for readjustment upon one region makes its achievement more difficult, since it involves cutting more deeply into the former pattern of trade. The bilateral deficit of Europe with the United States of about 38 per cent (approximately $1·3 billion) might have been greater in the absence of restrictions.

While the gold change has made the dollar crisis more intense for OEEC Europe than elsewhere, that region has had, simultaneously, another post-war trading problem of greater quantitative importance. Loss of invisible income and worsened terms of trade have made it necessary for Europe greatly to increase its exports to the rest of the world as a whole in order to buy the same imports as before. For such countries as the United Kingdom and France, the increase of exports required has been some 60 per cent. (In the worst year, 1951, this figure rose to 85 per cent for the United Kingdom.) This has meant a strain upon the manufacturing capacity of those countries and set off inflationary pressures, which in parts of the period had other causes also.

The most important of the various causes for the worsened terms of trade is probably the great increase in manufacturing output throughout the world, and notably in the United States, which entailed increased requirements for materials and a rise in their relative prices. In searching for differences in the pattern of trade in the period 1950–mid 1952, compared with that of 1936–38, it is well first to multiply figures for the latter by 3. The index of world dollar prices had risen to 225 and the volume of world trade by about one-third ($2\frac{1}{4} \times 1\frac{1}{3} = 3$).

In the attempt to close the dollar gap, OEEC Europe has had some success in increasing exports of manufactures to the United States. The United Kingdom has cut imports severely, by direct restriction; continental Europe has restricted in some lines, while purchasing fairly freely, as intended by ERP, in others. An alternative method of curtailing dollar imports is to invest outside the dollar area in the production of commodities now bought from the United States.

If a true multilateral equilibrium of trade is to be reached, it is probable that OEEC Europe should not close the main part of the dollar gap by either of the methods mentioned in the preceding paragraph, but by the capture of dollars in multilateral trade. It is important to observe that not much progress can be made along this, the most fruitful, line, until OEEC Europe has secured a firm overall balance with the non-dollar world, for, until that point is reached, she can be paid by third parties for the most part in her own currencies. Thus, the establishment of an overall balance is a prior condition for the best solution of the dollar imbalance. From this point of view, the further deterioration in the European terms of trade between 1948 and 1951 was unfortunate.

It has been suggested that it should not, eventually, be more difficult for Europe to settle her accounts with the United States, since in the 'thirties also she had to have an over-balance with the non-dollar world wherewith to buy the gold to remit to the United States. It is further suggested that, since the United States has increased the value of her imports more than three times, there are additional dollars available for Europe to capture in third-party markets in lieu of the gold formerly bought there. But there is a big difference. It has been seen that the United States has increased her purchases outside the Western Hemisphere less than three times (see Table 3) ; it is only in Canada and Latin America that she has provided additional dollars. But the gold previously came mainly from the sterling area, with which Europe had well-established trading relations. While Europe was involved in post-war difficulties, the United States was able to meet demands in Canada and Latin America arising from and supported by their additional dollar earnings. It was clearly much easier for Europe to have a large over-balance outside the Western Hemisphere, which could be earned and paid for by newly-mined gold, than to establish an equivalent over-balance with Canada and Latin America by displacing U.S. exporters. For this process to go forward it would be necessary that the Western Hemisphere countries should not, themselves, be in overall imbalance.

Meanwhile, all these developments have to proceed against the background of increased world demand for U.S. exports. The balance of grain supplies has shifted ; there has been an abnormal increase in the world demand for industrial equipment, and other countries have not been able to increase supplies as quickly as the United States ; meanwhile, all along the line, the United States has shown marked progressiveness and efficiency, of which her abnormal increase in the export of textile manufactures is a notable manifestation. These trends make the task set for Europe of capturing dollars by displacing U.S. exports in third-party markets more difficult.

Local inflations, both in Europe and elsewhere, played an important part in creating a dollar imbalance in the post-war quinquennium. Their importance in the overall picture has now diminished considerably, but continued vigilance is necessary to prevent recurrence.

E

For the world-wide dollar imbalance, the prevention of inflation in the various countries is an essential remedy. For the special problem of Europe, it is not a sufficient one. The secular growth of U.S. imports will provide an easement for this, both because it will allow a rise — although not a relatively large one — in direct European exports to the United States, and because it will provide additional dollars around the world for Europe to earn, if she can generate and maintain continuing competitive pressure. How far Europe can go beyond this and win additional dollars in third-party markets by displacing existing U.S. exports must remain a doubtful question. But if she cannot do this on a rather considerable scale, then in the near future she will have to curtail U.S. imports in order to be in balance. This may be achieved in part and in due course by investment in the production outside the United States of commodities now bought from that country. There being no other source of U.S. dollars, it does not appear probable that direct discriminatory restriction of dollar imports can be avoided by Europe in the near future. The question of an expansion of U.S. capital investment abroad has not been considered.

Study of the large size of the post-war maladjustments, notably those connected with the displacement of gold, and with the need for Europe in her general trade to export so much more in order to pay for the same imports as before, has a two-fold moral. (1) We need not think that seven years, complicated as they have been by the Korean outbreak, the post-Korea inflations, and the rearmament programmes, constitute a long period for the attainment of balance, even taking into account the generous aid provided ; nor need we therefore despair of the eventual achievement of an equilibrium in which discriminations and restrictions are no longer necessary. (2) On the other hand, the large size of the adjustment still to be made must make us sceptical of the possibility of the quick demise of various protective devices.

POSTSCRIPT ON GOLD

The problem of gold has been in the forefront of my mind ever since my work in the International Monetary Fund. I have written upon it from time to time, but no further papers are included in this volume.[1]

In the report, gold appears mainly because the diminished commodity value of accessions to monetary gold stocks was found to be the principal component of the imbalance of payments that persisted for a number of years after the war. But it is not on this account that the importance of gold has figured so prominently in my mind since then. Its more fundamental and lasting importance is connected with the shrinkage in the amount of liquidity available for countries as international reserve, and I insisted on putting in a short passage about this in my report (see pages 17-21), although it was not strictly relevant to its subject.

I believe that the gold question is by far and away the most important of any in relation to problems of international balances of payments. But I have found that a deaf ear is turned to any discussion of it. It is a subject on which there appears to be inspissated prejudice. There must be something peculiar about gold. For many years the 'gold standard' was considered so sacred that rational discussion of it was ruled out. Now discussion is taboo for the opposite reason : gold has become so disreputable as to be beyond the pale of discussion by civilized people. I feel sure that Keynes, who was largely responsible for toppling gold off its former pedestal, would be deeply distressed by this recent development.

My main reasons for feeling strongly on the subject are the following :

1. This is a case where economic opinions are formed without reference to the *quantitative* aspect of things ; this is a sign that most economists have not yet been converted to submitting themselves to the discipline of the dynamic, as distinct from the static, approach ; for the former of its *essence* requires a quantitative assessment, while static economics requires qualitative argument only. If the dollar price of gold

[1] My principal contributions were : 'Plan for Restoration of Full Gold Convertibility of the Dollar together with a Revision of the Gold Content of the Dollar'. Hearings before a sub-committee of the Committee on Banking and Currency, U.S. Senate, 33rd Congress, Second Session, 30th March 1954. 'The Role of Gold To-day', South African *Journal of Economics*, March 1958. 'Why the Dollar Price of Gold must Rise', *Optima*, Johannesburg, September 1958. 'World Monetary Liquidity', *The Irish Banking Review*, March 1959.

was raised in line with the dollar prices of commodities, this would mean adding at once about $40 billion to the reserves of central banks, as well as raising the annual accession of gold by, probably, more than a billion dollars a year. What is the use, by comparison with this, of raising quotas in the International Monetary Fund by 50 per cent (less than 5 billion dollars) just for once ? In relation to this great big thing, the theoretical arguments about the price of gold, to the extent that any are vouchsafed at all, are finicky. If, for reasons not specified, we really have to take the question of altering the price of gold to be taboo, then why do not the various monetary authorities realize that they ought to get together and substitute some other *great big thing*, to take the place of gold ? The whole question has been allowed to go by default.

2. Having been trained by Keynes, I am a believer in the importance of liquidity, both national and international. There may be some misconception about his attitude, because in his theory 'liquidity preference' figures as a 'bad thing', to the extent that it may be a drag upon investment. But he did not blame people for desiring liquidity, and his mode for preventing liquidity preference being a drag was to give people as much liquidity as they wished to have. He was a liberal, not a governess. The value of liquidity is that it gives freedom for manœuvre and therefore encourages enterprise. In the international field a sufficient amount of liquidity is required if nations are to engage in multilateral trade and not clap on restrictions on every occasion of some small oscillation in their balances. I am sure that the post-war difficulties would have been greatly reduced, had liquid reserves been larger. This remains a problem.

In regard to Keynes, who has been praised for his share of responsibility for the International Monetary Fund, the situation is rather pathetic. For many years he had believed that the expansion of world production and of international trade was hampered by the lack of liquidity, and at the time of the World Economic Conference (1933) he proposed the issue of international gold notes, to supplement it. It is to be observed that at this time, when Keynes was at the height of his revolt against orthodoxy, he wrote, 'at all stages of the post-war (*i.e.*, First War) development, the concrete proposals which I have brought forward from time to time have been based on the use of gold as an international standard, while discarding it as a rigid national standard'. The most important object that he had in mind in his proposal of a Clearing Union — it is to be noted that the new currency he proposed was to be called ban*cor* — was to increase world liquidity. How galling it would have been for him, had he lived, to realize that the increase in liquidity due to the inception of the I.M.F. was small indeed compared with the decrease in liquidity due to the changed position of gold. Although prescient in many respects, in 1944 he had not tumbled to the prospective effect on liquidity of the decline in the commodity value of gold.

I am not aware of any argument that will bear inspection against raising the dollar price of gold in line with the general rise of dollar prices that has occurred in consequence of the war.

If one talks to non-Americans, they reply that it is idle to discuss the subject, since the Americans will never agree. If one talks to Americans, they reply that it is idle to discuss the subject, since their Treasury will never agree. This implies that what, in my own mind, is the most important thing that could be done to increase the economic strength of the free world, is the subject of dictatorship by half a dozen Americans — no more. I resent this. I may add here that I believe that I have a very good record in *not* pronouncing on what the Americans ought to do — in liberalizing their tariff, investing more abroad, prolonging their aid, etc. I have usually taken the view that that is *their* business. But the dollar price of gold is not their business ; it is world business. Gold is the international medium of settlement and reserve. The accidents of history have put the Americans into a strategic position in respect of gold holdings. They allowed the commodity value of the dollar to depreciate during the war and after it ; the question of what ought to be done about a consequent re-rating of the gold value of the dollar should not be for Americans alone to decide, but for the whole world. In fairness to the Americans, one must add, that there does not seem to have been a lively interest in this topic in most other countries either.

I have added this note, precisely because there is little reference to the gold question in what follows, and in order that it

CHAPTER IV

THE CONVERTIBILITY OF STERLING

I was for a period deeply depressed by the result of my researches with the International Monetary Fund. *Always on the assumption that we ought not to bring the possibility of a continuance of American aid into the reckoning*, it seemed likely that it would take a good many years before those vast shifts in trade would occur that would be needed to secure a balance. Accordingly in my writings in the following period I was apt to stress that quantitative import restrictions might continue to be needed for a considerable time. I believe that some economic colleagues, who had since the war shared my faith in the feasibility of moving towards greater freedom of trade, felt that I had weakened on this point of cardinal importance ; they may not have studied my I.M.F. paper carefully.

In regard to convertibility, however, my spirits soon revived. I advocated giving priority to the restoration of convertibility, while retaining, and even strengthening, import restrictions for a further period. This did not accord well with American thinking, which regarded the return to convertibility and the dismantlement of restrictions as having parity of importance, being addressed to the same aim, namely the re-establishment of multilateral trade in the most advantageous channels. To me, the restoration of convertibility seemed to have greater urgency.

I strongly dissented, and continue as a matter of economic principle to dissent, from the point of view that I found prevalent in certain American circles, namely, that any imbalance of trade could be cured by either deflation or devaluation. I strongly held in 1952, a year in which Europe was suffering from a mild recession and one not far removed from the excessive devaluations of 1949, that neither of these remedies would then be appropriate to cure the European imbalance.

It was under these influences that I composed some lectures on the dollar in the course of 1953. Referring to the inconvertibility of the dollar after the American Civil War, I wrote : [1]

> 'Her (viz. the British) struggle against Hitler may perhaps be compared in intensity with the American Civil War, the strain and burdens of which must not be under-rated. By this analogy, Britain should be expected to restore sterling convertibility in 1959. If we may press the analogy even further, Congress finally enacted the restoration of convertibility in 1875, naming 1879 as the date for its coming into operation. This would give Britain until 1955 to make its final decision, with a further four years' grace thereafter to bring the thing into effect.'

We may take Britain's 'final decision' as signalized by her intervention in the free markets to support transferable sterling in February 1955, whereby she established the *de facto* convertibility of sterling. It is pleasant to think that the dates given in the two arms of this little essay in prediction (namely 1955 and 1959 [2]) were both correct.

My reasons for returning to the advocacy of sterling convertibility in 1954 were two. 1. By then, it seemed clear that rising overseas military expenditures by the United States would suffice to secure a world dollar balance, *without* bringing into the reckoning any forms of 'aid'. While one naturally hoped that the need for such expenditures would disappear, owing to the re-establishment of perfect international goodwill, it did not seem realistic to suppose that this happy outcome would occur at all quickly. In some quarters it was argued that we should not restore convertibility, until we saw the U.S. external payments in balance *net*, not only of aid, but also of overseas military expenditures. This struck me as positively perverse, for how were the Americans to undertake such expenditures, which we certainly did not wish to see stop, unless they had a sufficient balance on trade account to finance them ?

2. The conclusion of my I.M.F. paper began to work in

---

[1] The Dollar (pub. Macmillan), p. 30.
[2] Actually the unification of official and transferable sterling appears to have occurred on 29th December 1958.

my mind to suggest that an early return to convertibility should be regarded as a matter of urgency ; for, according to that conclusion, to get a balanced pattern of trade in the world, it would be needful for Europe to earn more dollars from third parties in multilateral settlement. But it would never succeed in doing so unless the European currencies were themselves convertible. Accordingly, the breathing space provided by the continuance of U.S. overseas military expenditures should be used to re-establish convertibility without further delay, and thus prepare the way for the arduous process of winning dollars in multilateral settlement.

I call attention to the first article in this chapter, entitled 'Towards a New Pattern'. It contains two points, both of which I have continued to regard as of outstanding importance.

1. The view had gained ground in authoritative British quarters, which appears to have been endorsed by the Commonwealth Conference in the autumn of 1952, that, if convertibility was to be restored, it would be expedient to have wider margins within which sterling could fluctuate. And there were some influential persons who held that we ought to have a 'freely floating sterling'. (This would not be 'convertibility' at all according to the historic usage of that word ; by a revolution of a language, some were beginning to use the word 'convertibility' as merely meaning that holders of sterling should be legally permitted to sell it in the market for whatever price they could get. This was the condition obtaining in the period 1931–39, when sterling was deemed to be 'inconvertible'.) It was believed that a country with a narrow reserve and a precarious external balance could adopt convertibility with wide margins with less risk than convertibility with narrow margins. I consistently expounded the opposite view. Eventually, the authorities appeared to have been converted to it.

As for a 'freely floating sterling', I do not dissent from Professor Meade that this might be an ideal system in a world which had already achieved a balanced structure of trade, where the trade cycle was largely under control and confidence was good. But those have by no means been the conditions in the last decade. The idea that it would be easier, or less attendant with risk, or require less reserve, to have a freely floating currency than to have one fixed within narrow margins, I regard as downright fallacious.

When it appeared in February 1955 that the British authorities were determined to hold transferable sterling within the 'commodity shunting point', *i.e.*, to maintain *de facto* convertibility within narrow margins, it seemed that this battle had been won. In the light of this, the British announcement at the OEEC meeting in Paris four months later that, in the event of official convertibility, we should desire larger margins, seemed both unintelligible and disastrous.

2. In 'Towards a New Pattern' there is also argument about the use of the interest rate structure in relation to the maintenance of convertibility in post-war conditions on the one hand, and to the needs of the domestic economy on the other. This problem remained uppermost in my mind in the next five years, and I watched developments closely from this point of view. It seemed to me that lessons were being learnt all the time and that progress was being made in the understanding of how external and internal requirements could be reconciled. This struck me as a central problem in the working of our monetary system. I was accordingly in due course to be deeply depressed on finding that the Radcliffe Committee appeared neither to have formulated the problem to itself nor to perceive that anything could be learnt from the five years' experience.

3

Towards a New Pattern [1]

ONLY the authorities can profitably try to guess whether the incursion of funds that occurred some two months ago was influenced by the fact that short-term interest rates were higher here than in New York. Even the authorities cannot know the answer to this question for certain, nor can they definitively assess its relevance for the future. It may be that the high interest rates did exert some pull only because their influence entered into combination with other forces operating at that time, and that they could not be relied on to have an influence in other circumstances. Further experience will throw more light.

[1] *The Financial Times*, 5th July 1954.

If high interest rates really did exert an influence, this was a notable event in monetary history ; for it would be the first time that any such influence was exerted for nearly a quarter of a century — since 1931. The use of the Bank Rate to exert a short-term effect upon the external balance of payments was a prime method of management for many decades during the heyday of sterling. Consequently, any sign that it might be possible in the widely different circumstances of to-day to revive this instrument of management should be watched with extreme attention. No doubt the authorities will do so in the period to come.

The matter is one of great relevance for the problems that lie ahead. We are now approaching by cautious stages a period of great decisions, including those concerning the convertibility of sterling. We must not regard the establishment of convertibility in isolation, but also frame some notion of the new pattern of things that we hope to see realized in the following period.

This interest rate question has a close connection with the proposal to have more flexible exchange rates. It is important to notice that we have here *rival* methods of coping with short-period disturbances in the balance of payments, whether due to seasonal or chance causes, or to the first impact of a recession. For the Bank Rate weapon cannot work unless a lower limit to the foreign exchange rate is rigidly fixed. We are concerned here, of course, only with means of tiding over short-period disequilibria ; neither method can be expected to see the country through a protracted recession in the outer world.

I suspect that if a choice between these two methods is available, preference should be given to the Bank Rate method. We have long experience of it. There were special reasons why the other method worked reasonably well during the 'thirties. But the scene has changed again. We have now a curious mixture of great disorderliness in international monetary arrangements on the one hand, with new aspirations for international co-operation which must not be ignored.

I believe that the Bank Rate method of coping with short-period disequilibria would fit in better with the world-wide pattern of currency arrangements as it may develop in what we hope will be a period of greater order ahead. If it is to be used, then we have to reject too great a widening of the limits within which the foreign exchange rate is officially permitted to fluctuate. We certainly have to reject the notion of a 'freely floating' pound.

Now the minds of many will at first react strongly against the idea of reviving the Bank Rate mechanism. Whatever is decided, it is important that the decision should represent a national policy of a bi-partisan character. We aim at a durable arrangement. Therefore many points of view must be taken into account.

There are old memories of a deflationary policy being introduced at times when it tended to intensify domestic unemployment. It is true that there has recently been a change of opinion — not unchallenged in certain quarters — favourable to a flexible Bank Rate policy. But this change of opinion and this difference of opinion relate to an entirely different matter to the one here under discussion, namely, to the use of a tight credit policy to check any tendency towards internal inflation. This was out of vogue after the war ; it has recently come into vogue again, and, although there are certain murmurs, there is no really strong opposition to the view that a tight credit policy is quite a sensible method of checking internal inflation, and that it should be used again if there is a recurrence of the disease. The use of a tight credit policy solely to correct an *external* imbalance is an altogether different matter. The situation might arise when there was no internal inflation and indeed when conditions were getting depressed. For instance, a world-wide recession might have the double effect on Britain of creating unemployment and putting her external balance wrong.

It would be almost universally agreed that the method of deflation and tight credit was an utterly unsuitable one for dealing with such a situation, on the ground that it would tend to intensify internal depression. No pundits now, not the Bank of England or anyone else, could persuade the public to accept a deflationist policy at a time when unemployment was increasing, merely on the ground that it was needed to correct an external balance. There must be a quite clear understanding about that. At first sight this might seem to tend towards a rejection of the use of the Bank Rate for correcting an external imbalance.

But it is necessary to examine the matter more carefully. And it is appropriate to recall the views of Keynes, whose thinking has had such a profound influence in regard to all these matters. In 1931 he had his classic debate with Montagu Norman at the Macmillan Committee. Keynes pressed the view that it should be possible to continue to use interest rate policy as a delicate mechanism for adjusting external payments (short-term capital movements) while simultaneously having a different policy for the internal situation.

It should be possible, he argued, to maintain in appropriate circumstances a relatively high rate of interest for influencing international payments, while having easy credit for business at home. Such a combination would be appropriate to a recession. This proposal met with an absolute and repeated negative from Montagu Norman. He held that it would be altogether impossible to discriminate between external and internal policy in the way proposed. Speaking with the full authority of Governor, he carried weight.

But much has happened since 1931. Would the authorities subscribe to Montagu Norman's verdict to-day ? Is it not possible to revive Keynes's idea ? Could we not indeed have a policy for shaping short-term interest rates to produce the right effect on the external balance, while screening the internal economy from the effects of high short-term rates at times when an internal disinflationary policy was inappropriate ?

Economists have come to doubt if high short-term rates do have a strong influence on the level of internal fixed capital investment. As regards inventories, there will not be much tendency to increase orders in a time of falling prices whether short-term rates are high or low. For the thermostatic control of the internal economy greater stress is laid on other weapons. We have the idea of Budget deficits, unthinkable in 1931. It is to be hoped that the authorities have many plans for capital outlay in nationalized industries or by the local authorities, in readiness against the possible onset of a recession.

We have also such weapons as the adjustment of depreciation allowances. We have had much experience of management for securing a discrimination between various rates of interest ; we have had the Treasury bill rate separated from the commercial bill rate ; we have had long-term rates rising while short-term rates were held at a low level, and long-term rates falling while short-term rates were held at a high level. Is it not possible that the vast and complex experience of these kinds of management enables us to alter the verdict of Montagu Norman ?

I suggest that we should study most carefully as a possible objective a system by which short-term rates can be moved up and down in accordance with exigencies of the international balance, while the thermostatic control of the internal economy, by ease or stringency in the domestic capital market, proceeds independently. May this be the new pattern for the future ?

4

Convertibility Problems [1]

THE path of virtue does not always run smooth. In many respects the present situation is propitious for a restoration of the convertibility of sterling. The British external balance has been favourable ; the world balance against the dollar area has been favourable, even if we exclude economic 'aid' and the provision by the United States of military end items ; it has depended, it is true, on overseas expenditures by the United States and offshore procurements, but the flow of these has seemed likely to continue unabated for at least another two or three years ; few think that the American authorities will allow their economy to run into a steep recession at a time when the high level of domestic defence expenditure makes it comparatively easy to prevent one ; the modest recession that recently occurred has not had calamitous effects on the non-dollar world. By the re-establishment of commodity markets the British have taken steps to make sterling convertible for some purposes without untoward results ; sterling has been strong in free markets.

As against all this the French vote on EDC has been a setback. Until new arrangements are made that are commonly deemed to fill the gap adequately, there will be uncertainty about the continued flow of U.S. defence expenditures overseas ; any diversion from Europe, where the central core of the dollar

[1] *The Bankers' Magazine*, October 1954.

problem is located, would be awkward. We may hope that matters will be patched up in a way favourable to Europe. But there will be a period in which uncertainties are too great to allow a major move like the restoration of sterling convertibility to be undertaken. A General Election also casts before it, for a certain distance, a shadow of uncertainty. I am confident that if a Labour victory occurred at a time when convertibility was already an established fact, the new Government would do its best to support the policy, seeing, as it would, how much depended, for the Commonwealth and for the British standard of living, on its success. But it might be politically impossible for Labour leaders to give such an undertaking in advance, and, failing a decisive statement by them, the world would remain uncertain. In the period immediately following the restoration, the boat is bound to be heavily rocked. That will have been foreseen and prepared for. But it would not do to have a season of Election campaigning, with its exaggerated and often irresponsible statements, fall within that period. Thus there is a very nice problem of timing.

Amid those short-period perplexities it is always salutary to remind ourselves of basic issues and to clear our minds about the objectives and mode of operation of the system that we envisage when we use the word 'convertibility'. All the more so, if fundamental thinking still needs to be done. The problem of convertibility is not simply that of attaining conditions that will make a return to it possible, but of developing in new circumstances and with new objectives a system of managing our monetary affairs that shall be relatively stable, relieve us of recurrent crises, carry its own criteria for guiding day-to-day policy and be, so far as is possible in the world of to-day, permanent. And if we are anxious to move over from our existing system to a convertible system, that is largely because we know that our existing system, which at times appears to be jogging along sufficiently comfortably, cannot be permanent. If a widespread scepticism developed about our resolve finally to return to convertibility, the existing system would begin to deteriorate.

The old system of convertible sterling had its heyday before 1914, but operated also between 1925 and 1931. Although sterling was the foremost currency in international dealings and was in truth a world currency, we maintained its convertibility on the basis of a very narrow, one might almost say microscopic, gold reserve. This was a conscious and deliberate traditional policy. But we had a secondary reserve of large dimensions consisting in the volume of our short-term overseas loans on London bills, which could be rapidly reduced by a rise of the Bank Rate. Any temporary imbalance in our external payments could be rectified with great speed and efficiency. This was excellent.

But the establishment of high interest rates might have a depressing effect on business at home, causing serious unemployment ; it was on this feature of the gold standard that Keynes made his classic attack. There are those nowadays who doubt if monetary stringency has as strong an effect on activity and employment as used to be supposed, and these might question whether the raising of the Bank Rate, together with all its financial consequences, were really responsible for the bouts of depressed activity and unemployment that used to occur. Even if that is correct, it can still be held as an indictment against the old system that it contained no corrective against the generation of massive unemployment through a decline of foreign trade activity. The first impact of a shrinkage in overseas markets would be looked after by the reduction of lending abroad (via the higher Bank Rate) ; then the country would swing into a condition of depression to match the depression occurring overseas ; the consequent reduction in its need for raw materials and in the availability of incomes for spending would reduce imports in line with the fall of exports, and a rough balance of external payments would thus be achieved automatically.

It cannot be too much stressed that, convertibility or no convertibility, there is now no question of a return to such a system. All parties envisage that in the event of a depression developing overseas, whether originating in the United States or elsewhere, we should apply correctives to sustain employment here ; our activity would not be allowed to swing down to match what was proceeding abroad ; still less would active deflationary measures be employed. It is true that there is still occasionally to be heard in certain circles talk of the 'old medicine' ; those are mere idle words ; responsible persons know that ; any attempts to apply the 'old medicine' to-day would be the surest recipe for getting full-blooded socialism to-morrow. The system for securing our external balance by keeping resources idle is recognized as uneconomic, irrational and unacceptable. It must not be supposed that rejection of the 'old medicine' is merely a matter of political expediency. Might it not be worth while, it is sometimes plausibly argued, to let national income run down for periods from time to time, if that were the price of getting a system that worked smoothly and automatically ? That question might be worth considering seriously if the loss of income were widely diffused and evenly borne; but, unfortunately, those thrown out of work are partic-ular people, many with dependent families. Such a victimiza-tion of the few is now rightly rejected by the social conscience.

Thus the system underlying, as distinct from the mere fact of, convertibility will have to be different in certain funda-mental respects from that of olden times. In the period from 1931 to 1939 we lived under a somewhat different system. Sterling was inconvertible, but marketable at a freely floating rate, which was, however, heavily doctored by the authorities. (Sterling was always considered at that time to be 'incon-vertible', but by the new-fangled jargon by which some pro-pose that sterling should be made 'convertible at a freely-floating rate' we are invited to reverse the usage of many generations and pronounce sterling to have been convertible during the classic periods of inconvertibility.) In 1931 we were driven helter-skelter off the gold standard, partly because an important section (the German) of our external reserve was immobilized ; we had no thought-out system to put in its place ; it did not look impossible in the autumn of 1931 that sterling might fall to a very low level. But things turned out differently ; the havoc of the slump was world-wide and Britain was not in fact one of the great economies that were worst hit ; this was soon appreciated and confidence in the future of sterling revived. At first, hopes in Britain were pinned to the favourable effects of the depreciation of sterling on exports ; but it must always be remembered that, unlike the depreciation of 1949, the depreciation of 1931 was short-lived, owing to the action of President Roosevelt in devaluing the dollar in 1933. Thus this period is not one in which we can learn much about the effects

F

on trade of devaluation ; nor is it one in which we can learn much about the rectifying effects of a freely-floating rate, since in fact after 1933 the rate was held fairly steady until the menace of trouble from Hitler became immediate. What particularly characterizes that period is that we gave up the use of the Bank Rate to level short-period discrepancies in our external balance of payments and instead had what was by British precedents a very large gold reserve, mainly held by the Exchange Equalization Account and actively used. The low Bank Rate and easy money conditions were required at home to stimulate employment. The period does not give a decisive lesson in favour of the view that such moderate oscillations as were allowed in the exchange rate were adequate by themselves to preserve an even or favourable external balance in varying conditions ; and reserves were larger then than they are now in relation to the annual value of current payments.

During the war things were kept going in Britain by severe restrictionism and control, some measure of bilateralism, aid in various forms, and the piling up of open obligations in the shape of sterling balances. Meanwhile the Atlantic Charter was a call to the authorities to consider the face of things to come. The Americans felt that restrictionism and bilateralism were inimical to world prosperity and thereby to peace, that multilateralism and the freeing of trade from administrative shackles should be the goals, and that some stability and order should be reintroduced into the foreign exchanges. But it was recognized that the governments of nations sorely stricken by the war would not be ready to cast down barriers quickly nor restore currency convertibility, whether owing to their grave genuine difficulties, to a faint heart, or to some perverse inclination towards administrative meddling and manœuvre. It was recognized that a move towards unshackled trade could not be encompassed without some new form of financial support. And there also on the scene was Keynes, having by now full British support and much influence on the American negotiators, setting his face against any system of convertibility that had as its corollary the need for periodic deflations.

From the discussions there emerged, after much give and take, the International Monetary Fund plan. In considering how this was to provide a currency system for a brave new world, it is well to consider the thought behind it, rather than the actual Articles of Agreement. Three points may be mentioned. First, there was to be a kind of super-reserve which would provide ample liquidity for all members and relieve them of the necessity for restrictionism and jiggering with exchange controls to meet temporary difficulties. Secondly, there was to be the possibility of an agreed alteration in the exchange rate of a nation in which costs and prices had got hopelessly out of line with those outside. Thirdly, if a nation tended to be in a chronic disequilibrium of payments, whether on the debit or credit side, it would have to take special remedies. The debit nation would presumably — though there was some lack of clarity here — have to impose restrictions ; for the chronically credit nation the 'scarce currency' clause was designed, which would entitle all other nations to discriminate against it in an orderly way.

I recall attention to these principles because they represent the last attempt to devise a system which should enable currencies to function smoothly without periodic resort to deflation and severe unemployment. And, if a number of countries come towards the verge of making their currencies convertible, it behoves us to consider whether it is indeed these principles that will be applied or whether there are other remedies for external imbalance, tried or untried, available for countries of convertible currency to use in place of the 'old medicine'.

The International Monetary Fund is still with us. The fact that it has so far been to a large extent inactive is not by itself evidence that it is unusable for its purposes. Post-war maladjustments and difficulties have exceeded all expectations : nations have fallen victim to inflations that have made it impossible for them to play the rules of any game, new or old, in foreign exchange policy. And in these conditions it was impossible for the International Monetary Fund to play its prescribed game either.

Many of the post-war clouds have cleared away, although there are still serious maladjustments due to the war. But it can hardly be claimed that these are of a kind to preclude the introduction of an orderly workable system for adjusting disequilibria, if one can be found. Indeed a good system should have power to rectify maladjustments. The time has come to take a long view. The urge to convertibility in various quarters is a symptom of that.

How, then, do we stand in regard to the three IMF principles? First, it must be said frankly that the Fund cannot be regarded as a super-reserve. The British always thought that it was much too small. They may have held, and I believe that in the beginning some of its American sponsors held, that it would be better to let Congress take two bites at the cherry. After all, if the Fund had been working actively and successfully for two or three years, the Americans would not have been likely to let the whole scheme break down for lack of replenishment. The additional sum needed would, by comparison with the sums involved in Marshall Aid, have been modest. It is quite a different matter to consider replenishment for an institution which has been inactive and, by ordinary standards, lacking in success. Furthermore, since the inception of the Fund all currencies, including the dollar, have undergone a great inflation, so that even had the reserve indeed been adequate for its prescribed tasks in 1945, it would be grossly inadequate now. Thus, the existence of this reserve fund makes far less difference to the situation confronting us than the war-time planners hoped it would. It does not follow that we need despair.

In regard to the second principle (currency devaluation), I believe that this was not sufficiently analysed at the time and that views about it have since changed rather considerably. There are circumstances when devaluation is a proper and indeed the only available remedy, for instance if a nation's costs and prices have got quite out of line with those in the rest of the world. It is not practical politics to expect all wage- and salary-earners to allow their emoluments to be scaled down, in the hope of a corresponding fall in the cost of living. This was essentially the case against the upward revaluation of sterling in 1925. I believe that in 1945 devaluation may have been thought of as a remedy of wider application. It was believed that if a nation proved to be in chronic difficulties with its balance of payments, devaluation was a panacea. Some British had it in mind that Britain's relative recovery in the 'thirties had been due to the devaluation of sterling in 1931, forgetting that in that part of the period when recovery was marked — after 1933 — sterling was not devalued relatively to the dollar, owing to Roosevelt's devaluation of the dollar.

There are conditions, other than a rise of internal costs, that may cause balance of payments difficulties. For instance, a country that has been mainly dependent on a single export may find that world demand has declined, owing to the discovery of a substitute or otherwise. Currency devaluation cannot then be regarded as a sure remedy for its external problem. Or a war, by temporarily cutting off certain channels of trade, may cause large changes in the pattern of world production and consumption that are not readily reversible. There is still what is known as a 'structural' imbalance between the dollar and non-dollar worlds, masked in the recent period by U.S. military expenditures overseas and by discriminatory restrictions on dollar imports in a number of countries. It is not likely that a change in the rate at which the dollar is exchanged for other currencies would suffice to correct this. Britain in particular maintains a number of restrictions on dollar imports. Few still believe that a change in the dollar-sterling rate would enable her to dispense with these. Some have supposed that there is some rate of exchange at which trade must balance ; this is a fallacy. In certain circumstances the depreciation of its currency may so turn the terms of trade against a country as to make its balance worse rather than better. Revaluation of currencies, as allowed by the International Monetary Fund, may be advisable in carefully defined conditions. It should not be regarded as a panacea, and too much reliance may have been placed on it by the founders of the Fund.

To proceed to the third principle, the fact that a chronic debtor must in the last resort take special measures to improve its balance is a platitude. On the other hand, the idea that a chronically credit country should be put in the dock was a great novelty. In regard to the possible working of the 'scarce currency' clause in future, one must have two misgivings. The action of the Fund, if ever it took it, in giving members official authority to discriminate against dollar imports would be bound to cause annoyance in the United States. In the period since the war, even a Fund on which the Americans had no votes would have been wise not to give this annoyance at a time when the Americans were so generously disposed to fill the dollar gap in other ways. The future is another question. There is doubt whether the Fund would adopt this measure readily, as occasion might require. According to the British intention members of the Fund were to be entitled to draw out their quotas as of right, just as an individual uses a banking overdraft facility already granted, or members of the European Payments Union have obtained credit from it without discussion to the limits allowed by its rules. If this procedure obtained at the Fund, its hand would be forced in a time of world-wide dollar scarcity, since it would in fact run short of dollars and have to declare them technically 'scarce'. But the Fund has adopted the different procedure of only allowing a drawing after discussion — save for 'stand-by credits' to meet exceptional cases which are themselves subject to discussion. By discretion in the granting of credits the Fund has it in its power to prevent the dollar becoming 'scarce' in the technical sense.

There is a more formidable difficulty. It was the British idea that on the occasion of 'scarcity' all members should restrict their dollar expenditures, no doubt on some proportionate plan but having regard also to special needs. But at a late stage in the negotiations a clause crept into the 'Articles of Agreement' disallowing restriction to particular members for whom dollars are not in fact in short supply. This introduces a bilateral element into the plan entirely inconsistent with the multilateral philosophy of the Fund. Some might hold that it renders this famous 'scarce currency' clause almost nugatory, since the nations individually short of dollars would be bound to limit their dollar purchases in any case. (On the other hand it might be held as a saving grace that it gives official sanction to their confining their restrictions to dollar imports, as distinct from imposing general import restrictions, which would transmit the trouble in ever-widening circles.) Far different was the original conception that all should join together in limiting the purchases of a scarce currency and thus sharing the burden widely, instead of throwing it all onto those countries which happen, by the accident of the multilateral pattern of trade, to be in normal dollar deficit. Furthermore, this objectionable clause is reminiscent of war-time bilateralism, with its distinction between hard and soft currencies, from which the Fund was supposed to be about to rescue the world. When all currencies are convertible, as was planned, there is no meaning in distinguishing between the countries in good supply of dollars and those lacking dollars ; as viewed by any particular country the dollar is, in that case, the same as any other foreign currency. What happens when the dollar approaches the point of scarcity in those conditions is that in the various free foreign exchange markets of the world it rises to the point at which it becomes cheaper to remit gold (and at the same time becomes scarce in the Fund). In those circumstances, which particular country is in good supply of dollars and which country lacks them depends on the mere accident of which has done what last in the arbitrage markets.

There is an even graver aspect of this question. A fully multilateral scarce currency clause would not only be unpopular with the Americans, but also with those countries which are normally in bilateral dollar surplus. For they would be asked to restrict dollar purchases when it was not strictly necessary for them as particular countries to do so. They could only be persuaded to do this if it was clearly presented to them as their required contribution to a general scheme, which was in other respects working smoothly. How far away we are from all that.

And so it has regretfully to be admitted that for nations contemplating a restoration of convertibility the existence of the International Monetary Fund does not make that great difference to the likely modes of working of currency relations that was intended by its founders. It may indeed be able to perform valuable service, but its existence cannot be held to justify a crucial change in the principles that should govern a nation's foreign exchange policy.

In the face of vast losses and new burdens Britain has maintained solvency since the war — not without American aid — by various methods which may be broadly classed under two heads. (I omit domestic measures to promote exports.) On the one hand, she has maintained severe restrictions on imports; on the other, she has created a kind of protection for her exports to certain markets by limiting the transferability of non-resident sterling and particularly by not allowing its transfer to the American account area. Both modes of self-protection have also been hurtful to her, the former obviously, since it is hurtful not to be able to acquire desired goods at the best price, the latter in more subtle ways.

A currency subject to limits on the right of transferability is in that respect inferior to one having no such limitation. This is a handicap, although, as events have shown, not a fatal one, to the building up of various forms of 'invisible' exports. For a highly populated country of limited natural resources, these are the best of all kinds of exports, since the qualities in the last analysis that make the foreigner willing to pay for them are intelligence, integrity, and reputation for gentlemanly conduct in business relations.

There is another even more important point. If the world ever settled down to a natural pattern of multilateral trade, and it is slowly moving in that direction, it is probable that the direct bilateral account of Britain, and even of the whole sterling area, with the dollar area would be adverse, the deficit being met from a surplus with the third-party world, whose exports to the dollar area are expected to rise in the coming decades. This implies the winning of dollars by Britain in multilateral settlement. But it may be taken as an axiom that third parties will not in the long run and as a regular practice be willing to give a convertible currency in discharge of an obligation expressed in an inconvertible currency; Britain cannot expect to exchange her sterling for dollars in multilateral settlement, unless she is regularly willing as occasion arises to give dollars for sterling. This is a simple point, but it is absolutely fundamental.

Finally, it must be said that the protection to Britain's solvency that has been given by inconvertibility cannot be expected to endure for ever. It endured during the confused period of transition, and it has endured recently because there is confidence in the future of sterling; the wide use and acceptance of transferable account sterling and its high quotation in free markets have been heartening symptoms of confidence. But once grave doubt gained ground as to whether Britain intended to carry the matter further, a reversal of tendency would occur. The protection given by inconvertibility is based on the fact that a third-party country, finding itself short of dollars, is willing to impose sterner restrictions on dollar imports than on sterling imports, thus giving British exporters an advantage. But there is always some restiveness, and a hope that this will not be a permanent state of affairs. If there was grave discouragement as regards the prospects of eventual convertibility, nations would be less willing to accept sterling in settlement and Britain would find herself subject to progressively greater pressure in bilateral negotiations for settlement, in whole or in part, in gold or dollars. In fine the long-run alternatives are for Britain herself to take the initiative by making sterling convertible at the appropriate time, or to have a piecemeal convertibility forced on her by others, step by step, to the accompaniment of a whittling away of the international position of sterling.

Thus it should be her aim to work clear of both of these two forms of post-war protection (import restriction and inconvertibility), as soon as the time is ripe. But there is a difference between the two processes. The reduction of her own import restrictions can proceed gradually according to circumstances, as it has already proceeded, and the movement can even be reversed if necessary, albeit, one hopes, always reluctantly ; but the establishment of convertibility for non-residents would be a large once-over move, the reversal of which would be disastrous. As its consequences cannot be measured, it is evident that the decks must be cleared for it, and round about the time of its occurrence progress with the other forms of dismantlement must be cautious. Our American friends are right in arguing that the removal of restrictions and the establishment of convertibility should be regarded as complementary moves towards the multilateral ideal. But they will readily understand that if a sudden large move is to be taken along one line, a temporary halt may be necessary in progress along the other.

In regard to import restriction, unhappily, something more fundamental has to be said. In the earlier part of this article I have been at pains to make a number of negative propositions. It cannot be taken as axiomatic that a nation's external balance will adjust itself automatically in the face of large changes. We have seen that what I have called 'the old medicine' (deflation, or simply allowing unemployment to develop), which appears to have been sufficiently potent to adjust our external balance in the old days, is now utterly unacceptable. The hopes pinned to devaluation or freely-floating rates appear to have been excessive. The creation of the International Monetary Fund has not, as its founders hoped, provided a radical remedy, although it may well be of considerable service. It is hard to escape the conclusion that, so far as our wisdom has at present taken us, reliance will still have to be placed on import restriction as the cure of last resort for an external imbalance. This is particularly true of the period, of which we have unhappily not yet reached the end, in which the pattern of world trade has not adapted itself to a post-war equilibrium.

A gold (or foreign currency) reserve should be adequate to cover sudden shocks (including that of convertibility!) and to see a country through the first stages of a longer-term mal-adjustment. But it is futile to suppose it possible to build up a gold reserve large enough to finance a continuing deficit on current account, such as some change in the external scene can cause. The only reserve against that is to have a margin of unnecessary imports that can be cut down. This must not be thought of as being in general a restrictive doctrine. Quite the contrary. A country should aim at having in fair weather a large amount of imports not strictly necessary. This gives it the only known reserve against bad weather.

In all international negotiations Britain should make it plain that this is the position, reserving her freedom, and should also seek the co-operation both of the sterling area and of Europe. The way is not yet clear for permanent unconditional liberalization commitments (although within the family of European countries these commitments should be hard).

But in regard to convertibility I hold that, subject to what I have written in the opening paragraphs (EDC and General Election problems), we should be thinking in terms of an early restoration. It is a British interest, and of course a world interest, that sterling should be convertible. Confidence is good now and might with prolonged delays begin to decline, which would make the technical operation more perilous. We have the advantage of overseas American expenditures, which are likely to continue for some time. The great unknown is the increased dollar expenditure that would occur, if the various nations removed their remaining discriminatory restrictions on dollar imports, a process which sterling convertibility would undoubtedly have some tendency to expedite. Mr. Triffin, a high authority, has estimated that if all such discrimination were removed, the increase in world dollar expenditure would only be £725 million. (*Quarterly Review of Banca Nazionale del Lavoro.*) That may be optimistic. Even if the figure were somewhat larger it would not, given the maintenance of U.S. military expenditures, cause any great pressure to obtain dollars via sterling. I do not think that the fact that the great underlying problems of international equilibrium remain unsolved should deter us. The fact does entitle us to maintain the right to use discrimination, as and when required, despite American pressure in the opposite sense. But we want convertibility on its own account and for our own sake. It would be very disappointing if we had not achieved it at the end of another quinquennium. Looking at that period as a whole, we may well judge that the circumstances are more favourable for taking the initial shock now, or soon, than they may be later.

5

Comment by Dr. Erhard and Rejoinder

TO THE EDITOR OF 'THE BANKERS' MAGAZINE'

SIR — Although I am not sure whether your readers will be interested in another letter on Convertibility Problems after having read Mr. Harrod's brilliant article [1] and the instructive discussion between Mr. Hawtrey and the author,[2] I should very much like to say a few words about these problems.

I believe Mr. Harrod did a very useful thing when he raised the question of the new currency system 'that shall be relatively stable, relieve us of recurrent crises, carry its own criteria for guiding day-to-day policy and be, so far as is possible in the world of to-day, permanent'. It will not be convertibility alone that will bring about this new system, although it will largely contribute to an equilibrium of the balances of payments of countries and to the liberalization of trade. The European

[1] 'Convertibility Problems', by Roy Harrod, *The Bankers' Magazine*, October 1954, pp. 299-307.
[2] *The Bankers' Magazine*, November 1954, pp. 393-394, December 1954, pp. 482-484 and January 1955, pp. 5-8.

Payments Union, which has introduced a kind of regionally limited non-resident convertibility, has been and still is a considerable support for the multilateral liberalization within the OEEC area (that is to say, with the defects which are necessarily part of a regional system).   It will not be different for the whole world when European currencies are convertible, that is to say, when they will also be convertible into dollars.

But I am in full agreement with Mr. Harrod that the problem of convertibility is not simply one 'of attaining conditions that will make a return to it possible'.   If I understand him correctly, Mr. Harrod's claims quoted at the beginning of my letter imply neither more nor less than a currency system which will give us *to-day* 'in new circumstances and with new objectives' what Peel gave us *in his time* with the Banking Act.   I am only afraid — and here I am in agreement with Mr. Hawtrey — that Mr. Harrod knows the new system no better than others.   The resort to import restrictions — even as a last expedient for achieving an equilibrium in the balance of payments — perturbs me.   Are import restrictions really a remedy which we must consider, and is it not dangerous to remind ourselves of their existence while at the same time we in Europe are making every effort to remove, not merely exchange control, but all quantitative restrictions as well ?

If we leave aside exceptional circumstances such as, for instance, those which we experienced after the war, we know that difficulties in the balance of payments of one or of several countries, and consequently also difficulties of maintaining convertibility and a free international trade, can only come about if countries differ in pursuing an expansive or restrictive policy.   We know from bitter experience in the 'thirties that the maintenance of a system of convertible currencies enforces an international interdependence in business activity and that a deflationary policy in a country which is important for world economy must initiate a correspondingly restrictive policy in other countries, which in fact is neither possible politically nor sensible from the economic point of view.   But are we not still too much influenced by bad experiences in the past when considering the future of convertibility and of free trade ?   Is it still necessary to reckon with economic crises of greater extent, and can we not hope, after the recent recession in the United

States, that minor fluctuations in the business activity of one country can be without serious consequences for others ? Surely the new system of international payment relations will not be characterized by a lack of sophistication and automatism, as before 1914, and the future convertibility of currencies will presumably require certain administrative aids. The International Monetary Fund and the European Fund which has just been discussed will be able to perform useful services in this respect.

When aiming at convertibility it will be necessary to accept once again this interdependence in business activity regardless of the form which the future currency system of countries will take. One could even go as far as to define convertibility as a system of international interdependence in business activity. But, much more so than before 1914, this new international community would have to *think* internationally — rather as an organized equilibrium, perhaps, which is achieved by a mutual international adjustment of the economic development in each country. Already, an encouraging beginning has been made, especially in OEEC, which ought to be further developed. The good creditor and debtor policies must be discussed jointly in an organization of creditors and debtors, and must be achieved by one method or another. There seems to be no alternative. This may seem to involve a considerable willingness on the part of nations to renounce a part of their sovereignty, but it would involve no more self-restraint than states have imposed upon themselves in former times by observing the rules of the classical gold standard.

Yours faithfully,
LUDWIG ERHARD,
Minister for Economic Affairs of the German Federal Republic

Bonn/Rhine,
Germany,
21st January 1955

TO THE EDITOR OF 'THE BANKERS' MAGAZINE'

SIR — In regard to Dr. Erhard's letter in your issue of February I need say little more than that I am in almost complete agreement with it. I am sure that your readers will feel it to be a most important and encouraging contribution.

I appreciate his point that, at a time when we are striving to terminate restrictions, too much talk about the ultimate need for restrictions in hypothetical conditions endangers a weakening in the all-important resolve to get rid of them as quickly as possible. But there is another side of the matter. The Americans, who are helping us in so many ways, attach great importance to the dismantling of restrictionism; and it is a point of honour that we should be most careful, in statement no less than in commitment, not to raise hopes that might later be incapable of realization.

There are still two contingencies in which that might happen — an unexpected and abrupt termination of U.S. expenditures overseas and an American slump. In regard to the former, the international situation *unhappily* makes it improbable that the contingency will arise in the near future. In regard to the latter, I have a good record since 1945 in deprecating both the notion that there must be a severe American slump, and the notion that a slump, if it comes, is most likely to originate in the United States. None the less, this is a contingency which we still cannot dismiss from our minds. It might, if it arose, make it desirable to have concerted restrictions on imports from the U.S. on the lines envisaged in the Scarce Currency Clause of the International Monetary Fund; it might also happen, if there were practical difficulties in regard to that Clause, that it would be desirable to concert restrictions by other methods.

There is one final point that should be mentioned in this context. Dr. Erhard is no doubt aware of British anxieties about the apparently strong adhesion on the part of Latin American countries to a bilateral system of settlement. This may render more difficult the achievement of that unrestricted multilateral trade that we all desire. It is natural for the countries of Europe, taken as a group, to have a direct bilateral deficit with the dollar area; before the war this was settled without difficulty by the shipment of newly-mined gold, coming mainly from the sterling area. That mode of payment having shrunk to small dimensions, the most natural method of multilateral settlement would be for the European countries to earn dollars in Latin America. The prospects in this respect still seem poor. Unfortunately, if one channel in a multilateral system is blocked, that may necessitate a restriction, however undesirable, in other channels.

Frankness requires that these difficulties should be mentioned. But they should not diminish our efforts towards removing restrictions in the present favourable circumstances.

I am, etc.,
ROY HARROD

POSTSCRIPT

When it was announced, on 20th February 1955, that the British authorities would intervene to support transferable sterling in the free markets, I uttered a loud whoop of joy. This struck me as the most important step in the history of British reconstructive efforts since the war. But almost at once I met a sage and discreet friend, whose views I was bound to treat with the utmost respect. While sharing my opinion of the importance of what had been done, he informed me that it would not be helpful to the British authorities to underline this for the time being. Accordingly I felt inhibited from publishing my sense of joy.

I venture to call attention to my restraint on that occasion. From time to time I have expressed views that have been obnoxious, and even embarrassing, to the authorities, and I can hardly hope that occasions will not again occur when I shall feel impelled to do so. But I have always made it a rule to consider whether saying anything embarrassing to the authorities might be harmful to the national interest, and on such occasions I have refrained. This was a case in point.

I was told that the article to appear next did cause some embarrassment ; but I had no compunction on that occasion.

CHAPTER V

THE BRITISH BOOM, 1954–55

On 30th November 1954 I went, after a busy day, to a banquet given by the Institute of Certified and Incorporated Account-ants. I was there informed, to my surprise, that an article, which I had published that morning in *The Financial Times*, had caused a set-back in the gilt-edged market. This allegation subsequently appeared in several newspapers. I was surprised, but also pleased, as an upward movement in the gilt-edged rate seemed expedient on the occasion of a gathering investment boom tending towards inflation.

I am not so pleased by what has happened since. I little thought at the time that the set-back of that day would prove a landmark visible for many years thereafter. Gilt-edged prices have never since recovered to their level of 30th November 1954, but have continued on a long course downwards.

What was in my mind then was the use of the monetary weapon as a delicate instrument. I assumed that a short and sharp shakedown would suffice to curb inflationary tendencies and that, when this phase was past, the authorities would stage a recovery. But in the years that followed, a tribe of deflation-ists, whom one had supposed defunct, emerged from their lairs.

Meanwhile, other things have happened. The fall in the yields of good equities below gilt-edged yields, not in itself undesirable, has set a new problem for monetary management, via the 'interest rate structure', which has not yet been solved ; indeed serious thought about it has hardly begun.

In retrospect, the following article seems rather mild in relation to the strength of the boom that had developed. I referred to the deflationary measures for which I asked as being 'quickly reversible', and to the possibility of moving in the opposite direction 'next spring'. But it has to be observed that, despite the admirably docile behaviour of the gilt-edged market in relation to my article, the steps for which I asked in it were not taken by the authorities at the time. Had they been taken promptly, it is quite possible that fairly moderate measures would have sufficed. That is the whole essence of the art of monetary management. Policy should be flexible. If one acts very promptly, then the action may not have to be drastic. It may be, however, that the situation had got already a little more out of hand than I allowed for in my article. If that was so, the authorities, who presumably had much more information at their disposal than I had, should have known it.

The delay of several months transformed the situation. By mid-1955 the boom had gathered a tremendous momentum, and far more drastic steps were required than would have been necessary nine months earlier. It is true that the Bank Rate was raised by $\frac{1}{2}$ per cent in January 1955, but this was regarded as derisory. It was raised by another 1 per cent at the end of February, but this was partly actuated by the motive of supporting the *de facto* convertibility of sterling, referred to in the last chapter. There was a certain tightening in monetary policy in the spring of 1955, and I believe that this had a salutary effect.

6

A Drift Towards Inflation? [1]

ARE we drifting into a condition of semi-inflation ? Even one who is by no means inclined towards austerity and deflation at every turn, but rather the contrary, may feel some anxiety at present. In this business of monetary management timely action is of the essence. It is an old adage that the only effective way of curing depressions is to check the antecedent booms. In the course of a boom the pattern of activity gets progressively shifted, with a piling-up of orders upon producer goods industries. The further the shift goes, the greater the readjustment required afterwards, and, while no one wants to carry the subsequent deflation to the point of causing significant unemployment, the readjustment in the depression will be much more difficult if the previous expansion has been allowed to go too far.

[1] *The Financial Times*, 30th November 1954.

G

There are further advantages in early action. If the inflationary tendency has not gathered great momentum, the pressure required to correct it may be slight; and if events show it to have been undue, it can be quickly reversed. But if the authorities show any inertia in dealing with a situation tending towards inflation, the lapse of even three or four months can aggravate it considerably. The circumstances and criteria for action now are quite different from those of the old gold-standard days. But it is well to remember how frequently the authorities then, although working for somewhat different objectives, altered the Bank Rate. The mere fact that it was a Thursday morning created a flutter of interest in the City.

Signs of incipient inflation cannot now be culled from the movement of general prices. But long ago, in the 'twenties, the Federal Reserve System recognized that to wait for general price movements before correcting an upward or downward tendency would often mean waiting too long. The state of the labour market is important. A visible indicator is the number of 'unfilled vacancies', which has been rising substantially during the year and stands at a higher level than it has reached since the change in coverage of the figures in March 1952. This is supplemented by increasing reports of labour shortages. Deliveries of certain classes of steel are becoming protracted. This can easily have a snowballing effect, for once the fear of delivery trouble becomes at all widespread, one can easily get that tendency, to stock up as an insurance against expected shortages, which was so disastrous in the period before 1951–52. In the old days great attention would have been paid to the comparative weakness of sterling in foreign exchange markets. While we may accept as correct the obvious diagnosis that this is mainly due to the impression that the D-day for sterling convertibility has been put back somewhat, it would be unwise to assume that the old link between sterling quotations and an inflationary tendency has been completely severed.

I am not suggesting that more than a mild dose of disinflationist medicine is required at present. For this purpose the monetary mechanism is presumably appropriate. Hopes are now placed on the combined influence of monetary and fiscal policies being sufficient to iron out the trade cycle. The fiscal weapon must be regarded as the more slowly working remedy ; the British are used to their annual Budgets, and we cannot reckon on an immediate response to tax adjustments. I do not argue that we must necessarily acquiesce in this ; it is not inconceivable that investment allowances could be turned into a short-period stabilizer by making orders placed within certain months ineligible for the allowance or eligible for only a proportion of it ; this could prove a stabilizer of terrific potency. Accountants, tax authorities, and others concerned with the details of such adjustments would raise their hands in horror at such a 'fancy' proposal. We should not be too much deterred by such expostulations ; we live in a scientific age ; awkward arrangements demanded by scientists in a factory are often regarded as 'musts', and similar awkwardnesses may in due course have to be imposed on those concerned with accounts by the science of economics.

But for the moment these are pipe-dreams, and we must revert to the Bank Rate mechanism. A small rise of Bank Rate, reversing expectations earlier in the year of a further downward movement, would have a psychological impact ; it would be noted as signifying that the authorities endorse what many people are already 'feeling in their bones' about the inflationary element in the present situation. But the symbol is not enough by itself. The traditional method of open-market operations is available, by which the cash supply of the banks can be reduced. This in turn can be reinforced by suitable advices. The instructions given to banks during the 1951-52 episode had their effect ; various orders on capital account were suspended.

Some may hold that, while it is comparatively easy to get a strong instruction carried into practice over a wide area on the occasion of an admitted national crisis, it is more difficult to introduce fine shades into such instructions. We do not now need a drastic curtailment of orders, but only a moderate amount of postponement by those in doubt, in fact by the 'marginal' orderers. We need the banks to be a little more severe for a short period in granting accommodation, until existing pressures ease off. The difficulty of introducing fine shades into such instructions is not a good reason for not trying to do so. Full employment policy, executed by monetary and fiscal pressures, is still in its infancy and on its first trial. The bankers up and down the country, who alone can make such a policy effective, have to be trained in their new task. It is essential that the policy should be flexible and quickly reversible. This is an apt moment for experimenting with the mechanism ; the economy is at present in a condition of fairly robust health and no great harm can be done. The harm may come later if nothing is done now.

If the authorities find it desirable to move in the opposite direction next spring, that would not justify *ex post* criticism of a certain stiffening now. We may recall the experience of the Federal Reserve System in 1953 ; in the preceding winter the arms programme of the United States seemed still to be engendering inflationary pressure, and brakes were applied by the Federal Reserve System ; by the late spring of 1953 the engines were reversed, and a large-scale enlargement of the cash basis, including a reduction of legal reserve requirements, was undertaken by the system. This did not imply a contradiction, but a quick response to a changing situation.

It will be said, in objection to the proposal for a stiffer monetary policy now, that it would make no difference to the policy or action of the great majority of producers. That is quite correct. We only need to affect a minority. All we need is to give an additional reason for delay to those who are in doubt. In a situation such as the present a curtailment of total orders by no more than 2 or 3 per cent might make all the difference.

In some quarters there is undue anxiety lest such a policy might reduce investment by British industry. Since 1945, 'investment' has become something of a fetish ; it is quite wrong to give an unqualified blessing to investment as such, which may often be wasteful and often postponable without detriment. All depends on the kind and quality of the investment. It is of vital importance to make British industry more ready to undertake cost-reducing investment, to experiment promptly with new ideas, to push forward rapidly in all spheres where technological improvement is possible. We need much more thought about measures of long-term influence to encourage progress of that kind. But the greater part of investment is not of that kind. Furthermore, a disinflationary policy can be useful in discouraging additions to stock — which by creating shortages can have a vicious spiral effect. Long-term considerations about investment should not be allowed to interfere with restraints and encouragements designed to keep the economy on an even keel and avoid inflationary or deflationary tendencies. The success of such a policy will, in its turn, help long-term planning.

7

Bank Rate [1]

MANAGEMENT of the Bank Rate cannot, unhappily, be based on an exact science. Judgement is required to interpret trends that cannot be exactly measured. The title of Mr. Hawtrey's great classic *The Art of Central Banking* indicates how matters stand. Policy could not be reduced to rules of thumb even if we had exact daily figures for everything that we require in theory to know. For behind the figures are motives, and these too have to be assessed. The entrepreneurs, whose various orders serve to determine the recorded figures, are actuated by various motives, often mixed and not always clear-cut, which have to be interpreted. We have not at any moment full insight into their minds, and many would be unable to give a precise and absolutely reliable account themselves. The authorities have to use their skill in interpreting the general situation.

There is one cardinal maxim for the authorities : early action is indispensable. Mr. Hawtrey has himself done much over many years to expound and explain the importance of this. If matters are allowed to drift in an inflationary or deflationary direction, the corrective will be more difficult and more liable to have harmful repercussions.

In some circumstances the authorities may be reasonably reluctant to take early action. If they are uncertain whether a corrective is needed, and if they fear that the corrective will make the shoe pinch somewhere, they may be understandably reluctant to move. In this regard we are in a happy position in Britain at present. It would be difficult to argue that in existing conditions a tightening of credit would cause hardship. Thus

[1] *The Bankers' Magazine*, March 1955.

the choice almost seems made for us. To allow a drift towards an inflationary situation to continue always has evil consequences in the end ; to exert a moderate restrictive pressure on an economy so buoyant as ours is at present, cannot inflict serious injury. Indeed there is something to be said for the maxim that it may be expedient to move somewhat in a restrictive direction, even if one has no great apprehension that things are getting out of hand, simply to be better placed for action later ; for example, for applying the stimulus of credit relaxation. It may be something of this sort that the American authorities have recently had in mind. Unemployment there is still considerable and it must have been quite a hard choice to decide to abandon the policy of 'active ease'.

There is one respect in which our notion of how the art of maintaining stability should be exerted has changed in recent years. We no longer believe that the automatic repercussions of Bank Rate changes and open-market operations are as decisive in influencing a given situation as their advocates used to believe. Much has been argued about the unresponsiveness of the economy to these changes. Professor Shackle surveyed some aspects of this controversy in a recent issue of *The Bankers' Magazine* (June 1954).[1] But if we are more dubious of the automatic effects of certain measures, we are also better placed to supplement them. It is understood that the whole banking system is willing, by an agreement reached through discussion, to modify its lending policy in the directions of greater stiffness, or of greater ease, as the situation requires. A stiffening was executed by this method in 1951–52 and had salutary effects. What is required now is not only a stiff Bank Rate, but an agreement by which the banks will, for the time being, make accommodation somewhat less easy to obtain. We want to see an actual thinning out of orders placed by firms. This does not mean that all or most firms will change their policy in any way ; the great majority will no doubt proceed as they intended ; but if a number of firms near the margin are influenced by accommodation difficulties to postpone certain orders, that is the effect we require.

It can be argued that it might be difficult to get the whole

---

[1] 'Bank Rate and the Modernisation of Industry', by G. L. S. Shackle, *The Bankers' Magazine*, June 1954, pp. 553-556.

banking system to move together first in one direction and then in the opposite direction from time to time. In 1951 it was understood that we were involved in rather a special crisis of greater magnitude than anything confronting us to-day ; this no doubt influenced the willingness to co-operate. Reluctance to try to carry the banks along in rather frequent changes of policy is understandable, but misplaced. It would no doubt be easier if the high authorities in the Bank of England, by adjusting their levers from time to time, could do all the required work in glorious isolation. But we do not now believe that they can. We have entered a new era in which we are taking the full-employment policy very seriously. A corollary of this is that we have to widen the sphere of understanding and co-operation, and bring a larger number of people into a knowledge of the diagnosis which requires prompt and rather frequent changes of direction. It will be a privilege for the banks to co-operate actively in this great enterprise, and not merely be in the position of passively reacting to the manœuvres of the central bank. Their staffs should be trained to expect more frequent changes of directive in regard to granting accommodation than they have been used to previously.

We may remind ourselves of the evils which flow from allowing boom-like conditions to develop too far. There is the obvious evil, all too plain to consumers, of a rise in the cost of living. This may have the further consequence of increasing the tempo of wage demands, and thus setting up a vicious spiralling tendency which, even although quite moderate, may do harm. There is the obvious harm to the saving propensity, which has so happily been reviving lately, that results from a progressive deterioration in the standard of value. More urgently important is the need to maintain sterling easily and without strain at a rate no lower than $2·8 to the £. Any doubt or difficulty on this score, such as might be caused to some extent by a tendency to an upward price movement in Britain, would have disastrous effects in many directions.

There are less conspicuous evils inherent in an undue development of boom conditions. The further this goes, the more inevitable and the more dangerous does it make the subsequent readjustment or recession. In the boom there is a special stimulus to the production of producers' goods. Certain parts of industry expand at a greater rate than the remainder. But this high rate cannot be maintained and requires a readjustment later. The readjustment has to be twofold. In the first place, the tempo achieved during the boom being too great to be maintained permanently, the industries affected have to readjust downwards to a lower and more normal rate of demand. Secondly, the aftermath of the over-expansion will be excess capacity in certain quarters, and so for the time being demand for producers' goods is suppressed below its normal rate. Unemployment will be created in these industries, and the problem of reabsorbing those thrown out may be difficult. This is where the danger comes in. We have to deal not merely with the awkwardness of the readjustment itself, but the possibility that the temporary unemployment may disseminate a widespread recession in demand, generating a rather widely diffused unemployment. These are well-known dangers ; we must not forget them.

Furthermore, there are dangers connected with the price and profit development that occurs during the boom period. Firms may be encouraged to add something to price by the abnormal strength of demand. Even if this is not frequent, the mere negative point that prices are not reduced by as much as the increase of turnover would allow, has a tendency to swell profit. In the boom process, the high rate of profit is at once a consequence of the boom and the means by which it is carried forward. The high rate of profit is needed to finance that very rate of expansion of capacity which we suppose to be abnormally great. There is no need to frame an exaggerated picture ; in the task of maintaining full employment we have to be on the look-out for rather fine maladjustments ; these may do harm. When the abnormal rate of ploughing back the high level of profit comes to an end, a gap in total purchasing power appears. Again this may be dangerous unless a readjustment can be effected quickly. Some readjustment of prices and of profits becomes expedient, so that consumption can be encouraged to the greatest possible extent. But the downward process must not go too far. There is a right amount of downward price adjustment ; but if this is overdone, prices may get out of line with costs. These troubles are the aftermath of allowing the boom process to proceed too far.

It has other evils also. If a labour shortage develops, there may be difficulty in getting labour deployed in the places where it is most needed. We were all too familiar with this difficulty in the unhappy five years after the war. A tendency to over-order for stock may also creep in, partly as an insurance against future price rises or shortages. The British import account is apt to be strongly affected by any such tendency. It is to be hoped that the British position is now strong enough for short-period fluctuations in the external balance not to cause panic measures of restriction. If stocking-up worsens the trade balance, that has the corollary that it will be improved later. None the less, Britain has not so wide a margin that she can be altogether free from anxiety if big swings in the external account occur.

These being the undoubted evils of letting a boom develop too far, we have to be very vigilant. It has to be admitted that symptoms at present are not acute, but they are there. The figure for 'unfilled vacancies', substantially higher than it was a year ago, is reinforced by fairly widespread reports of labour shortage. It is true that this figure may contain some padding, but that very padding is an unhealthy symptom. It is always satisfactory that employment is good. One must not be thought to be subscribing to the obnoxious doctrine that a certain amount of unemployment is healthy if one holds that the margin of available labour should not fall below the level required for the passage from job to job ; such a margin need not entail any real hardship. The expansion of employment in 1954 has been greater than the fall of unemployment and greater than the normal increase of the working population owing to a substantial pull of women into employment. There may be a trend for a larger proportion of women to find paid employment, and this is not necessarily unhealthy. In the last six years more women have come into employment than men and as the total amount of women in employment is less than half that of men, this represents a fairly marked tendency for a larger proportion of our women to take jobs. But in 1954, the tendency was accelerated, 218 thousand women coming in as against the annual average of 95 thousand in the last six years. It is not likely that this high figure will be maintained permanently. The situation of 1951 is now repeating itself.

This is rather ominous. The art of maintaining full employment requires not only what those words indicate, but also that care be taken that the rate of expansion of employment keeps fairly steady; expansion for too long at a rate that cannot be maintained carries in its train that aftermath that has been outlined in our discussion of a boom. Plans for new factory building seem to be very high; it is to be feared that these do not represent so much an intensification of the drive to modernize British industry as an over-optimistic calculation of the rate at which additional capacity will be needed. This over-optimism may have been given a fillip by the recent relaxation of hire-purchase regulations, leading to a temporary upsurge.

Not much can be gleaned from movements in the official price indices. The recorded rise in the official retail price index in 1954 was 4 per cent. This may be compared with an increase of the wage index of 4·3 per cent. Imported materials, as a category, have barely risen in price. As there are undoubtedly elements in cost which are more static than wages, and as there has been some increase in labour productivity, it does not seem that the rise of prices, which is also to be found in the wholesale price indices of materials used and produced by British industry, can be fully, or mainly, accounted for by a rise in basic costs. Rather it appears to have been 'demand-induced'. It is not a formidable upsurge, but it is unsatisfactory.

In considering the expediency of restraining methods, the external situation is relevant. It is a very happy thing that in recent years the American trade cycle and the European trade cycle have been out of phase. This fact helped the United States in her recent recession and, still more, helped Europe not to be badly affected by it. If the rest of the world is fairly buoyant and not subject to forces making for recession, that is an opportune moment for a given country to take disinflationary medicine; it will not at that point have a tendency to create difficulties abroad or promote a vicious downward spiral of world scope. From this point of view, this is a most happy moment for Britain to take a little such medicine. The United States is recovering. It is an ideal time to purge our system of its inflationary tendency and thus safeguard ourselves from the necessity of having to make a more serious and dangerous readjustment later.   This implies not only Bank Rate policy, but also an agreement among the banks to make accommodation less easy.

_____

The article next to be quoted was influenced by our unfortunate *démarche*, already referred to, in Paris during June. I continued thereafter to return to the charge, adjuring the authorities to make up their minds and explicitly repudiate the idea of wider margins for sterling.

Although I remained convinced that 24th February 1955 would be accepted by economic historians as the critical date on which we returned to *de facto* convertibility, I sometimes slipped into the habit of referring to 'convertibility' as something still to come, both to comply with my sage friend's request, referred to above, and also to conform to current journalistic usage, which implied that 'convertibility' was not yet achieved.   Official convertibility came at the end of 1958, and flags were duly put out ; but February 1955 remains the more important date.

8

Foreign Exchange Policy [1]

THE time is approaching for a decision in regard to foreign exchange policy.   Prior to the decision, the British attitude is bound to be equivocal, and that is a source of weakness.   Early in 1954 prospects for sterling convertibility looked fair, but the U.S. recession created uncertainty, and free sterling accordingly began to weaken.

It was inevitable that at the September 1954 meeting in Washington the Chancellor of the Exchequer should make a delaying speech.   Words seem to have a greater effect in these days than a plus or minus in the monthly trading account, and there followed a more serious deterioration in free sterling which was only corrected in February of this year.

Then came the two simultaneous operations at the end of February of an additional rise of 1 per cent in the Bank Rate and official intervention in the free sterling markets.   The

_____

[1] *The Financial Times*, 19th July 1955.

combined effect of these worked wonders. Sterling stood up marvellously to a General Election and to the onset of two very serious strikes. It weakened in June. Careful study of the timing makes it impossible to hold that the strikes were the main cause of this weakness. These markets react quickly and would not just have failed to notice the existence of the strikes for a week or two. Once again the determining influence there appears to have been words.

In the OEEC discussions the British were reported to be taking the line that rather wide margins of flexibility would be required for a convertible sterling, if certain European arrangements were put into effect. Judgement cannot be pronounced on the wisdom of this in the absence of fuller information. Suffice it to say that it is impossible to expect world confidence in a certain bottom quotation for sterling to be sustained, if it is implied that on a restoration of convertibility the official lower point would be substantially reduced.

It is unnecessary to look beyond this to account for the June weakening of sterling. But the continued apparent inoperativeness of Bank Rate on the home front may have contributed to reduce foreign confidence. For these reasons a clearly defined foreign exchange policy is becoming rather urgently needed. The price of ambiguous attitudes and statements may become rather heavy.

And so now we are face to face with the straight issue — are we in our regular policy under convertibility conditions to rely on Bank Rate policy or on flexible foreign exchange margins as our normal weapon for correcting short-term maladjustments in the external balance of payments ? We cannot do both — let there be no mistake about that. If the allowed foreign exchange fluctuations are too wide, Bank Rate becomes inoperative as a weapon for adjusting the external balance.

First, it must be said that there is no harm in having the foreign exchange margins somewhat larger than we were used to before 1931. Then the maximum swing in the dollar rate was in the neighbourhood of 0·6 per cent, now it is 1·43 per cent ; no one need object to 2 per cent. But 5 or 6 per cent would be an altogether different matter.

In recent years there has been a good deal of City opinion favourable to a flexible sterling. This is vaguely associated in the minds of some with the principle of economic freedom and the working of the price mechanism. There is a paradox in this. In the 'twenties this same proposal was regarded by capitalistic persons as a piece of the blackest (or reddest ?) socialism.

The reason was that flexible rates imply more 'management' by the authorities. That remains true. Under any system whatever the Exchange Equalization Account — before 1932 the Bank of England — has to intervene frequently ; otherwise there would be chaos. Greater flexibility in the exchange rate gives the authorities greater scope for interference in adjusting it.

To-day, the issue will not be settled on any such grounds. Everyone accepts 'management' in this field. The issue will be settled simply and solely by reference to whether one method or the other will be more efficient in delivering the goods, that is, in preventing recurrent balance of payments crises.

Recent experience with Bank Rate appears to be encouraging. Despite the unfavourable conditions — incomplete convertibility of sterling, the relative narrowness of the international short-term capital market, the large size of the sterling balances, the prospect and fact of a General Election, uncertainties about future British policy — the reaction was good. It is a curious paradox that European bankers seem to have understood the true significance of the rise of Bank Rate much more promptly than did our own industrialists and City.

Would a flexible exchange rate have been equally effective ? It seems doubtful. What it boils down to is this : could a fall of two or three points in sterling be relied on to make a sufficient number of foreigners bulls of sterling on a 90-day prospect ?

Advocates of flexibility may remind us of the success of the arrangements in the period 1932 to 1938. But it must be remembered that from 1932 until a few months before Munich there was world-wide confidence in sterling as the best currency in existence, not excluding the dollar, which was then undermined by uncertainties connected with the New Deal and a continuing U.S. slump of great severity.

Only wishful thinking can posit sterling as likely to be thought a *better* currency than the dollar in the five or ten years ahead, which are what we are concerned with now. Failing that, it is doubtful if a flexible exchange rate would have the desired effect.

Consequently, contrary to widely-held views, it is likely that, on the occasion of an adverse turn in the balance of payments, it would cost more gold to support sterling within wide margins than within narrower margins. In the latter case assistance could be rendered by a high Bank Rate, in the former, not.

The important point on the other side is the fear that in certain circumstances there might be a conflict between external and internal requirements in regard to the Bank Rate. For instance, there might be an external deficit combined with growing unemployment at home. The latter would call for an easy money policy. In most cases, such as the present, the external and internal situations require the same policy ; but the opposite case might occur.

However, surely our experience has now shown that, despite what was thought twenty-five years ago, it is possible to devise a policy with different impacts on the external and internal situations. For the external impact it is the actual rate of interest — say, on Treasury bills — and that alone, that matters. For the internal impact this rate by itself is of minimum significance; it is all the surrounding circumstances — attitude of the banks to advances, and so on — that count.

Indeed, the experience of the last few months, regrettable as it is on its own account, proves that it is possible to have a high short-term interest rate, without producing marked deflation at home. In different and appropriate circumstances this possibility could be put to good use.

Thus, relatively narrow foreign-exchange margins can be commended because they enable Bank Rate policy to have an effect on the external balance. Further advantages are that they are more in line with the International Monetary Fund arrangements and would make co-operation with our European neighbours easier.

9

The Truth about the Crisis [1]

BRITAIN has been passing through one of the phases which seem to be becoming almost periodic, of lack of confidence

[1] *The Director*, October 1955.

abroad.   The position has entirely changed since the early months of this year, when foreign confidence in her was running high.   There are certain specific reasons for this, of which by far the most important is uncertainty about the Government's plans for the future of sterling.   It is to be hoped that this will soon be put right.

But behind this trouble is another one.   It is felt abroad that Britain has some internal difficulties, and this is true ; but it is also felt that she does not know what to do about them.   It is the latter point that is fatal to confidence.   After all, our difficulties are by no means insurmountable.   Productivity has been rising well and is expected to continue to do so.   But if one does not diagnose one's own difficulties clearly, then one may not apply the right remedy and the difficulties may get greater.   And if one does not *seem* to know what to do about them, then the foreigner, who is unable to make a close diagnosis himself, must be expected to infer that they will probably get worse.

There is an analogy from the events of 1949, when the Government declared roundly that sterling would not be devalued, yet seemed at a loss for other measures to rectify the situation.   The position is much better now.   The Government has a definite policy, embodied in the credit squeeze and ancillary measures, and has adopted an attitude of confidence and resolution in regard to that policy.   None the less, the situation is not altogether satisfactory.   Expert comments on why that policy is necessary, on what it is supposed to achieve, and on what it is likely to achieve are not free from ambiguity. It is in this ambiguity that our weakness lies.

I will therefore put the matter very precisely, as I see it. In the spring of 1954 there was a great increase in the pace of industrial investment.   Factory building 'starts' may be a good index of this.   In the year following, these stood at 62 per cent above the previous year and 59 per cent above the average of the five preceding years.   No economy could stand so large a sudden increase in so important a sector without serious trouble. The consequences have been long order books, shortages of skilled manpower, and failure, owing to unacceptable delivery dates, to get our proper share in rising export markets.   That is the crux of the trouble.   The credit squeeze is designed —

admittedly in a rather roundabout, but not therefore inefficient, way — to reduce the total of new orders for factories and equipment to more manageable dimensions.

When discussing this point with industrialists, I sometimes find an utter unwillingness to believe this to be so. This excellent spurt of factory building is entirely welcome, they plead ; we are modernizing ourselves ; the effect will be to scrap obsolete factories, reduce costs, and make British industry more efficient. It just cannot be the case, they argue, that the authorities are so wicked as to wish to curb the pace at which all this admirable work is proceeding. One is bound to have sympathy with such an attitude, but it is out of touch with reality.

May I draw an analogy with the attitude of advocates of 'welfare' ? The more starry-eyed of these sometimes put forward schemes which, for the time being at least, are too grandiose to be manageable. We answer them by saying, 'Your schemes are excellent in themselves, we do not disparage them, but there just is not the money to pay for them. You must proceed more gradually ; you can have all those things in due time.' To which the starry-eyed reply that our attitude is inhuman, that man has an inherent right to a certain minimum of welfare, that the matter does not brook delay, and that the money has just got to be found ; finance should be the servant, not the master. To which again we reply that if you do proceed on such a wide front so quickly you will merely cause inflation and by the consequent rise in the cost of living take away with one hand what you are giving with the other.

What is good for the goose is good for the gander. All the plans for re-equipment recently projected may be admirable in themselves — although some may have been flavoured by a pinch of optimism. But there just is not the money to pay for them all. And if it is said that it is absolutely necessary for the future of British industry that they should all go forward and that finance must be found somehow, the answer is that this will cause inflation, and that the inflation will cause delivery delays and manpower shortages which will impede the implementation of the plans. Much better not to have more plans at any one time than can be executed without inflation. They can all be carried out in due course, if patience is shown.

The statement that 'the money is not there' does not quite cover the ground. It might be proposed to have a heroic savings drive to find the money. There is the incidental difficulty that no savings drive is likely to be able to induce private persons suddenly to step up savings by a large percentage in one particular year to the detriment of their normal standard of living.

Waiving this point, a heroic increase in savings in one particular year would not solve the problem, which is partly physical. There are not the basic tools and skilled personnel available for a sudden increase greatly out of line with trends. The limitations on the rate of expansion were painfully seen in war-time. The Exchequer was not short of money to expand the Air Force overnight to the size required. But there was a physical limitation to the possible rate of expansion in the availability of gauges and jigs and the skilled men required to make them, and in trained pilots needed to train other pilots.

One may put this further question to the indignant industrialist. If all the factories started in 1954-55 are demonstrably vitally needed for industry, why were not some of them started in 1952 or 1953 ? And, if it was not fatal to delay them until 1954-55, can it be proved that it would be fatal to delay some of them to 1956 and 1957 ? It would be a pity to lose foreign markets meanwhile, perhaps in perpetuity, and to undergo the more widely diffused evils of inflation merely for the sake of a hurry that makes no haste.

Newspaper comment, including expert comment, has recently been putting the spotlight upon wage increases as the main cause of the present inflation. This is an error. There is no doubt that in 1954-55 wage increases have been running slightly, although not greatly, ahead of increases in productivity. It is vitally important that wage increases should not get out of hand. Export markets are becoming ever more competitive, and we need to be in a position to offer lower prices, and not the other way round. This is crucial, and we must wish all strength to the elbow of those, not excluding trade union leaders, who are trying to educate the rank and file that it will not benefit them in the long run to have too steep a rise of wages in relation to productivity. Nothing said here is intended to belittle the importance of this.

H

Undesirable as excessive wage increases are and desirable as modernization of plant may be in itself, it is no good being led by these facts into making a false diagnosis. To argue that because one thing is undesirable in itself and the other desirable anyhow in its long-run consequences it must be the former thing that is the cause of our present embarrassments, is an example of thinking that may properly be characterized as woolly. In the year ending July 1955 wage rates went up by about $7\frac{1}{2}$ per cent and wage earnings per person but little more ; in the first half of 1955 manufacturing output was also about $7\frac{1}{2}$ per cent above that in the first half of 1954 ; output per person employed in manufacture, however, went up about $4\frac{1}{2}$ per cent. Thus the wage increase was somewhat too great. But this discrepancy is of very small order of importance compared with the huge increase in orders for equipment. In such matters it is useless to argue from mere theory ; it is essential to bear in mind the orders of magnitude involved. People sometimes go astray by thinking of consumption as of vast dimensions compared with the demand for capital equipment. In fact, the value of the total output of goods, excluding food, drink, and tobacco, for the whole wage-earning class is substantially below that of the output of industrial equipment. Thus an increase of $7\frac{1}{2}$ per cent in the purchasing power of the former must have a small effect indeed in causing inflationary pressure compared with a 62 per cent increase in the demands on the latter account. The aggregate consumption of all classes only appears to have risen about 5 per cent in the same period.

The faulty diagnosis has this bad effect. The average foreigner watching us probably thinks that we have got into an inflationary spiral owing to uncontrollable wage demands backed by sundry strikes, and is accordingly sceptical of our power, despite the Chancellor's brave words, to get out of our difficulties. We ourselves think that British good sense will lead to an abatement of these evils in the coming year ; the foreigner cannot be expected to share this faith. He accordingly believes that we are powerless to overcome our difficulties, which must therefore get worse.

But if it is the case — no one who seriously examines the figures can deny it — that wage increases have played a very minor part in causing inflationary pressure, and that what we are suffering from is a perfectly ordinary industrial boom, then of course, it is entirely within our power to check the tendency.

What we ought to do is tell the world in the plainest terms that for good or ill we have allowed an industrial boom to develop, that this is causing inflationary pressure and weakness in our external balance, that we have weighed the situation well and do not think it needful to press deflation to the point of causing work now in hand to be suspended — we intend to 'restrain', not to 'halt' (the Prime Minister) — that consequently we are bound to have a weak external balance for a year ahead, that we will pay out what gold is needed, having an ample reserve for that purpose, that we think it better to spend some gold that way rather than promote an acute deflationary crisis now, but that meanwhile we are imposing a severe check on the starting of any *new* work, so that we expect to get into good balance again in the course of 1956.   That would be a simple story and a true one, and would restore confidence.

10

Sterling and the Second Budget [1]

IN recent times there have been two central themes in our financial development — the industrial investment boom of 1954-55 and the question of sterling convertibility.   Naturally, they interact at many points.   Some might argue that behind them is another theme no less important — the question of whether wage rates will continue to be pressed up more quickly than productivity increases, and thus lead to a long period of downward movement in the value of the currency.   I have some doubts as to whether this last danger is as great as is sometimes feared, although every effort should be made to meet it. The wage increases in 1954-55 were too great, but it must be remembered that these occurred in a phase of unusually strong inflationary pressure, with a very long schedule of unfilled vacancies and a quite abnormal increase in the aggregate demands for labour.   It has not yet been proved that the temper of labour is such as to insist on excessive increases when

[1] *The Director*, December 1955.

these exceptional conditions are absent. If we take the last eight years, the other period of excessive increases was that following the devaluation of sterling, when the increases were justified by the movement in the cost of living, and were desirable. The increases in 1952–54 were more moderate.

The 'Second Budget' of 1955 belongs much more to the convertibility story than to that of the current inflationary pressure due to the investment boom. Its main purpose was to reinforce confidence in sterling abroad, and on the first round it appears to have achieved that purpose. It may seem odd that matters so domestic and intimate as taxes on pots and pans should be mainly related to the question of foreign confidence ; none the less, this is the proper interpretation. These taxes are likely to have the most marginal influence on internal inflationary pressure (unless, as we hope will not be the case, they have the wrong kind of influence by stimulating wage demands). There were indeed features in the Chancellor's Budget statement more directly relevant to the internal inflation : namely, those bearing on the restriction of capital outlay, whether by the central government, the local authorities, or the nationalized industries.

To understand the full significance of current events, one usually has to take a backward glance. The plan for convertibility projected at the Commonwealth meeting in the autumn of 1952 ran at once into heavy weather. But prospects improved rather rapidly in the later part of 1953. From November 1953 to September 1954, transferable sterling was inside the commodity shunting point ; the steps taken early in 1954 to extend and unify the transferable account system, further strengthened the position. By one use of language, and that a perfectly reasonable one, it would be possible to say that sterling was convertible during this period of about ten months. For some months in the spring of 1954 transferable sterling was inside the lower gold point for official sterling. But even when it was not, a difference of one or two cents could not be regarded as a serious detraction from convertibility. Non-resident holders of sterling were able to get dollars for it, if they wished, at a minimal loss. That holders of sterling balances did not seek to do so on a large scale was a great sign of strength, and pointed to the feasibility of making sterling convertible *de jure* as well as *de facto*. Hopes were high at that time that something of this sort would be done before very long.

There is a strong prejudice against convertibility in certain British quarters. The argument used at this time was that it was all very well to have sterling strong when the Americans were making such large disbursements overseas by way of aid and military expenditures, but that the time would not really be ripe for convertibility until it could be shown that the world was in dollar balance net of these disbursements. This is a difficult and awkward argument. It is no doubt important to assess what may happen when the large U.S. disbursements tail off. On the other hand, it is quite wrong, and indeed absurd, to look to the rest of the world getting into balance with the dollar area net of these disbursements prior to the disbursements coming to an end. For if that happened the Americans would be unable to make the disbursements — a most unwelcome eventuality — except by dipping into their gold reserves in a big way ; and if they had to do that, Congress would look with great disfavour upon any continuance of the disbursements. In fine, so long as the disbursements are to continue, it is desirable — one might almost say necessary — for the United States to have a net favourable balance of payments on all other accounts ; consequently, to say that one will not have convertibility until their net balance on all other accounts is equal, is tantamount to saying that one will not have convertibility until the Americans cease to spend anything, whether by way of aid or on overseas military account.

Believers in convertibility argue that the continuation of the U.S. disbursements, which are not likely to have come to a rapid end in one given year, or even in two or three years, provides a good occasion for convertibility ; at present there are enough disbursements even if we leave out of account 'aid' in the strict sense ; they give us a breathing space in which the pattern of other payments may alter. From the British point of view two favourable results would follow convertibility : it would be easier for us to earn dollars in multilateral settlement, and the leadership of sterling might induce other currencies to become convertible, so that the brunt of a world dollar shortage, if one reappeared, would not have to be borne exclusively on British shoulders.

Be that as it may, the hostile argument was still carrying weight in 1954 ; but in the early part of that year there was a more decisive factor — the American recession. Most American experts endeavoured to assure us that this recession would soon 'saucer off' ; but it was impossible, even as late as September 1954, to be sure of this. If the American recession had deepened, that would have been an embarrassing time to resume convertibility.

Accordingly, the sum of circumstances was such that when the Chancellor went to the meeting of the International Monetary Fund in Washington in September 1954, he felt bound to utter words which seemed to imply an unfavourably long postponement of official convertibility. There was even reference to a condition that the Americans must adopt a more liberal commercial policy ; any reference to this condition seems to suggest a postponement *sine die*. The *de facto* convertibility then came to an end, and transferable sterling fell below the commodity shunting point.

We do not know how much gold was lost by commodity shunting during the following winter, but it is believed to have been substantial. Meanwhile, internal inflationary pressures were getting more severe. At the same time the authorities braced themselves to take action, which had resounding success. After an increase in the bank rate of $\frac{1}{2}$ per cent, it was put up by another 1 per cent on 24th February and on the same day it was announced that the authorities would intervene in the transferable sterling markets. The combined effect of these two measures was electric. With extremely little expenditure of gold, transferable sterling came up, as by magic, well inside the commodity shunting point. This was a great triumph, the brightest day for sterling so far.

But in June the situation deteriorated. The British delegates in Paris, in order to counter certain unwelcome suggestions by continental representatives, spoke of wider margins being needed, should sterling become convertible. This was, of course, destructive of confidence in the rates for sterling, official or transferable, which the authorities had been so successfully and easily holding since February. This was a contradiction in policy, the occurrence of which we may attribute to the distracting influences of the General Election and two strikes.

It is just possible, I suppose, that there were some who seriously thought, despite the evidence of the preceding three and a half months pointing in the opposite direction, that it would be desirable to have considerable flexibility when sterling became officially convertible.

The *de facto* convertibility of sterling remains to this day, but since June it has cost gold. It is impossible to decide how much of this is due to the words uttered in Paris and how much to the loss of export trade due to the strikes. It is likely that the former had a much more profound influence ; the strikes were over fairly soon and everyone could see that, while our exports had been temporarily damaged, they had not received lasting injury. But the attempt to hold sterling at a certain rate, while allowing it to be believed that in due course the rate will be fixed lower, is clearly a Sisyphean task.

The Chancellor has striven nobly to counteract the effects of the Paris attitude, and, in particular, he used firm language at Istanbul. But, by then, things had gone so far that it seemed expedient to make a demonstration on the home front, showing that the country was prepared to make sacrifices to uphold sterling. Hence the 'Second Budget' which thus belongs to the sterling story.

Basic inflationary pressures were just as severe between February and June, when sterling was strong, as they have been since June. Indeed it may well be that the basic situation has been considerably less critical since June, because the higher Bank Rate established in February, even though it may not have acted as quickly as some hoped it would, served to reduce the tempo of industrial expansion. By June we had already begun to correct our situation. But, of course, foreigners cannot diagnose our situation accurately. A boom generates a momentum of talk and rumour, which may increase in intensity even when the boom has begun to decrease in intensity. Such talk catches the ear of foreigners, as do Ministerial speeches and Prime Ministerial speeches. While the basic cause of the weakness of sterling was what was said in June, much chatter and indeed expert comment have served to reinforce that cause. Most foreigners have a misconception of the nature of our inflationary pressure ; they suppose it to be the effect of uncontrollable wage demands, reinforced by strikes. Hence the increase in purchase taxes might be calculated to impress them ; and if the Labour Opposition uttered loud cries, that was all very helpful, because it suggested that the authorities were manfully imposing sacrifices that would be felt.

But the real solution of this part of our troubles is an even more decisive and final clarification of our policy in regard to sterling than that given by the Chancellor at Istanbul.

11

The British Boom, 1954–55 [1]

IT is central to the method of economics to give precise definitions to certain aggregates or categories of phenomena by means of expressions that usually consist of, or are compounded from, the terms of common speech. These may, however, sometimes be given a special twist, in order to adapt them to the purpose in hand. Examples of such expressions are factor of production, velocity of circulation of money, aggregate demand. One essential skill of the good economist consists in his choice out of all the vast multiplicity of aggregates or categories which could in principle be defined precisely, those particular aggregates or categories, the precise definition of which serves to clarify one's understanding of that *galimatias* of heterogeneous events that constitutes the economic life of the community. These expressions, having served their purposes as tools of scientific thought, are often handed back into circulation in ordinary discourse. The fact that these and not other categories were chosen for naming, thus being rendered eventually into familiar concepts, has its influence in turn on the direction taken by discussions about public policy.

In the study of inflation and of the trade cycle, the general price level has been an important concept. Analysis has concerned itself with the causes of its oscillations, and policy with preventing them. Some might regard a 'disinflationary' policy as essentially meaning a policy directed to preventing the general price level from rising (or to causing it to fall back after an antecedent rise). In recent years there has been firmly placed at the centre of the systematic study of these matters the

[1] *Economic Journal*, March 1956.

notion of general level of activity. I do not suggest that nine-teenth-century economists were unaware of fluctuations in this general level or that they gave it no attention; but it was not used as a concept of central significance, whether as cause or effect, in the strict analysis of the economic equilibrium and disturbances thereto. Students of the trade cycle were bound by the very nature of their subject to give it increasing atten-tion; gradually, they came to treat it more systematically; the work of Sir Dennis Robertson constituted an important landmark in this process; finally, Keynes, by the vigour of his impact, rendered a systematic treatment of the causes and effects of changes in the general level of activity common form in trade-cycle analysis.

I would suggest that the 'time interval between order and delivery' is a concept of no less central significance than the 'price level' or the 'level of activity', and that it should play its part in analysis, namely, in the functional equations that we set out as purporting to account for the course of fluctuations. It will no doubt be held that economists are well aware of the fluctuations in this time interval. But they have so far tended to regard them as a by-product of more fundamental changes, just as the older economists tended to regard the fluctuations in output as a whole as a by-product of the price oscillations which were their central theme.

I would suggest further that the increase in this time interval has been the most important feature, both as regards cause and effect, in the British boom of 1954–55, and that increases in the price level and in the level of activity have played relatively minor roles. Unfortunately, precise and com-prehensive information on this important magnitude is lacking, and the availability of information may, naturally and properly, have much influence on the direction in which economists turn their attention. In the nineteenth century there was more information on prices than on the level of production; now that has been remedied. It would be very helpful to economic studies, and thereby improve the quality of the advice that economists may see fit to tender in times of perplexity, like the present, if the authorities would obtain information for publication under this head by means of recurrent sample enquiries.

It is a familiar fact that Keynes, when analysing the causes tending to produce over-full or under-full employment, gave more attention to the latter alternative, having regard to the circumstances of the time. He argued that there was a possibility of equilibrium with under-full employment. What would happen if the propensity to invest, the rate of interest, and the multiplier had values such that aggregate demand exceeded the supply potential ? It is not clear whether he conceived that there would be a corresponding equilibrium at the high level. To elucidate this one may turn back to his earlier work, *A Treatise on Money*. In the terms which he then used, an excess of investment over saving caused a proportionate rise in general prices. This generated 'windfall profit', which sufficed to finance the excess investment. The same price rise curbed consumption, thus imposing what in the language of other writers has been called 'forced saving' on consumers. The difference between what they would, in the absence of inflation, have consumed, and what they do, in the face of higher prices, consume, constitutes a reduction in consumer command over productive resources, and this command is transferred to entrepreneurs undertaking investment. The excess of investment is financed, whether directly or via intermediaries, by this windfall profit, which automatically suffices for the purpose. If entrepreneurs take any of this windfall profit out in the form of higher consumption, prices will rise still higher, and by the doctrine of the 'widow's cruse' windfall profit will rise accordingly, so that those bent upon investment have their way and funds are found for them.

This doctrine of the boom appears to be carried forward in essentials into the *General Theory*. When there is unemployment, an increment of investment has its main effect in expanding employment ; but as we approach a full-employment ceiling the increase in demand, due to the increment of investment and to its operation through the multiplier, has a divided effect, increasing employment somewhat but also raising prices ; finally, at the point of absolutely full employment, any further increment of demand has its whole effect in producing a price rise. The excess of aggregate effective demand over the supply potential may be called the 'inflationary gap', and prices will rise to, and presumably stay at, a level such that aggregate expenditure exceeds the aggregate cost of production, including a normal profit, by the amount of the gap.   This might be conceived to be a position of equilibrium.   This inflation of prices is independent of any increase in rates of factor rewards ; if these are also raised (*e.g.*, if the money value of the 'wage unit' goes up), the whole price structure will be raised accordingly, but, in the absence of any new forces acting upon the propensity to consume or the propensity to invest, the 'gap', viz., the excess of aggregate expenditure over aggregate costs, including normal profit, will remain the same.

When the war came and gave us practical experience of inflation, the operation of such an inflationary process as that postulated above was deliberately obstructed by war-time controls.   We might describe a system in which prices were allowed to rise in the manner described above as 'open' inflation and the war-time system as 'suppressed' inflation.   While such measures as taxation and the restriction of private investment tend to narrow the 'gap', price controls and rationing, formal or informal, do not do so.   The former types of control may be said to cure or reduce inflation at the source by reducing the 'gap', while the latter only 'suppress' its consequences ; they ensure that the gap that remains, instead of finding expression in a certain rise of prices, finds expression of equivalent value in unsatisfied demand.   At the consumer end we have consumers queueing outside shops and some arriving too late to obtain what they require, while within the productive process we have delayed delivery in respect of orders placed.

These symptoms of 'suppressed' inflation continued after the War, and were then supposed to be connected with the continuance of controls in the form of price regulation, the allocation of materials, and, in certain cases, rationing.   The essential feature of suppressed inflation is unsatisfied demand, and the continuance of this was supposed to be bound up with the controls that prevented the operation of what is regarded as the normal function of the price system — to equate demand and supply.   (The other types of control were also continued in this period, viz., those tending to reduce the gap, such as controls over new investment and budget surpluses.)

In due course the symptoms of suppression tended to disappear, and controls directed to 'suppression' were removed at about the same time.   By 1953, delivery dates were in the majority of cases normal.

But then in 1954 the old symptoms began to reappear within the field of producer goods, although the system of controls had not been reintroduced.   Even in the earlier period we may judge that the delays were not fully accounted for by the controls.   We now have to consider the proposition that such delays, hitherto regarded, not as the effects of an inflationary gap, but as the effects of measures designed to suppress its consequences, are part of the normal functioning of an inflationary economy, even when no deliberate attempt is made to suppress the inflation.   If an inflationary gap appears when employment is very near the full-employment ceiling, as in 1954, it may be that, normally, it is not wholly, or even mainly, reflected in a proportionate rise of prices, but rather in a growth of delivery delay, and thus of unsatisfied demand.

There is some connection between this analysis of an inflationary situation and doctrines that have been discussed in the very different field of entrepreneurial price policy in conditions of imperfect competition.   Hot on a new track, the early proponents of the theory of imperfect competition supposed that entrepreneurs would equate marginal cost with short-period marginal revenue.   Further consideration showed that in the majority of cases they were unlikely to do this, if it meant raising prices substantially above the cost of production ; they would bring long-period marginal revenue into account, and this would mean a lower pricing policy.   So in the analysis of inflation the idea that the inflationary gap would find full expression in a proportionate rise of prices implied that the representative entrepreneur would, as the inflationary situation developed, raise his price sufficiently to equate demand to supply and keep his order books of normal length.   It is reasonable to suppose that he does nothing of the kind.   He pursues a conservative pricing policy and allows his order book to lengthen.

There is nothing irrational in this.   For in imperfect competition the paramount consideration is the bad effect on long-period marginal revenue entailed by the loss of a customer.   Now it is quite true that the quotation of long delivery dates may lose custom ; it has been losing custom in British export markets during the last year. None the less, it will not lose so much custom as raising prices sufficiently to keep order books short ; by definition such a policy would involve shedding all customers whose needs cannot be met within a normal delivery period ; if every effort is made to retain those customers by letting delivery delays grow, some will indeed be lost, but not so many as by raising prices enough to equate short-period demand to short-period supply ; the fact that the length of the order book does grow is a proof of that. Therefore, if the prime object is not to alienate customers, the entrepreneur, faced by a choice of evils, will tend to let his order book grow.

We may ask how this phenomenon will affect the balance between investment and consumption. It appeared that, by the Keynesian analysis of inflation beyond the ceiling of full employment, investment would win ; the forced saving induced by the rise of prices would enable resources to be diverted to the financing of the investment plans. Perhaps this argument should not be pressed too far. A steep rise of prices, involving producer goods as well as consumer goods, might cause some investment projects to be abandoned even in the heyday of a boom. Yet, on the whole, this analysis implies that it is consumption rather than investment that is squeezed out by the inflationary process.

The matter is altogether different if the inflationary gap finds its expression mainly in unsatisfied demand. In this case it is more probable that investment will be squeezed and consumption win through. Once again one must be careful not to be too categorical. On the whole, it seems that the phenomenon of delivery delays is more prominent in the sphere of sales to producers than in that of sales to consumers. In the phase since controls were largely abandoned in Britain, delivery delay to the final consumer has been less prominent, although there have been notable exceptions, as in the provision of a telephone. One reason for this difference may be that consumers are less specific in their requirements ; they go shopping and take the varieties of goods available as the ultimate data ; if they cannot find precisely what they may remember buying before the war, they accept substitutes. In the field of investment, the requirements are usually more specific ; a producer must perforce wait for the equipment that he needs for his productive process. The extent to which delay obtains in the two fields may depend also on where the new inflationary force has arisen. If, after a condition of near-equilibrium, there is a sudden spurt in investment demand, then one may expect the phenomenon of delay to obtain mainly in the sphere of investment goods. Symptoms of suppressed inflation will appear in the sphere in which the supply potential is inadequate to match the new demand.

By the autumn of 1954 it was evident that the British economy was becoming subject to severe inflationary pressure. After a period of fair balance between supply and demand long delivery delays of the kind so familiar between 1945 and 1951 reappeared. The expression 'delivery delay' has a twofold meaning : there is the time interval involved in the date for delivery actually quoted by the firm which accepts an order, and there is the failure of the firm to deliver at the quoted date. The former kind of lengthening became especially notable in the second half of 1954. The lack of precise statistical data in this field has already been mentioned ; industrial reporting is not always reliable, but in this case it was so widespread as to be broadly trustworthy. It is supported by one notable published series. In the year from July 1954 to June 1955 orders for metal-working machine tools were 88 per cent above the annual rate in the preceding eighteen months, but production rose by only 5·7 per cent between those periods.[1]

Our next task is to enquire into the cause of this increase of pressure during 1954. The published figure for factory building 'starts' indicates that we then became involved in an industrial investment boom of very great magnitude. It is not the building aspect of this figure that is important, since new factory building is but a small part of the total demand upon the building industry. What is important is the associated demand for industrial equipment. Furthermore, the figure for starts, representing the final decisions to push on with

---

[1] Orders in a given year are taken to be equal to deliveries in that year plus orders on hand at the end of the year minus orders on hand at the end of the preceding year. By this reckoning orders for machine tools rose from the annual rate of £48,064,000 to £90,725,000. (Figures from *Monthly Digest of Statistics*.)

extension plans, may be taken as an indicator of the still wider class of decisions to acquire new equipment, whether these were associated with new building or not. There is no reason to suppose that there was a greater propensity to order new factory building than to order new equipment generally. The figures for industrial building starts measured in square feet are set out in Table 1. The increase shown in the final figure is spectacular. If this is a fair indicator of the increased tempo of orders for new equipment, it would be clearly impossible for the economy not to run into strong inflationary pressure. A sudden increase in a large sector of demand amounting to almost 80 per cent in one year is clearly quite unmanageable.

TABLE 1

INDUSTRIAL BUILDING STARTS *

	Square Feet (index numbers)
1949–53 average	100
1949	106·2
1950	121·6
1951	110·5
1952	64·8
1953	96·8
1st July 1954–30th June 1955	177·3

* *Monthly Digest of Statistics.*

These factories will take various times to build. It appears that a fair average figure is in the neighbourhood of two years. Orders for the associated equipment may in some cases be placed before the building starts ; others will come along during the course of the building. We may accordingly expect the economy to be subject to acute pressure for some two years after the end of 1954. And this pressure will take the form mainly of delivery delay, since it would be impossible for the engineering industry to expand supply by 80 per cent. This delivery delay has an unfortunate effect on the external balance ; it means that currently Britain is not furnishing supplies promptly, and it also means a loss of custom, which may be permanent, since, if delivery dates become too lengthy, foreign buyers seek other sources of supply. Indeed, it is well known that they have recently been doing so ; thus the increase in orders as recorded understates in such circumstances the total increase in demand. The delivery delays also entail waste and inefficiency in productive processes at home.

In this connection it is important to make a distinction which is not always fully appreciated by commentators. Those who claim that it is important to curb investment do not seek to reduce at all the amount of investment that is occurring ; on the contrary, it is probably desirable for Britain in her present phase to expand investment year by year. What it is urgently important to reduce is the quantity of *orders on investment account*. It is the excess of orders on investment account over the maximum supply potential of the industries making the investment goods which causes the inflationary pressure, the delivery delays, and the loss of export markets. It may be well to have orders on investment account running slightly ahead of the supply potential of the relevant industries, so as to keep them under a constant incentive to expand. This incentive seems to have been lost during the recession of 1952. But if the increase in orders goes far beyond any possibility of expansion, then nothing but harm is done. Indeed, it is probably true to say that by reducing orders upon investment account (very drastically indeed) one would increase the amount of achieved investment. Delivery delay is bound to cause inefficiency if essential components are not forthcoming. Associated with this is the impossibility of expanding really skilled man-power sufficiently to meet requirements, so that firms are retarded by the lack of availability of skills ; those available do not always, in a time of acute man-power shortage, find their way to the places where their skills are most needed in relation to the efficient operation of the economy as a whole.

There can be little doubt that this sudden expansion has been the main cause of the inflationary pressures ; the strain has been concentrated upon manufacturing industry. Attention has been called to the increase of consumption. This may have been a little too great in relation to the increase of production, but its contribution to the inflationary situation has been relatively trivial. This is shown in Table 2.

It is not fair to compare the increase of consumption expenditure with the production index, because various kinds of services play so large a part in the former, and the consumption of these may not have expanded as much as that of material objects. The increase in the consumption of household goods and clothing is given in the second column, because these items are shown separately in the *Monthly Digest of Statistics*. However, in considering the balance between consumption and production one should not consider only the direct consumption of material goods, for part of the demand going from consumption on to manufacturing industry is constituted by

TABLE 2

CONSUMPTION AT 1948 PRICES, AND INDEX OF INDUSTRIAL PRODUCTION *

Date	Consumption Expenditure	Consumption of Household Goods and Clothing	Production Index
	Percentage increase over same quarter in preceding year		
1954 :			
1st quarter	+3·4	+ 4·2	+7·2
2nd quarter	+3·6	+ 6·5	+7·5
3rd quarter	+4·3	+10·2	+6·5
4th quarter	+6·3	+10·6	+5·7
1955 :			
1st quarter	+4·8	+ 7·7	+6·1
2nd quarter	+3·1	+ 3·3	+5·7
3rd quarter	+2·7	+ 2·1	+3·3
	Percentage increase in whole year from fourth quarter 1954 to third quarter 1955 (inc.) over preceding year		
	+4·3	+ 6·0	+ 5·4

* *Monthly Digest of Statistics.*

the demand for various material goods required by consumers' services. The true index of consumption for a proper comparison with the index of production probably lies somewhere between the first and second columns shown in Table 2. The abatement in the increase of consumption shown after the first quarter of 1955 is welcome. However one regards these figures, it is clear that the increase in demand on consumer account is quite small by comparison with the 77 per cent increase in demand on investment account shown by Table 1.

In this connection there is a point of first-rate importance which should always be borne in mind. There is a widespread impression that aggregate consumer demand is very large by comparison with the demand on account of new equipment, so that an excess demand on the former account of 1 or 2 per cent might have an effect of comparable magnitude with that of a far greater percentage increase in demand on investment account ; and when we are thinking of a strain on manufacturing industry, we have to exclude that part of investment demand which comes under the heading, building and construction — including, of course, residential building. Our tireless authors of *National Income and Expenditure*, to whom all economists owe so great a debt, have recently been publishing an input-output table, which throws a light upon this matter. The table in the current issue (1955) relates to 1950. The pattern has no doubt shifted since then, but the figures there provided may serve to give us rough proportions, which are all that we need for the argument. From the data there provided (Table 17) I have constructed the following table by a method described in the footnote.[1]

TABLE 3

DISTRIBUTION OF PRODUCT OF MANUFACTURING INDUSTRY, EXCLUDING FOOD, DRINK, AND TOBACCO, IN 1950

Consumption	39
Government	9
Fixed capital	19
Exports	33
	100

[1] We are concerned with the output of items 3, 4, 5, and 7 of Table 17. The distribution of the final output between persons, public authorities, fixed capital, and exports is shown clearly. Stocks have been omitted, both because they are not large enough to affect the broad proportions that we seek to ascertain and because their changes in 1950 would not be representative of other years. The intermediate output has been distributed by reference to the information given in the left-hand side of the table. Let total sales by 3, 4, 5, and 7, as shown in column 1 (£183 million), be x_1. Let the amount of the output of 1 distributed to intermediate output, persons,

From this it appears that, if we exclude food, drink, and tobacco, the total demand made by all consumers on manufacturing industry is only about double that made by the provision of manufactured equipment for industry. Accordingly, an increase of orders on the latter account approximating to 80 per cent has a far greater effect in imposing a strain on manufacturing industry than an increase in consumer demand of the order of 4 per cent or even 7 per cent.

In general comment much importance has been attached to the rises in wage-rates and wage earnings. There is no doubt that any tendency for wages year by year to rise more than productivity would be very injurious to the economy, and there cannot be too much effort of education and propaganda to drive this point home. The figures, however, do not indicate that wages had so risen prior to the end of 1954 ; but by that date inflationary pressures were already operating in full force. Consequently, up to that point, wage increases can be ruled out as a causal factor. During 1954 the index of wage-rates rose by 4·3 per cent and wage earnings per person rose by 7·3 per cent ; during that period the index of manufacturing production rose by 9·6 per cent, and it can be calculated that productivity per person employed in manufacturing industry rose by 6·7 per cent. To get a broader basis it may be well to compare 1954 as a whole with 1953 : wage-rates rose by 4·3 per cent, wage earnings by 6·1 per cent, the index of manufacturing production

---

public authorities, fixed capital, and exports respectively be called a_1, b_1, c_1, d_1 and e_1. Of the output of 3, 4, 5, and 7 sold to 1, $\dfrac{x_1 b_1}{a_1+b_1+c_1+d_1+e_1}$ has been assigned to persons, $\dfrac{x_1 c_1}{a_1+b_1+c_1+d_1+e_1}$ to public authorities, $\dfrac{x_1 d_1}{a_1+b_1+c_1+d_1+e_1}$ to fixed capital, and $\dfrac{x_1 e_1}{a_1+b_1+c_1+d_1+e_1}$ to exports, leaving a residue of $\dfrac{x_1 a_1}{a_1+b_1+c_1+d_1+e_1}$ still unassigned. A similar procedure was then applied to the intermediate output, x_2 ($=£83$ million), of 3, 4, 5, and 7, as shown in column 2, which was distributed in like manner, leaving a residue of $x_2 a_2$. A similar procedure was applied to all ten columns. This left a residue of $x_1 a_1 + x_2 a_2 \ldots + x_{10} a_{10}$. This total amount ($=£624$ million) was then distributed between persons, public authorities, fixed capital, and exports in the proportions shown in line 14 of Table 17. The procedure clearly implies approximation, but the error should not affect the proportions shown in the resulting table in the text sufficiently to frustrate its purpose in the argument.

by 8·1 per cent and productivity per person employed in manufacturing industry by 5·4 per cent. The wage increases between
1952 and 1953 were of the same order ; between 1950 and 1952
the wage increases were somewhat larger, but this was the
inevitable and, given the event, the desirable result of the
devaluation of sterling in 1949. Right to the end of 1954 no
chronic tendency for wages to outstrip productivity by an
appreciable amount can be found. It is true that if wages
continue to rise fully in proportion to manufacturing productivity, the cost of living will tend to rise, since distribution
and other services are not likely to increase their 'productivity'
as much as manufacturing industry, but nevertheless have to
share the burden of wage increases, which they are unable to
'absorb'. For instance, with the rise of 8·1 per cent in manufacturing production between 1953 and 1954 may be compared
the rise of 4·3 per cent in the gross domestic product at constant
prices, as calculated for us by the Central Statistical Office.[1]
For this reason it might be regarded as undesirable for wages
to rise so fast ; but a rise of wages of this amount should not
affect our power to compete overseas, since it is the British
ex-factory prices that matter, provided that wage developments
in foreign competitor countries are similar.

In the spring of 1955 there were excessive wage increases.
Between April 1954 and April 1955 the index of wage-rates
rose by 7·9 per cent, average wage earnings by 9·4 per cent,
while manufacturing production rose by 8·6 per cent and
productivity per person by 5·5 per cent. Thus there was an
'excess' rise of wage earnings of 3·7 per cent. If we are considering the causes of inflationary pressures in 1955, then we
can say, having regard to the proportions shown in Table 3
above, that even the wage increases in 1955 were only of trivial
importance by comparison with the investment boom involving,
as it did, an increase of the order of magnitude of 80 per cent.

There has been a tendency to overstress the importance of
the wage increases. It is natural and even justifiable to over-
stress an evil, if it may have very injurious consequences in the
long run, as a chronically excessive rate of wage increases could
have. But in this case the effect of that over-emphasis has been
unfortunate. Foreigners, lacking full information about the

[1] *National Income and Expenditure* (1955), Table 12.

British investment boom, came to believe during 1955 that the British troubles were mainly due to their being the victims of uncontrollable wage increases, reinforced by strikes, and that these might render another devaluation of sterling necessary. This undermined confidence in sterling in the later part of the year. We have shown that so far there is no evidence of a *chronic* tendency for an excessive rate of increase. The great inflationary pressures of 1955 rendered that year exceptional. The rises in wages that occurred in the winter of 1954–55 may be attributed at least as much to weak employer resistance as to the strength of labour demands ; employers were inclined to grant the increases readily on account of the extreme labour shortage and the urgency and profitability of business in a time of large excessive aggregate demand. It is important to note that even if there are one or two further rounds of excessive wage increases — for the avoidance of which we devoutly hope — sterling is still undervalued by so substantial a margin, owing to the devaluation of 1949, that foreigners can rest assured that, even if the worst happens on the wages front, a further devaluation will not come into question for a long time.

Accordingly, the nature of the British boom of 1954–55 may be stated in very simple terms as follows. In 1954 entrepreneurs made simultaneous decisions to expand capacity by an amount that was far in excess of what could possibly be supplied. This resulted in a great lengthening of delivery dates and delivery delays and an acute man-power shortage. Investment on the proposed scale has not, of course, been achieved ; that was quite impossible. Meanwhile, the external balance has suffered and domestic waste has been caused by the delivery delays. Exports have not indeed fallen ; on the contrary, they have risen ; but they have not risen in proportion to the expansion of world markets, so that the British share has been declining, and they have not risen sufficiently to purchase the imports required by an expanding economy or to provide that excess of exports over imports that is needed to finance overseas investment.

We may ask why this spurt suddenly occurred in 1954. It would be agreeable if we could find the cause in the normal working of the 'acceleration principle'. The figures shown in the three right-hand columns of Table 4 have some tendency to support such an explanation. The accelerated rise in consumption began in 1953, but in the sphere of manufacture did not yet overtop the highest preceding year.

Econometricians have claimed that they do not find swings in investment as large as would be required by the acceleration principle. Those of us who have argued that the acceleration principle plays an important causal role in the trade cycle would not expect such swings. It is not to realized investment that one must look to see a reflection of the acceleration principle,

TABLE 4

CONSUMPTION AND EXPORTS AT 1948 MARKET PRICES *

Year	1948 = 100		Percentage increase over highest preceding year		
	Consumption Expenditure	Consumption of Manufactures, excluding Food, Drink, and Tobacco †	Consumption Expenditure	Consumption of Manufactures, excluding Food, Drink, and Tobacco †	Exports
1948	100	100	—	—	—
1949	100·2	108·5	+ 2·2	+ 8·5	+ 12·0
1950	104·5	113·8	+ 2·3	+ 4·6	+ 13·9
1951	103·8	106·4	—	—	+ 5·2
1952	102·7	103·8	—	—	—
1953	106·4	112·7	+ 1·8	—	—
1954	111·3	122·6	+ 4·6	+ 8·8	+ 3·4

   * *National Income and Expenditure* (1955).
   † This index has a wider coverage than that supplied in the second column of Table 2.

but, in a boom, to unfulfilled orders on investment account ; and in the slump one sees its reflection in the growth of redundant capacity. It is not the amount of realized investment but the difference between this and investment *orders* that exerts the dynamic force in the upward phase. It is depressing to find in general treatises a reiteration of the alleged negative result of the econometricians' investigations, since the idea that this has significance is based on a complete *ignoratio elenchi*. In the present boom investment has shown a healthy trend of increase ; but it is in unfulfilled investment orders that we must seek a manifestation of our disequilibrium and of the effect of the acceleration principle.

It would not, however, be sensible to attribute exclusive causation to the acceleration principle. A wider view should also be taken. One may once again think in terms of a representative entrepreneur. For a number of years after the War he was beset with special problems, including multifarious shortages and controls. Then came the Korean outbreak and the new defence programme. The crisis of 1951 was followed by a minor depression in 1952. Thereafter he experienced a period of relief from controls and of steady progress, free of crises. During this period he may at last have had the leisure to get round to taking longer views ; he had reason to hope that markets would continue to expand, and various projects of modernization had matured in his mind. It is not unnatural that by 1954 a large number of entrepreneurs were ready to go forward at about the same time. Unfortunately, these decisions, coming all at once, were more than the economy could stand.

It has been expedient to check the boom for two sets of reasons. First, there are the immediate reasons that have already been indicated : the congestion has an unfavourable effect on the external balance and causes inefficiency at home. The situation is not so bad that it is expedient to bring the expansion to a sudden and violent halt, leaving factories half finished. Rather it is important to prevent the inception of new plans until the existing backlog has been cleared off. Unfortunately, the figure for factory building starts shows but little sign of abatement in the second quarter of 1955,[1] so that a sharper squeeze was evidently needed to curtail the level of new decisions to expand. It is not to be expected that restrictive measures will purge the system of inflationary pressure at all quickly. It hardly seems that we can expect much easement until fairly late in 1956.

Secondly, important as it is to rescue the economy from the disadvantages of inflationary pressure, there is a still graver issue at stake. What of the succeeding slump ?

We may set out three possibilities in ascending order of gravity. I am not able to have an opinion about which is the correct one.

1. It may be the case that as many new factories will be needed every year as were started in the period from July 1954

---

[1] After full returns are in, it may prove to be above the first quarter.

to June 1955. This would be the most favourable possible assumption. Even on this assumption, the sudden spurt in 1954–55 was bad and restraint is desirable. If it is really true that, as a permanent feature of our economy, about 80 per cent more new factories should be built every year than were actually started on an average in the five years before 1954, it would still be wrong suddenly to increase the rate of starts by 80 per cent in one year. The stepping up to a higher tempo of investment should proceed more gradually, say, at 10 or 15 per cent or even 20 per cent per annum. On this hypothesis, restraint now is needed on the principle of *reculer pour mieux sauter*. It is idle to suppose that the situation could be met by a campaign for the drastic reduction of consumption in the national interest ; for to offset the increased investment orders consumption would have to be reduced by more than 35 per cent, and that did not happen even during the Second World War. Furthermore, the resources could not be switched from the production of consumption goods to investment goods in one year. Physical limitations make the expansion of investment of the magnitude now being attempted utterly impossible.

2. An alternative hypothesis is that all the factories that have been started will be fully needed but that there will not be a need for so many new factories every year in future. In this case we have to face the possibility of a serious slump in the engineering industry when present plans have been completed. Furthermore, much of the expansion of capacity is within the industries making producer goods.

3. A still graver hypothesis is that the investment boom to date has been spiced with optimism and that markets will not suffice to give full employment to all the new factories.

The boom has now become world-wide. We have to face the possibility of a world-wide recession within the next two or three years. Having regard to the fact that, as shown in Table 3, one-third of the output of our manufacturing industry goes abroad, this would be a seriously aggravating factor.

In connection with the three possibilities listed above, attention should be given to the man-power situation. In recent years the population within the age group from fifteen years of age to sixty-four has been almost exactly stationary and will remain so — save in the event of massive immigration — for a quinquennium. Even afterwards the increases will be only small. But what is called the 'working population', that is, the employed and the unemployed taken together, has by no means been stationary in recent years. This is because persons previously unoccupied have been drawn into paid occupations. The majority of these have been women, but men have also made a substantial contribution — presumably mainly by the deferment of the retiring age. It is possible that the inflow of women will continue for a further period ; but there can hardly

TABLE 5

INFLOW INTO PAID OCCUPATIONS *

	Population of U.K. from Fifteen to Sixty-four Years of Age (inclusive)			'Working Population'		
	Male and Female	Male	Female	Male and Female	Male	Female
June 1948	100	100	100	100	100	100
Dec. 1952	99·8	99·9	99·8	102·3	101·4	104·1
June 1953	99·8	100	99·7	102·6	101·5	105·1
Dec. 1953	99·8	100	99·6	103·1	101·7	106·0
June 1954	99·8	100·1	99·6	103·4	102·0	108·0
Dec. 1954	} No Change Probable			104·6	102·5	109·0
June 1955				104·8	102·6	109·5

* Monthly Digest of Statistics.

continue to be a substantial inflow of men. The increase in working population, male and female together, has been running at about 1 per cent during the last 2½ years, with an acceleration in 1954. The likelihood of a slowing down in this rate of increase gives rise to serious reflections.

It is claimed that the new factories are in many cases intended to replace obsolete factories which will be scrapped, and that they are on balance labour-saving. It is just possible that the aggregate of the nation's industrial plant, as enlarged by this very high level of recent factory building, will require no more personnel to man it fully than did the old. But it is impossible not to be uneasy on this score. May it be that stands are now being created which there will not be personnel to fill ? This will not necessarily lead to a still more acute man-power shortage than we have at present, to be shown by a rising figure for 'unfilled vacancies', for it is necessary simultaneously to look at the demand side of the picture.

The rate of increase in consumption that has been occurring recently is in part associated with the rising number of persons in paid occupations. If the creation of capacity has been at all geared, in accordance with the acceleration principle, to the rising trend of consumption, and if in the coming phase there is no substantial increase in the number of persons in paid occupations, there will be disappointment on the demand side.

TABLE 6

CIVIL CONSUMPTION AND EMPLOYMENT *

	Number in Civil Employ-ment at June	Consumer Expenditure Whole Year	Percentage Increase in Consumer Expenditure over preceding Highest Year	Consumer Expenditure per Person in Civil Employ-ment	Percentage Increase in Consumer Expenditure per Person in civil Employment over preceding Highest Year
1950	100	100	—	100	—
1951	101·0	99·3	—	98·3	—
1952	100·6	98·3	—	97·7	—
1953	101·1	102	+ 2	100·9	− 0·9
1954	102·8	106·4	+ 4·3	103·6	+ 2·7

* *National Income and Expenditure* (1955), and *Monthly Digest of Statistics.*

Table 6 shows consumer expenditure per person in civil employment. While this has shown an increase, the increase is not so strong as that in consumer expenditure. This suggests that, if it proves impossible to pull a still higher proportion of the population of working age into paid occupations, there may be a disappointment on the side of increasing markets.

It appeared to me in November 1954 that monetary restric-tion had become expedient.[1] It is possible that economic experts, who have access to all the information available at the

[1] See R. F. Harrod, 'A Drift Towards Inflation ?' *The Financial Times*, 30th November 1954.

centre of government, might have been in a position to perceive that investment orders were becoming excessive at a somewhat earlier date. The Bank Rate was raised in February, but the credit squeeze was not severe. Certain subsequent hesitations on the part of the banking system to react as expected have now become a familiar story. It seems likely that the monetary policy, although not inducing much restriction of plans, did avail to prevent a further expansion. Orders for machine tools ceased to expand in May.[1] Unless reporting is very much in arrears, factory building starts did not show a normal seasonal rise in the second quarter. The railway strike, however, may also have been a factor here.

It is possible that some reluctance and hesitation in the restraint of investment may have been due in part to an attitude of some economists in recent years, which has been decidedly favourable to investment. There is debate whether economists, as such, ought ever to give advice. I believe that it is incumbent upon them to do so. But it is arguable that it should be confined to cases where the grounds for the recommendation can be perceived only by one who has a professional understanding of the working of the economic system. There are other kinds of advice, such as to work hard and live soberly, which, although no doubt conducive to economic prosperity, do not belong to the special province of the economist, since, without being an economist, one can appreciate the value of these maxims. It seems that what has almost amounted to a crusade among certain economists in favour of a greater tempo of investment belongs to this category.

Even the economists' crusade in favour of saving, which was so characteristic of the nineteenth century, was somewhat more professional ; for while each individual might understand well enough that saving would advance his long-run interests, it was not so clear, save to the professional, how his saving also conduced to the increase of the wealth of the whole community. It surely is clear how investment conduces to wealth.

There is a further distinction between the nineteenth-century crusade for saving and the recent crusade for more

[1] There was a revival in the winter of 1955–56, after this was written, and in the two months, January and February, 1956, the May 1955 level was exceeded. Thereafter there was a continuing decline.

investment. In the great majority of cases saving is homogeneous ; one saves by compressing expenditure in terms of pounds, shillings, and pence below income, and the residue can be applied to a wide variety of purposes. Investment, by contrast, is heterogeneous ; one has to invest in this or that particular piece of capital. Consequently, an overall exhortation in favour of investment may lead to inappropriate investment, or to investment at inappropriate times. It must be remembered that in the ordinary course of things less critical vigilance is applied to expenditures that can be entered into a capital account than to current expenditures. Accordingly, there is a greater propensity to wastefulness in the investment field than in the consumer field. Some reporters have urged that the British have much to learn from the Americans in this matter, that the Americans have developed a more rigid economy in relation to investment items than we have, and that this may be one factor in their superior efficiency. The somewhat indiscriminate advocacy, in certain quarters, of investment as being a good thing as such, may have had a bad effect in retarding the development and enforcement of an official policy designed to check the excessive tempo of investment in the crucial period of the winter of 1954–55.

There have been cross currents in policy during 1955 owing to the presence of the sterling problem. The rise in the Bank Rate in February was in part designed to have a favourable effect in the markets for official and transferable sterling by providing an incentive to encourage non-resident holders ; and in this regard the policy was highly successful for the time being. The good work was, however, to some extent undone during the discussions in Paris in June, when it was suggested that the margins for sterling might be widened at a later date. This produced a most unfortunate effect on the markets. The British Chancellor subsequently felt impelled to make statements to restore confidence, and notably a strong statement in. regard to margins at the meeting of the International Monetary Fund at Istanbul. It appears to have become evident there that, in order to restore confidence abroad, it would be expedient for the authorities to impose some plainly visible sacrifices on the British public. Hence the 'Second Budget'. This should be regarded as belonging rather to the chain of events connected with the sterling markets than to those connected with internal inflationary pressures. In relation to this former purpose it appears to have been successful.

Those without access to the very latest figures cannot judge how effectively the credit squeeze is working at present (November 1955). One would suppose a considerable intensification to be desirable. Its purpose would by no means be to reduce the tempo of investment, but rather to reduce the vast excess of investment orders over the supply potential, however greatly that be stretched. It should do so by causing a growing number of firms to have sufficient anxiety about their own liquidity to postpone for the time being the inception of extension plans that they are otherwise ready to make. Inceptions should be deferred until such time as the congestion created by the violent spurt in starts in 1954–55 has been reduced.

12

Tripped up by the Printing Press [1]

It is reported that the credit restriction is now really beginning to bite. But recorded global figures that would be evidence of this process are not yet available. We still do not know if current cut-backs or postponements of capital outlay are great enough to meet requirements.

Looking back over more than a year, we are bound to judge that the restriction has gone forward somewhat haltingly and inefficiently. Little blame for this can be ascribed to the authorities, given the framework within which they had to operate. But it is most important to consider the obstacles presented by that framework, for new thinking is needed and large changes are required as a matter of urgency.

In a monetary restriction there are two aspects : the rise in interest rates, and the reduction in the volume of money (in the strict sense of bank deposits and currency notes). The rise in interest rates has been very marked indeed, but not the decrease in the volume of money. Bank deposits have fallen only by about 5 per cent. This does not look like a very formidable squeeze.

[1] *The Director*, June 1956.

If only one can get acute stringency without too great an increase in interest rates, that is all to the good. High interest rates are burdensome to the taxpayer and, when there is a large external liability (sterling balances), burdensome to the external balance of payments.

One may get to the heart of our recent problems by asking why it was that the authorities did not reduce the volume of money more strongly. There is no technical difficulty in reducing the cash basis of the Joint Stock Banks by as much as one likes, and the authorities could in principle have reduced it much more sharply than they did. The difficulty arises at the next stage. The first normal reaction of the banks to a squeeze at their base is to reduce their call money and holding of bills. If their cash base is reduced very strongly and if they meet that by a correspondingly strong reduction in their second line liquidity, then they are faced with the situation of having an unbalanced list of assets, and are compelled by common prudence to cut down their investments and advances with corresponding severity. But it really is not practicable to impose a drastic squeeze upon the cash basis, impelling a drastic curtailment of call money and bills, unless the Government can simultaneously make a big reduction in the volume of Treasury Bills that it requires the market to take up.

Suppose a different course of events. Suppose that in the spring of last year the Government had been able to make a sufficient reduction in the flow of (tender) Treasury Bills. The discount market would not have had to put up rates substantially, since, despite its diminished resources, it would have been in a position to take up the issue without resort to the Bank of England. One could then have had a sharp cut in the banks' cash basis, a correspondingly sharp cut in the second line liquidity holdings of the banks — without any great rise in interest rates — and then the banks would have been compelled, whether they liked it or not, to make a sharp cut in their investments and advances. The element of voluntaryism would have been taken out of their procedures last summer. The banks would have had to cut down advances ; they would not have feared that by doing so in an alleged national interest, they might be handing over business to their competitors, because they would have had certainty that their competitors would be simultaneously acting in the same way, not for the sake of the national interest but out of sheer necessity. It would have been quite unnecessary for the Chancellor of the Exchequer to address a letter to the Governor of the Bank of England.

All this happy process was rendered impossible by the fact that the Government could not reduce the flow of Treasury Bills sufficiently. The reasons for this are well known. In the early part of the year it had to finance big spending by the local authorities, and in the later part of the year it had to finance the nationalized industries. The transfer by certain nationalized industries at that time from overdraft to public issue may have actually done harm ; for their issues had to be supported by the transfer of Treasury Bills from tap to tender and this inevitably led to an increase of liquidity in the banking system at the very time that the authorities were trying to reduce liquidity by their credit squeeze. It made it quite impossible to squeeze really hard. Pressure from the local authorities has been reduced by the new arrangements made last autumn. The problem of the nationalized industries is by no means solved. The Chancellor's new arrangement has the great advantage of giving him more freedom in his timing, but the fact remains that he has still, somehow or other, to find the money for the nationalized industries — just as, in effect, he had to before — and this may well continue to involve the financing of them by the printing press.

Now it might be thought that all these difficulties could be overcome by a sufficiently drastic policy of funding the National Debt. Could one not have funded enough not only to supply all these extraneous demands, but also to withdraw from the market a sufficient quantity of Treasury Bills ? It is well known that nominal funding has no economic meaning, if the new issues have to be taken up by government departments. Real funding means that the new issues must be fairly and squarely placed with private holders. But one cannot get such placing just because one happens to want to. One has to offer suffi- ciently attractive terms. This is essentially part of the story of how the given situation — the 'framework' — has been forcing up interest rates altogether out of proportion to the severity of the squeeze effected. Doctrinaire credit squeezers might argue that whatever the interest the Government might have to offer in floating new issues, it should face the cost, in order to make the credit squeeze effective. But there are limits to this. There comes a point when the further raising of the rate of interest on long-dated government issues is discreditable to the country — quite apart from the burden on the unfortunate taxpayer — and undermines credit abroad. In fact a point might come when one could rightly say that it was better to let up on the credit squeeze than to incur the discredit due to the spectacle of the British Government borrowing at exorbitant long-term rates.

And so we come back to the fundamentals of the situation. What has made the credit squeeze relatively inefficient has been the existence of large extraneous demands upon government finance. It is hardly putting the matter too strongly to say that one cannot have an effective credit squeeze unless one can simultaneously get a curbing of capital outlay by the nationalized industries.

One is bound to observe that a certain trend in recent years has been most unfortunate in relation to these circumstances. This is the trend of pension funds and other sources of finance to move over from gilt-edged into equities. I do not for a moment believe that the inflationary process will be with us for much longer. But it has already lasted too long for good health, and the idea of redistributing investment portfolios towards equities as a hedge against inflation has now bitten deeply in. Other things being equal, there might be no great harm in this. But other things have not been equal, and we are confronted with a tremendous paradox. In the old days most new issues were industrial, commercial, etc., the addition to the volume of gilt-edged in any one year being negligible or non-existent. But now a range of industries, responsible for some half of all new industrial investment, has been removed from the sphere of industry and commerce and is financed by the Government. So that just at the time when there has been a great wave of opinion against investing in government in favour of industrial equities, the Government has had to come forward, for the first time save in war, and find each year enough new money from the public to finance half the industrial investment of the country. The situation is impossible. No words less strong are adequate to describe it. It has hamstrung the credit squeeze. It will continue to make our capital markets, both long and short term, inefficient, and this in turn can have grave effects for the future of sterling as an international currency.

New thought will have to be given to this, and new solutions found. One way out would be to adopt the old idea and to implement it very rigidly and drastically : namely, that in a period of industrial boom the nationalized industries would have to cut their capital outlay right back. For instance, in the autumn of 1954 the nationalized industries could have been told that there just would not be finance for more than, say, two-thirds of their projected capital outlays, whether by bank overdraft, by new issue, by finance from the Exchequer, or in any way whatever. This is a possible solution ; some might think it too drastic. An alternative would be somehow to put the nationalized industries back, from the point of view of finance at least, on to an ordinary capitalist basis.

It is not known what the Chancellor intends when the two years of his present arrangement come to an end ; no doubt this problem will be given continuous thought at top level. If what investors require is a hedge against inflation, it is difficult to see how the nationalized industries can be brought back into the picture without reintroducing an element of profit ('equity'). One does not say this in a spirit of party politics. It is a problem of prime national importance, and Socialist leaders should be looking at it no less than others. If inflation ends soon, as we may hope and believe, this may abate the trend to equities, but is not likely to reverse it. Even apart from the trend to equities, the problem would be a grave one. If it is not solved, the future of sterling will be imperilled.

K

CHAPTER VI

THE BOOM DRAWS TOWARDS ITS CLOSE

13

New Thinking this Autumn [1]

THE fact that the indices of industrial production and manufacturing production have lapsed from their levels of last
autumn and even, fractionally, from their levels in the first
half of 1955, is greatly disquieting. It is disquieting, whatever
the reasons or justifications. We need to be able to rely on a
steady trend of increase, in order to fulfil the purposes we have
set ourselves. The amount of production is the cardinal
feature in the whole economy. A recession, or even a pause in
the upward trend, should actuate thought about needful
correctives ; it does so in the United States.

The main justification advanced is that this recession is the
necessary price we have to pay for the re-deployment of labour
— the shift from consumer to investment goods industries.
This needs close scrutiny. The numbers actually employed in
industry, and in manufacture in particular, were higher at the
end of June 1956, than at the end of June 1955 ; they were
only 0·5 per cent lower than at the end of December 1955.
Thus, the productivity per man of those at work has fallen.

Moreover, the new factories coming into commission have
been more numerous than in the preceding year ; these — at
least so we were repeatedly assured — were designed to raise
output per man ; it was hoped that they would be at least
tinctured, however slightly, with 'automation' compared with
the old factories, so that productivity should have been rising.

The plain fact of the matter is that output per man in
employment has fallen, because in important sectors overtime

[1] *The Financial Times*, 14th September 1956.

has been reduced or short time worked — more widely in reality than officially. It may be argued that this is but a temporary phenomenon and that after a further period the industries under pressure will have to abandon short time and cast many more hands on to the labour market — a slow, painful process, but a necessary one, so it is urged. But when we examine where those already displaced have proceeded, the picture is not altogether consoling.

Let us remind ourselves of the main objective of policy. It has been to release man-power (and materials) from consumer goods industries in order to aid the capital goods industries to catch up on their backlog and give prompter delivery to markets at home and abroad. One cannot make a perfectly accurate assignment on the basis of the Ministry of Labour classification, but those (temporarily) contracting industries with a broadly consumer slant seem to have released about 112,000 hands between the end of January and the end of June. But employment in manufacturing industry as a whole fell by 116,000 in this period. Though no doubt individuals who left consumer goods factories got employment in other factories, on average those who were displaced from those industries did not find employment in manufacture at all. It is true that 'food, drink, and tobacco' managed to absorb an extra 16,000 — very nice to contemplate, but not precisely to the point. The expanding sectors of the engineering and electrical group, which one associates broadly with plant and equipment, increased their employment by a beggarly 8,000.

The 116,000 released together with an additional 43,000 hands were absorbed into employment elsewhere. Twenty-six thousand were taken by transport, 35,000 by agriculture — no doubt seasonally — 40,000 by 'professional, financial, and miscellaneous services' — presumably more miscellaneous than professional. 55,000 went into building and contracting; this again was partly seasonal, but there were 30,000 more there in June 1956 than in June 1955. This is an undesirable trend, since from a long-term point of view there were too many there already. By all means let us speed the new factories, but they only take a small proportion of the building and contracting labour force.

Let us be frank; this re-deployment is not satisfactory.

It was quite right in the first instance to squeeze the consumer durables ; but we must proceed with moderation and circumspection ; fresh thinking will be required for this autumn.

There has been expression of regret in certain quarters on the ground that no sooner did British industry make a manful, and perhaps overdue, effort to re-equip itself, than a curb had to be imposed. In the last analysis the regret was not really reasonable, because it was not reasonable to suppose that the supply of plant and equipment could be doubled in little more than a year. That was not the fault of too much consumption or too little saving. It was physically impossible for the supplying industries to expand at so great a rate.

The main objective of the credit squeeze should have been to thin out the rate of the new ordering of equipment so as to reduce the queue of those waiting at home and abroad. It was quite sensible to seek to help the capital goods industries by releasing labour elsewhere. But it is no use releasing more labour than they can absorb (owing to other limitations on their rate of expansion) ; nor is it useful to have labour in slack employment in the consumer durables industries ; nor is it sensible to suppose that these latter should continue to be left in slackness for an indefinite period until they release still more labour. In the long run they will surely need the labour they now have ; how otherwise can our standard of living be doubled in twenty-five years ? We do not want to have a slow, grinding process of squeezing labour out of the consumer durables, only to have an equally slow process of getting it back shortly afterwards.

I have the impression that it is dangerous to hold the consumer durables industries at a low level for too long. What is vital for Britain is that there should be the greatest possible progress in the industries of quickly-moving technology. Very important, surely, in this connection are those industries just at the back of the consumer durables, the industries that make the capital equipment for the consumer durables. It is unwise and, indeed, reprehensible for an economist to touch on technological questions. But in this age one is surely not venturing too far if one utters the words electronics and plastics.

If one keeps the markets for the final products in the doldrums one will weaken the incentive for continuous research and development in the quickly-moving fields, where we can so easily be outpaced by our competitors. I would not have the labour force contracted in wireless and expanded in building and contracting, even though the latter has the grandiose name of investment and the former not. The really vital investment — from the point of view of the country's leadership — is only a small part of global investment, on which too much stress is laid.

While new factory starts began to slow down nearly a year ago and the capacity to provide plant and equipment is growing all the time, there will probably be need for restraining further starts for some time longer. It is arguable that the consumer durables should be given at least an orange light in the nearer future.

14

Time to Slacken the Reins? [1]

ATTENTION has been much taken up by the Suez crisis and the great issues involved.[2] The amount of economic dislocation entailed by it cannot yet be predicted. It is improbable that it will make a large impact on our chart of economic progress. A small mistake in our own economic policy could cost us more. We now enter a phase when there will be cross-currents and nice judgement will be required.

For nearly two years now we have had clear sign-posts. A great industrial boom gave rise to inflationary pressures; labour shortages, notably shortages of skilled labour, manifested themselves, and delivery dates fell far behind; this prevented our taking full advantage of the buoyant world markets for our exports or raising them enough to pay for the larger flow of imports that our increased industrial activity required; there may have been some unnecessary stock-piling at times; for a period in 1955 our external balance went into the red. The acute labour shortage caused many firms to offer wages far above trade union rates; and, finally, the standard rates themselves have been moved ahead of productivity. A vicious circle of rising wages and prices began to develop. All

---

[1] *The Director*, October 1956.
[2] This was written before the armed intervention.

these phenomena pointed unambiguously to the need for deflation.

The policy of deflation proper has had four main arms : the reduction in the actual quantity of cash ; appeals to banks to reduce accommodation by more than the actual reduction in the cash at their disposal made it incumbent on them to do ; measures, such as purchase taxes and the hire-purchase restrictions, specifically directed to reduce consumption ; a colossal budget surplus. The last of these was also partly motivated by the aim of reducing consumption, but the more impelling motive was the fact that, unless the large capital requirements of the nationalized industries were financed out of taxes, it would be technically impossible to reduce the amount of cash circulating in the economy or even to hold it down to the present level.

By orthodox criteria, banking policy should have its main effect in curbing investment ; but on this occasion, at least in its early phases, it seems to have had a more potent effect on consumption. The consumer, too, relies sometimes on an overdraft. It is not easy to gauge how far the delay in curbing investment was due to the lukewarm attitude of the authorities, who were reluctant to assert quite openly that the main cause of embarrassment was the too sudden upsurge of investment. They tended to take a rather Sunday School attitude to it, as being a 'good' thing — an attitude in which, it is only fair to add, spokesmen of the Opposition sought to outvoice them. None the less, it was quite clear that the inflationary symptoms listed above could only be cured by a curbing of investment orders. It was the orders on investment account which went zooming up in 1955 ; the increase in orders on consumer account was very moderate and below that of 1954.

However, in due course investment was affected ; and it is the precise timing of the effect that it will now be incumbent on the authorities to gauge. Factory building 'starts' appear to have passed their peak in the early autumn of 1955. This was some time ago. Indeed historians reviewing this phase in perspective may hold that our monetary policy was not so slow in taking effect as the Jeremiahs of free enterprise have this last year been complaining that it was. What was not at first appreciated was the extent to which the pure Bank Rate policy, first properly initiated in February 1955, was bound to be fettered on the home front — it had a quick success abroad — by the impossibility of getting an adequate reduction in the flow of Treasury Bills into the London market. It was only in July that a direct approach was made to the banks to reduce their accommodation. And it was not so very long after July that building 'starts' began to decline.

If the figure for factory building 'approvals' for the second quarter of 1956 has real significance — and one should not place too much reliance on it — the forces making for boom are already spent. The approvals figure is always much above the 'starts' figure (no doubt because it comprises many projects subsequently delayed or abandoned), but it has moved roughly in line with the general boom developments. If we allow something for the excess of approvals over 'starts', the second quarter approvals figure is quite manageable.

The pressures existing to-day are the consequences of decisions taken in the last two years. Many factories take a long time to complete. Moreover, the figures we have are not yet conclusive. Industrial reporting still suggests a fairly rosy attitude on the part of firms in relation to the future expansion of their business. It would certainly be premature to relax the tightness in capital markets. We are still too near the period of breezy exuberance through which the industrial world has been passing. There are indications that the industrial boom is still proceeding in full force in the United States — though possibly moderating in Germany — and in the former country restraining measures are likely to be intensified.

Meanwhile, there is another side to the picture. It has been a very proper part of policy not only to curb investment orders — because the excessive rate of ordering was causing confusion and inflation and loss of exports — but also to curb consumption so as to release men and materials from the consumer goods industries for re-deployment in the investment goods industries. While it is most desirable to reduce investment *orders*, when these are too great to be met and only cause inflation, it is not desirable to reduce investment itself ; on the contrary, it is probably the case — at least so we hope — that the country can profit from a good deal more investment. Consequently, in order to facilitate and speed up the process of expansion in the investment goods industries, the consumer goods industries have been asked — or rather circumstances have been created which has made it necessary for them — to curb their own current output and to release productive resources. This has been a sound idea in itself ; but it is possible to push this policy beyond the limit at which it still serves its intended purpose. It is likely that we have already exceeded that limit. In that case a rather important change of policy will be desirable, and indeed of vital urgency in the national interest, although it may be hard to square it with the Sunday School mentality. The plain fact is that if one is to conduct the affairs of the country wisely one has to advance beyond the Sunday School and enter the higher reaches of moral — not to say economic — study. It may be expedient soon to begin to relax the restraints on the demand for consumer durables.

The cut in the output of consumer goods has had two effects on labour resources. There has been a reduction of overtime working ; and in certain sectors much short time. This in itself is quite unhelpful. It might be urged that in due course these industries will have to discharge much larger numbers, including more of their skilled workers. But it is doubtful if this is desirable. After all, it is the industries producing durable consumer goods that are billed to have the greatest expansion in the decades ahead. It is very questionable whether one wants these industries in this, the last, lap of the deflationary process, to discharge many men whose skills are likely to be useful to them in future.

Secondly, only a small fraction of those who have already been discharged have proceeded to the investment goods industries proper, as was intended ; they have gone to other places. They have gone to food, drink, and tobacco, a sector of consumer goods against which differential measures were not taken ; they have gone to all sorts of miscellaneous jobs ; they have gone to building and contracting, which, though categorized as an 'investment' sector, already has more labour than it will need in the long term. Factory building, which is 'investment' in a more significant sense, only occupies a small proportion of the total labour in building and contracting. It need not be denied that the mitigation of pressure in the labour market due to the discharge of hands from the consumer goods industries in the last year has done some good. But it has been a mixed benefit, and one does not want to carry the process too far. Incidentally, the under-employment of those nominally at work may give rise to awkward wage troubles, which from another point of view it is so desirable to avoid.

The reason why the investment goods industries proper — engineering, electrical, etc. — have taken so small a share of the labour released is that their shortages are centred on skilled labour and the hands released are not necessarily of the right kind, and that there are *other* factors limiting their rate of expansion.

This is the negative case against an all-out policy of squeezing more labour out of the consumer durables. There is a more important positive case. In considering the need for more 'investment' in the country, we ought to concentrate on those sectors where technology is advancing rapidly, and we are racing with our competitors. In the decades ahead it is precisely the components of consumer durables and the capital equipment required to make these components that we should be seeking to supply to the world. If we allow our own consumer demand to go into the doldrums for a considerable period, this is likely to be frustrating to those who want to push actively forward with research and development. This is not a field in which one can pause and wait for two or three years ; the Americans and Germans will just go in and capture our markets.

15

Should the Bank Rate be Cut? [1]

It is nearly two years now since I ventured to ask in these columns for a rise in the Bank Rate. The request was not granted at once ; even when the Bank Rate was raised, the effective policy of disinflation remained rather weak ; it was technically impossible to make it strong, owing to the now all too familiar difficulties constituted by the dependence of local-authority finance, and, that having been put right, of nationalized-industry finance, on tender Treasury Bills.

When eventually the restrictive policy was strengthened,

<hr />

[1] *The Financial Times*, 30th October 1956.

partly with the aid of 'voluntaryism' — the Chancellor's famous letter to the Bank in July last year — its effect on the inflationary trend was, contrary to general belief, rather rapid. Factory building 'starts' passed their peak in the autumn.

If only stronger measures had been taken somewhat earlier, we should have been saved from many of our embarrassments in 1955. The expansion plans started in 1954, although excessive, could have been digested without great difficulty ; we could have proceeded with the expansion of our investment in a more orderly manner ; the wages spiral would not have set in, or not at least with such impetus ; above all we should have been saved from that weakening of world confidence that became so marked in the second half of 1955 and had ramifying effects. It is unfortunate that at the tail end of this episode of inflationary troubles, the Suez crisis should have supervened to revive world scepticism about Britain's future.

I now hold that the Bank Rate should be reduced. The credit squeeze has done its work. The economy has been shaken down. Undue optimism has been killed. The danger now is that in 1957 and 1958 the industrial capacity that we have taken such pains to create may be seriously under-employed. We must allow for time lags. It is important that in the coming year a sufficient number of firms should feel that prospects justify their making fresh plans for expansion.

In assessing credit policy one must keep attention focused on its aims. It is designed essentially to influence decisions — the decisions to make capital outlay, to spend on borrowed money, to consume. It is not well-adapted to curing the aftermath of an excess (or of a deficiency, for that matter) of decisions to spend. A boom in fixed capital investment, as ours has been, must have an inflationary aftermath. Labour and material shortages, slow deliveries, wage-price spiralling have inevitably to continue for some time.

But in relation to current credit policy what we have to ask is — are the decisions now being taken in this, the second half of 1956, excessively expansionist ? Do we fear that, if finance became a little easier, firms in the three or six months ahead would rush forward with fresh plans for expansion on a scale that would put the economy into an inflationary jam in the two coming years ? Expansion plans in the coming year *ought* to be considerably higher than they were prior to 1954, for in the meanwhile we have created industrial capacity, capable of coping with a higher level of orders for capital goods.

If the expansion plans of the coming six months are not likely to be excessive, then the Bank Rate should be reduced forthwith. There is no point in keeping it up. A credit squeeze should be regarded as essentially a short-term weapon ; when it has done its work, produced its shake-down, it should be terminated as quickly as possible. It is not desirable that high interest rates should become a habit in Britain. There has been talk in financial circles recently of this country never being able to get back to a 3 per cent basis. Why not ?

When the problem of the external balance is discussed, it is assumed without question that she ought to have a substantial balance on current account, in order to be able to finance some overseas investment ; but the corollary of that is that she should establish low interest rates at home ; it is almost a contradiction for a high-interest-rate country to set up as an overseas investor on a substantial scale. Being a mature (and moderately rich) country with a stationary population, it is natural for her to be an overseas investor.

She has a large National Debt, which will become progressively more burdensome unless interest rates are reduced. Furthermore, having nationalized the great capital-using industries, she has set herself the task of finding large sums for them, year by year, on a gilt-edged basis. All this points to the desirability of making 3 per cent the target for normal times. It should be understood, however, that this rate would be flexible, and liable to be raised promptly on occasions, like 1954–55, when an investment boom suddenly gathers an unmanageable momentum.

It should not be difficult to bring interest rates down without an undue increase in the quantity of money, provided that the flow of tender Treasury Bills can be kept within manageable dimensions. But it may well prove before long that easy money is not a sufficiently powerful recipe for keeping the economy in reasonably full activity. There are indeed some kill-joy people who would prefer to see people not producing at all than producing consumer goods ; but their views are not likely to prevail. Some re-stimulation of consumption will be required before long. But it need not be regretted if the easing of monetary conditions comes first.

The policy of compressing consumption in order to release man-power for the investment-goods industries has had no success in 1956. What has happened can be described in broad terms as follows. In 1954 and 1955 the man-power required for the trades that expand seasonally in the summer (agriculture, catering, building, etc.) was found — subject no doubt to some multilateral swapping of jobs — by persuading those not normally occupied to join the labour force or not to retire from it at their normal term ; in 1956 the required seasonal expansion in the summer trades almost exactly balanced the contraction in the trades producing consumer goods. There was no net increase in the working population. The reduction of employment in manufacturing industry was almost exactly equal to that at the consumer end of it, the investment goods sector of the industry making no net recruitment.

It is to be hoped that the needed reduction of the Bank Rate will not be impeded by the idea that it would be bad propaganda for the policy of wage restraint. This would be to play with fire. Credit policy is a delicate instrument, difficult enough in all conscience to manage ; it would be a first-class error to subordinate it to the exigencies of a campaign of 'moral suasion' in the wages field. That campaign must use its own appropriate weapons.

The external aspect is important. In this field the Bank Rate is an instrument of great value. Considerable credit easement could be produced without a large reduction of the Bank Rate, if this were thought dangerous from the external point of view. But in fact those foreign holders of sterling, who do not really need it, have probably already bolted out of it in consequence of the Suez crisis. If this is so, the position may even be a favourable one for testing out the external strength of sterling by a gradual reduction of the Bank Rate.

CHAPTER VII

THE WAGES PROBLEM

16

A National Wages Policy — the Problem [1]

IT was decided by correspondence that the subject with which you would best like me to concern myself this afternoon is the problem presented by the wages situation. It is in everyone's mind that we run the risk of being beset by a permanent problem of inflation owing to the tendency of wages to be raised too much. The words 'too much' carry no moral or political implications. We have to face the simple fact that if, on average, wage rates are increased at a greater rate than productivity rises, the excess increase must be translated into higher prices. Thus if, year by year, the wage increases are excessive, that must lead to a continuing rise of prices, in other words, to a debasement of the currency. I need not stress the evils that result from chronic inflation — the undermining of the incentive to save, the disturbance of contracts, and widely-diffused uncertainty affecting all forms of forward planning. We do not want to have chronic inflation.

It may be in the minds of some wage-earners that increases can be granted at the expense of profit. This is fallacious. The greater part of profit goes either to the Chancellor of the Exchequer, or to increasing the capital employed in the industry. If one sought to get higher wages at the expense of that part of the profit which goes to the Chancellor, he would have to recoup his loss by getting an equivalent amount of money from the wage-earners themselves ; thus they would

[1] Lecture given to the North-Western Students' Society, Stratford Town Hall, 24th November 1956. Institute of Municipal Treasurers and Accountants.

have no increase in spendable wages. If we attack that part of profit which is at present ploughed back, then either progress will be halted, or we should have to get the necessary funds from the wage-earners themselves as some form of enforced saving. What remains of profit, namely that part actually distributed in dividends, does not provide any source for a progressive rise of wages in excess of productivity. Suppose that it were decreed that no price increases were allowed to meet excessive wage increases, and those increases exceeded productivity increases to the extent that they have done in the last two years, the whole of this part of profit would be wiped out in two or three years. The system of private enterprise would come to a rapid and abrupt halt. Our problem therefore concerns what can be done to rid ourselves of the tendency for wages to rise too quickly and, by causing inflation, to frustrate the intentions of those who bargain for the increases.

Before proceeding, I want to draw a distinction between inflation that results from the causes we have here in mind, which may be characterized as a cost-induced inflation and inflation that is demand-induced. In the former case we envisaged the inflation occurring because producers are obliged to step up their prices in order to cover their necessary costs. Demand-induced inflation, of which we have had much during the last eleven years, works the other way round. There may be a condition in which the aggregate demand for all goods and services exceeds the maximum amount that the economy is able to produce. This tends to set up an increase of prices. This increase may be independent of whether there is at the same time any rise in costs or not. It reflects the old simple economic principle that if demand exceeds supply, prices tend to rise. That principle is often thought of in relation to a particular commodity ; but it applies equally well if we are considering the balance between an aggregate demand for all commodities and the maximum supply potential of the economy. I will say straight away that much of the inflation we have had since the war has been demand-induced ; wages have followed, not led.

There is no doubt that the demand-induced inflation may precipitate a cost-induced inflation. The demand-induced inflation may lead to a certain rise of prices, and then, if this stimulates wage increases, the demand-induced inflation may be reinforced by a cost-induced inflation. This has certainly happened. The demand-induced inflation stimulates wage increases through a number of channels.

First, there is the obvious point that a rise in the cost of living stimulates wage demands. Secondly, a demand-induced inflation is apt to cause an acute labour shortage. This has an effect both on employers and on employees. It makes the former more ready to grant wage increases, and it enables the latter to dismiss from their minds any fear that by asking for a considerable rise, they will thereby endanger their own employment. When a demand-induced inflation is proceeding, there is a long list of unfilled vacancies which seems to serve as an insurance against excessive wage demands leading to unemployment. Thirdly, when a demand-induced inflation is proceeding, profit is necessarily and automatically high. This again affects both employers and employees. The former have the wherewithal to pay higher wages, and they are most anxious not to lead to any interruption in their own labour supplies by quarrelling about wages. On the side of the employees, the spectacle of higher profit, which is visible to them, makes them feel that it is right and just that they should have their share in the form of higher wages. In such times profit often rises rather steeply, and wage-earners are greatly stimulated in their demands. There is yet another point. In these conditions the strongest firms very often offer wages far in excess of standard trade union rates. The spectacle of these high wages being paid by many firms, without causing them to go bankrupt, stimulates workers to think that other firms can well afford to pay higher wages too, and that it is high time that the standard rates were raised. Thus, while it need not be denied that in ordinary stable conditions, excessive wage demands may be made, there is no doubt that the special circumstances that are present when a demand-induced inflation is proceeding, are highly stimulating to excessive wage demands.

I have so far contrasted demand-induced inflation with cost-induced inflation, identifying the latter with wage increases in excess of productivity increases. But there is another kind of cost-induced inflation that has been of paramount importance since the war. In certain periods the prices that we have had to pay for our imports have risen steeply. These import prices are costs of production. They are a very important factor. More than a quarter of our total expenditure is devoted to expenditure on imports. If the prices of these rise steeply, that is bound to have a ramifying effect throughout the economy. Even if wages were static, even if there was no demand-induced inflation, we should none the less get a considerable overall rise in prices.

Now in order to put this problem of excessive wage increases in the right perspective, I shall go back over the post-war period. We need not concern ourselves much with the three years after the war. This was a period of strong inflation, demand-induced and cost-induced. Even if there had been no inflationary factors operating in Britain, we should none the less have had inflation, owing to the steep rise in the prices of our imports. The Americans largely removed war-time controls in 1946, and the consequence was a sharp rise of world prices expressed in dollars ; this meant a sharp rise in the prices that the British had to pay for their imports.

The figures that I shall give you, derived or calculated from official sources, are only approximate. They use index numbers which may involve some error, and there have been various changes in the basis of some of these since the war, which I have had to cope with. They will suffice for the purpose of a broad picture of events, which is all we need for our general problem.

From 1948 to 1950 was the period of restraint, and the index of basic wages only rose 2 per cent a year. Retail prices were rising fractionally more quickly, so that wage-earners were getting nothing in the way of an improved standard of living by the increase in basic rates. I believe that in this period retail prices were still adjusting themselves to the great post-war inflation. In the next two years (1950–52) the index of basic rates rose 8 per cent a year ; retail prices were still fractionally leading. Now these were formidable increases, by no means justified by rising productivity. But what we have to note here is that in these two years import prices rose by 50 per cent, and this was bound to have ramifying effects on the price structure of the whole economy. The rise in import prices was due in the first instance to the devaluation of sterling in 1949, and secondly to the world-wide inflation of dollar prices, due to the Korean outbreak. We were partly protected from the effect of the devaluation by bulk purchase arrangements, and by the fact that we were purchasing from areas that had devalued with us. From the short period point of view, the Korean war seems to have had a stronger effect on import prices. But from a long perspective it is clear that much the more important cause was the devaluation. I remain convinced that this was both premature and too large and had a very destructive effect on our economy. It entirely destroyed the policy of wage restraint. It is remarkable that wages did not react more strongly to a 50 per cent rise in import prices. In this period too the earners of basic rates got nothing in the way of an improved standard of living. In the next two years the scene changed. Import prices fell somewhat. Wage increases amounted to 4·6 per cent per annum and retail prices rose 2·6 per cent per annum. The increase in productivity was fairly good in this period and might have justified the greater part of the wage increases. I judge that the increase in retail prices, which was undesirable, was much more a readjustment to the devaluation of sterling than the effect of the perhaps slightly excessive wage increases.

Finally, we come on to the last two years. In this period the wage increases have undoubtedly been excessive, in the sense defined, the index rising by 7·7 per cent between mid-1954 and mid-1955, and by 7·2 per cent between mid-1955 and mid-1956. Retail prices rose 3·8 per cent and 4 per cent respectively, while import prices only rose 4 per cent in the two years. The rise in retail prices must in part be attributed to the excessive rise in wages. It is the development in these last two years that brings this problem into the forefront for our consideration.

But I must urge that in these last two years we have had a demand-induced inflation of considerable force, which has been due to the great investment boom proceeding. All those factors that I have mentioned as stimulating wage increase, when a demand-induced inflation is proceeding, were present. I think it would be a mistake to assess probabilities for the future by reference to the experience in these two years. The investment boom has induced the authorities to take corrective action, both

L

in the form of a credit squeeze and in that of allied measures. The index of standard wage-rates does not, however, tell the whole story.

Throughout the period from 1948, average weekly pay packets have risen considerably more than basic wage rates ; the rise has been cumulative. In 1948–50 they rose 4·7 per cent per annum, in 1950–55 they rose 9·3 per cent per annum, in 1952–54 they rose 6·6 per cent per annum, and between October 1954 and October 1955 they rose 9 per cent. It is interesting to observe, however, that in the period from October 1955 to April 1956, when standard rates rose 6·5 per cent — this being the season of the year when most increases occur —weekly pay packets only rose 5·3 per cent. This was the first time that the lead of the pay packet over the standard rate was not increased and this was doubtless one effect of the policy of disinflation.

There are various factors contributing to the lead of the weekly pay packets. It is difficult to tell whether a shift of workers from a trade or grade of low payment to one of a higher payment has contributed anything substantial. The increasing amount of overtime would obviously be significant. But most important of all is the growing tendency of many firms to pay wages far in excess of the trade union rates. In a time of labour shortage they are tempted to do this, if their profit position is comfortable, to make absolutely certain of their own labour supply.

If we look at the picture as a whole, only the last two years give ground for anxiety in regard to standard rates, and these years have been a period when, as noted already, the environment of strong inflationary pressure was abnormally conducive to wage demands. The problem of the high weekly pay packets is somewhat different. It has led to apparently contradictory attitudes. On the one hand, there is an impression in many labour quarters that wages have risen little more than the cost of living and that earners have not been getting their fair share of the rising output of the country. On the other side, there is the view that wage-earners have been faring exceptionally well and that they have been getting considerably more than their previous proportion of the national dividend.

I now present some figures for comparison. I repeat my

warning that these may be subject to error ; but about the broad pattern we need not doubt.

PERCENTAGE INCREASE IN 1955 OVER 1948
(APPROXIMATE FIGURES ONLY)

Gross domestic product	+23·9%	
Gross domestic product per person in working population		+18%
Consumer expenditure	+15·9%	
Consumer expenditure per person in working population		+10%
Manufacturing production	+37%	
Manufacturing production per person employed in manufacture		+21%
Index of basic wage rates divided by index of cost of living		+ 4%
Average weekly wage earnings divided by index of cost of living		+19·1%

It may be noted that consumer expenditure has risen considerably less than the gross domestic product. This is due to the fact that we have had to devote a rising proportion of our resources to production for export, to investment outlay and to defence expenditure. The slower increase in consumption is a mark of the austere spirit which the British have continued to show with a view to improving the economic conditions of the country.

Further, it is to be noted that the gross domestic product has risen less than manufacturing output. This is because the great technological improvements have been centred upon manufacturing processes, and it is not so easy to get increases of efficiency in distribution, transport, catering, recreation, and other miscellaneous services. The faster growth in manufacturing output per head is a widespread phenomenon and may be expected to continue. It introduces an exceedingly awkward element into the wage problem, as I will presently explain.

The figures given in the first 4 lines have been officially adjusted to allow for the rise in prices. The next 2 lines are in terms of volume. For the last 2 lines I have made the calculation myself, and this may be subject to error. Thus the various figures in the right-hand column are comparable. The small increase in the wage index stands out very strikingly against the other figures. It appears to give grounds for a grievance. On the other hand, if we look at the last line we see that the real purchasing power of the average weekly pay packet has increased fractionally more than the gross domestic product per person in the working population. We have not separate figures for consumption per wage-earner. But we may hazard a guess that if the purchasing power of average wages has risen by 19 per cent, the consumption per wage-earner has gone up more than the 10 per cent increase of consumption for the working population as a whole. This would justify the popular impression that wage-earners have been doing better for themselves than the rest of the population. It must be noted that this average rise of 19 per cent includes those who are getting no more than basic rates, the average position of whom is indicated in the preceding line, and must contain a great many workers the purchasing power of whose pay has risen by much more than 19 per cent.

None the less we have an awkward problem here. There may be many who are getting no more than their basic trade union rates. And these are very properly the prime concern of the trade union leaders. It is not for them to take more than a limited amount of cognizance of the fact that many of their members are enjoying wages far above the trade union bargain. They have to fight for their ordinary members. Seeing how small the increase in the basic rates has been — but of course the figure supplied is an average, concealing greater and smaller increases — they may argue that their ordinary unprivileged members are getting less than their fair share. This position has obtained for a number of years. It was not much more than a year ago that the index of basic rates caught up with the cost of living. Experts are not slow to point out that the inflation of prices, from which we all suffer, has been partly caused by the rise in the basic rates. This argument, stated by itself, seems sound enough. None the less the rejoinder comes that it is just this position that the workers object to. They would claim that it ought to be possible to give them wages representing a fair share in rising output, and that the wage increases ought not to be pushed on into the cost of living. On the other side it is contended that the wage-earners as a class are actually getting their full share in the

increase in national output, and more than their full share. I
have no doubt that it is this discrepancy between the level of
wages actually received and the level represented by the basic
rates that has made the wages problem so acute in recent
years.

A problem also arises when we subdivide the whole labour
front into sectors. Manufacturing workers might feel that, in
accord with the very doctrines that the experts proclaim, their
wages ought to go up as much as the average rise of productivity
per person in manufacture. But from the inflationary point of
view this is not so. If wages go up so much, the price of manufactured goods cannot fall ; the rise of wages will have to be
diffused through the whole economy among people of the same
degree of skill, or of lack of skill, but sectors other than manufacture may be unable to 'absorb' these increases, simply because their efficiency is not going up so fast. So that even if
wages go up no more than the rise in productivity per person in
the manufacturing industry, they will go up too fast from the
point of view of inflation ; that is, they will engender an
upward rise in the cost of living.

Then again within the field of manufacture there are great
differences ; in some sectors there may be rapid technological
progress, while others are fairly static. Wage-earners in the
more progressive sectors, seeing their own productivity rise,
will naturally tend to feel entitled to a proportionate rise in
their wages. But of course if this principle were allowed, it
would exacerbate the problem. If the most progressive sectors
set the pace for wage increases, then there will be increases
which the more static sectors in manufacture cannot 'absorb',
and there will be a rising tendency of ex-factory prices, taking
the overall average. It might be argued that the more progressive sectors should rapidly reduce their prices (keeping their
profit margin down severely) as their efficiency increases ;
this would prevent a demand for excessive wage increases in
the progressive sectors, and also cause a fall of prices which
would be an offsetting factor against the inevitable rise of prices
elsewhere. But the trouble is that in many cases these progressive sectors do not want to keep their profit down to a bare
minimum ; for it is precisely these sectors, which are the field
of rapid technological progress, that wish to make a fairly

substantial profit in order to be able to plough it back into investment and carry on their processes of modernization and adaptation at the quickest possible rate.

And so I come to the question of a national policy. If we could somehow persuade those concerned that such a policy was desirable, what would our criteria be ? If we were resolutely determined to avoid inflation, and that would be the object of the manœuvre, we would presumably lay down that the average of all wage increases must not be greater than the increase in the gross domestic product per person employed. From the above table it appears that this would be of the order of $2\frac{1}{2}$ per cent a year. It must be confessed that it would be extremely difficult to keep the workers in this strait-jacket ; yet only if we felt we were able to do this would it be worthwhile going in for a national wages policy. If our wages policy allowed for a greater increase, then it would, so to speak, be endorsing inflation, and our last state would be worse than our first. And it may be that even the $2\frac{1}{2}$ per cent is too great. The national wages policy would presumably be directed to influencing basic rates as agreed between Trade Unions and Employer Associations. But what about the firms that pay more than the basic rates ? Is our national wages policy to lay down not only minimum, but also maximum wage rates ? It would be difficult to get consent for that idea — even if it were desirable. But if we have to envisage some firms stepping wages up more quickly than the basic rates, then this has to be allowed for in the overall average. This means that if wages are to keep in line with the increase in the gross domestic product, the average of basic rates must not be allowed to rise by as much as $2\frac{1}{2}$ per cent. This involves severe restraint indeed.

But there are more awkward problems in store. I do not propose to-day to deal with the phenomena normally referred to as 'differentials'. By these we mean variations from wage rate to wage rate corresponding to the varying degrees and kinds of skill and responsibility. It is sometimes urged that many existing differentials are haphazard and due to the accidents of history, and that it ought to be possible to establish by so-called 'scientific' methods what the true differentials should be. I do not wish to deny that some tidying-up operation in this field might be of immediate advantage. But I am

not quite sure that there would be a net advantage in the long
run.   It is not sound doctrine that given differentials should
be frozen for all time.   At a certain phase in our economical
development some types of skill may be in high demand and
of special value.   In a later phase other kinds of skill may be
more important and the older differentials become meaningless.
We should need a constant revision of differentials.   Now in
fact this process goes on, although admittedly in an irregular
way, in consequence of adjustments made under the pressure
of bargaining and supply and demand.   It is not quite certain
that a national wages policy would not tend to freeze given
scales of differentials after they had ceased to correspond with
the economic facts of the case.   In what follows I propose to
abstract from this whole question of differentials, in this
particular sense of the word.

There is another kind of difference between wages more
germane to our immediate problem.   Wages may rise more
strongly in one trade than another because the former is
expanding more, or improving its technology more rapidly, or
showing a higher rate of profit.   Are these differences desirable
or not ?   If some wages are allowed to go up more than the
standard, shall we say $2\frac{1}{2}$ per cent, other wages will have to go
up less, if our anti-inflation criterion is to be observed.   The
economic function of these differences is to provide an incentive
to movement.   We want to get labour flowing towards the
expanding trades, towards the progressive trades, towards the
trades where profit is good.   Our free system does actually
achieve this to some extent, although not with streamlined
regularity.   Are we to incorporate this incentive element into
our national wage policy ?   Will those who, through no fault
of their own, happen to be in relatively static or declining trades
think it fair that under the aegis of a national wages policy,
they are not allowed to enjoy a proportionate share in the rising
output of the community as a whole ?   It would not be easy to
persuade them.

It might be argued that this incentive element is unnecessary.   In an economy in which there was full employment, but
not more than full employment, in an economy, that is, in
which the number of vacancies was roughly equal to the number of persons seeking jobs, employees would find their way

in the natural course of things to expanding industries, because jobs would be shutting down in their own industries and available in the other sector. But this presupposes that we can entirely escape from the situation, in which we have been for so many periods since the war, of over-full employment, namely, one in which the aggregate demand for labour exceeds the supply. In this situation there may be quite enough jobs in the static trades and more than enough jobs in the expanding trades ; it is then that the wage incentive is required to pull people over into the expanding trades, or the more progressive firms, which need the labour more acutely.

We shall probably be driven to the decision that the national wages policy just would not work in conditions of excessive aggregate demand for labour, that is, in conditions of demand-induced inflation. What we should then be asking would be for the authorities first to get rid of demand-induced inflation, in order to prepare the ground for the implementation of a national wages policy. Some may suggest that this would mean waiting till Domesday, although I am not so pessimistic myself. But this requirement does put a very severe restriction on the efficacy of a national wages policy to cure our troubles.

Furthermore, if we could get over our demand-induced inflation, it is not so clear that a national wages policy would be needed after all. I have already emphasized that it is the demand-induced inflation which sets up conditions that make the wage demands excessive. I would hold that we have not had enough experience since the war how the course of wages would go if we had full employment in the proper sense, that is, just enough demand for labour, and not an excessive demand for labour. It may well be that the wage claims made and granted would cease to be excessive to a degree that would give us serious worry.

There are undoubted disadvantages in a national wages policy. There is the great underlying issue of freedom of bargaining. Some might regard such a freedom as almost akin to a natural right, and hold that a national wages policy would be bringing us dangerously near to the conditions of totalitarianism. Is it quite certain that once one embarks on such a policy and is determined to carry it through, one will not find oneself driven to resort to some degree of direction of labour ?

I do not say that it is so, but these dangers loom in the background.

Akin to this issue is the question of profit. It strikes me that it would be very difficult to get the required agreement to a national wages policy without some kindred measures for a national profit policy. But this is exceedingly dangerous. It is not that one wishes profit takers to be in a position to get a rising share of the national output. One might well say that distributed profit, at least, should over the years be a declining fraction. Ploughed-back profit is another question. One can use taxation to keep distributed profits within the limits set by equitable considerations. By that method at least one can keep the overall average of profit within reasonable limits. But what is essential for private enterprise is that individuals should be free to make profits much above the average ; that is the essence of incentive. The man who works hard, who saves hard, who is more efficient than others and has his fair share of good luck, should be able to build a small concern into a great concern. It is not only a question of the money inventive. It is the incentive given by the feeling that by one's own efforts one can convert something that is small into something that is making a large contribution to the national well-being. It is a question of just pride in achievement. Therefore private enterprise requires variation of profit from firm to firm. How can that be squared with a national profit policy ? I believe that if one is going to contemplate any restriction of profit — apart from that involved in a given rate of taxation — one had better turn one's back on private enterprise completely. This is why I regard any idea of a national profit policy as highly dangerous ; but without one can we really get agreement for a national wage policy ?

This conclusion may seem pessimistic. But I would urge that we still ought to give the free system another chance. Almost throughout the post-war period special features have been present. First, we had the great reconstruction and re-stocking of the immediate post-war years ; then we had devaluation ; then we had the Korean outbreak and the re-armament programme ; then, after a short interval, we had the great 1954–56 investment boom. All through these phases we had strong inflationary forces at work which arose quite independently of wage increases, although admittedly the wage increases reinforced their effect on the cost of living. Furthermore, all through this period there has been the underlying grievance constituted by the figure I have given for the increase in the index of basic wages. Thus we have not had a fair chance to see how the free system works with full employment but not more than full employment.

In regard to the aforementioned grievance, we may hope for an easement through a greater flow of consumer goods. The trouble is that there just have not been enough consumer goods both to provide a considerably higher standard of living for the average worker who draws more than the basic rate and also a higher standard of living for the worker who draws no more than the basic rate. Other serious tasks have fallen on the economy, which have made it inexpedient to have an increase in the flow of consumer goods larger than we have had. But this condition will not obtain indefinitely. I am all in favour of the amount of investment in the country continuing to rise year by year. But in future years it will be possible to achieve that, and yet have a greater increase in the flow of consumer goods than we have had since the war. As this happens, the acute wages problem, with its inflationary tendency, ought to ease off.

I would make one observation in conclusion. It may be that we are still destined to have wage increases that are greater than we should like by our anti-inflation criterion, but let no one suppose that this will entail any danger of the devaluation of sterling. Happily, we still have a margin left over from the excessive devaluation of 1949. It is sometimes said that the rise of wages that has occurred since then has eaten into the whole margin provided by the devaluation ; wages have indeed risen by fractionally more than the amount of devaluation. But this is to ignore the fact that there has been a great rise of wages in the United States *since* the devaluation. U.S. weekly earnings rose by 48 per cent between 1948 and the end of 1955 ; the British weekly pay packets rose by 59 per cent ; we are thus still enjoying to this day a substantial part of the premium given us by the devaluation. It may be argued that American productivity per man has risen much more than ours since 1949, but this is doubtful. American productivity is far higher than

ours, but the figures do not seem to indicate that the percentage
increase has been much greater during the last seven years.
We may hope that the wage increases in the year or two ahead
will not be excessive ; but we should dismiss from our minds
the idea that, if this hope is not realized, the stability of sterling
will be in danger.

CHAPTER VIII

THE BOOM OVER

It will have been noted that the articles written during the autumn of 1956, when the boom was dying down, have some reference to the Suez crisis. These related to the earlier phases of the crisis, before it had been decided to take military action. Once this began, the situation naturally became obscure. One could hardly recommend credit relaxation at a time when one might become involved in heavy military expenditures. But this phase was soon over.

In the autumn articles I suggested that, in the programme of relaxation, priority should be given to consumer durables. Although orders on investment account had for long been falling and had probably fallen well below the capacity of the economy to meet them at their current rate, there was still a large backlog of unfulfilled orders, and it could be reasonably argued that investment should not be given the green light, until more of the backlog had been worked off. This is a nice point requiring more consideration than it has had. Owing to the wave of nonsense that mounted up in 1957, it became difficult to find a forum for debating it. I incline to the view that investment should be encouraged as soon as orders fall below capacity, even if a backlog is still present, on the ground that that is none too early a time to be planning new work to fill the gap that will arise when the backlog is finally worked off. But it would be unwise to be dogmatic on this point. It seemed sensible, in any case, to start reviving the demand for consumer durables, since there was admittedly excess capacity there, and the men and materials being released from the industries in question had ceased to be absorbed by the investment goods industries, doubtless owing to capacity bottlenecks in those industries.

Nothing was done about this at the time, but we have here another instance in which 'Nature' came to the rescue, policy failing. What happened was that consumers, after being set back by the hire-purchase restrictions, had got a second wind, having saved up enough money to buy the cars, etc., which they would have bought at an earlier date but for the hire-purchase restrictions. It seems as if we have in hire-purchase restrictions a weapon that operates on demand with welcome promptitude, but cannot be relied on to have a long effect. A weapon of this kind should be a valuable one within the armoury of measures — anything that has a prompt effect is particularly valuable — but a final verdict must await a further study of consumer behaviour. Prima facie, it seems quite wrong to list a variation in hire-purchase terms as a measure to be used only when the situation has already become critical ! The situation should never be allowed to become critical ; we need all serviceable measures to prevent that happening, and control over the terms of hire purchase appears to be one.

The revival of the demand for consumer durables was a valuable ingredient in the 1957 pattern.

17

Warning against Delay [1]

THE desirability of continuing the credit squeeze must be assessed by reference to its purpose. This was to remedy the situation that arose in 1954 and continued in 1955, when *orders* on investment account rose far above the level at which they could be met. The squeeze operated in three ways.

1. By imposing financial obstacles, it reduced the quantity of *fresh* orders that firms felt able and willing to place. 2. By reducing the rise in consumption (in which it was assisted by collateral measures), it lowered some of the forecasts that firms made about the capacity they would require in the coming period, and so again reduced the level of fresh orders. 3. By reducing consumption in certain lines, it released men and materials, notably steel, from employment in the consumer goods industries, thus making them available for the investment goods industries, with a view to the latter not being held back, for lack of man-power and materials, from expanding as quickly

[1] *The Financial Times*, 10th January 1957.

as they possibly could and catching up on their backlog of orders.

On all three lines the policy has had on the whole a marked success. Considering that there was a certain slowness in the take-off — seen in retrospect to have been mainly due to un-solved problems connected with the finance of the nationalized industries — the success was remarkably prompt. At the fundamental level of fresh orders placed, it appears to have been effective within a few months. It is important that this should be widely recognized as showing how utterly wrong were those persons, by no means confined to the ranks of doctrinaire Socialists, who were arguing in 1955 that it would be more efficient to proceed by direct controls.

Does anyone think that the rate at which fresh orders are being placed *now* is too high ? Does anyone think that it is such as to put an overload on the economy next autumn ? If not, what precisely is the credit squeeze supposed to be doing ? It is not a thing to be loved and treasured on its own account. It is costing the taxpayer much money and contributing sub-stantially to upset the Budget estimate of expenditure last April. It is imposing a burden on our external payments on current account at a time when we can ill afford that. The associated directives are deleterious to sound banking. I fully endorse the well-reasoned article by 'Lombard' in *The Financial Times* of 28th December, entitled 'Directives for Ever and Ever ?'

There is a danger that we may slip back into a plausible, but fallacious, attitude of caution, reminiscent of the bad inter-war period. It is argued that it cannot do any harm to wait a little longer before relaxing the restrictions, and that it would be prudent to defer action until it can be demonstrated with absolute certainty that the time is ripe. This is an altogether wrong point of view. Nothing can be demonstrated with absolute certainty in this field ; it is needful to act upon the best appraisal. It is just as dangerous and productive of sub-sequent misfortune to deflate when the situation no longer requires it as not to deflate when that is required. Policy must steer a middle course ; there are whirlpools on both sides, not on one only.

Some precepts, like 'not to live beyond one's means', apply equally well to the private person and the nation. But not all do. If one could single out one key point in the thought of the late Lord Keynes, to whom it is now customary to pay the lip-service of respect, I should say it was precisely that some private maxims are not applicable to the economy as a whole. If an individual is uncertain how his bank balance will stand at the end of the year, it will do no harm for him to 'err' on the side of caution ; if his prudence proves excessive, he will find himself with some money in hand at the end of the year, and be able to dispose of it fruitfully in due course. But this is not so if the nation — or those wise heads who do our economic planning — errs on the side of caution ; the money will *not* be in hand at the end of the year, because the goods will not have been produced. The productive resources of the economy will have run to waste. And worse may follow in the form of a vicious spiral of depression, which is very difficult to remedy once it has gathered momentum. Savings will have gone down the drain irretrievably. It is not too much to say that the praise-worthy efforts of the Chancellor to encourage small savings could, however apparently successful, be rendered totally abor-tive, and null and void in their effects, if he keeps on the disinflationary policy two or three months too long.

Some present hesitation may be due to the earlier lack of a frank and forthright recognition of what the besetting evil was two years ago — namely, an excess of investment orders. Instead there were references to some vaguely-conceived and ill-defined 'inflation', and much vagueness, too, about how disinflation was supposed to work. The consequence has been slowness to recognize that its task has been fulfilled.

It has been correctly pointed out that the squeeze has had a more potent effect on actual consumption than on actual investment. While the former has flattened out, the latter has shown a notable expansion, although at a reduced tempo recently. But in relation to credit policy it is to *orders* that one must look. If one does that, the paramountcy of its effect upon investment is evident; while orders on consumption account have done no more on the overall average than flatten out, although declining in certain sectors, orders on investment account have on the overall average declined by a very large amount.

It is sad to see our economy running below capacity. The

great investments that have been made do not seem to have raised productivity in 1956. It has been said that some under-employment is inevitable in the course of what the Americans call a 'rolling readjustment'. But that has now lasted long enough. The Suez aftermath will inevitably increase slackness ; the fall in the demand for cars will ramify out into many parts of industry and the shortage of oil and its by-products will also be damping. What is the sense of keeping a monetary damper in operation as well ? We need not be deterred by the idea that relaxation now might make the economy too active at some future date. The monetary policy can be reversed quickly ; in this field rapid reversals are a sign that the system is working well, and also help to make it work well by rendering the business world more alive to its meaning and quicker to take note of it.

Finally, there are fears related to sterling markets. Our reserves have now been replenished, and suffice, with a good margin, for all likely calls. There has already been a very thorough shake-out of reluctant holders of sterling. This is accordingly a specially favourable time for trying how our system of *de facto* convertibility works with a lower Bank Rate.

18

The First Signs of a Recession [1]

FOR more than a year now our index of manufacturing production has been below the level of the preceding year. In the eight months from April 1956 it was on average 2 per cent below the corresponding months in 1955 ; and the gap is gradually widening. We know from the course of employment that the shortfall must have been considerably more than 2 per cent since November. If this sort of thing happened in America, we should talk of an 'American recession', and begin to utter loud laments. (And the Americans would have been taking corrective measures.) Instead, our newspapers continue to refer to a 'plateau'. It is not a plateau, but the early, gentle premonitory downward slope of a recession. In the past this has usually got steeper and become a slump in the full sense.

[1] *The Director*, April 1957.

We can ill afford the loss of manufacturing output involved. We have to compare what we have done, not simply with the record of the preceding year, but with what we might have done had the upward trend of the last few years been maintained. It is true that we could not hope for our labour force to continue to expand, as it did in 1954 and 1955, and for that reason the increase of output could not have been so great as it was in those years. But, as against this, much new capacity has been coming into commission during 1956 which should be expected to raise output per man. Even if we take the cautious view that, despite this new capacity, the rate of increase could not be so great as the 7 per cent per annum achieved from 1952 to 1955, we may still think that the increase in 1956 could have been, say, 5 per cent ; and we might look to a further increase of this order in 1957. Our failure to achieve this increase may have been due in part to the quite normal working of the cycle of demand ; but we must certainly suppose that it has been mainly caused by deliberate restrictive measures.

We may pick out two main objectives of the restrictive policy. One was to reduce the flow of new orders on investment account, so as to check the continuing rise in the backlog of unfilled orders and the lengthening of delivery dates. This objective was achieved. Much has been done during 1956 to work off the backlog, and this has been all to the good. The other objective was to get an abatement of activity in the consumer goods industries, so as to release resources for the overloaded investment goods industries, the efficiency and expansion of which are so important for our economy.

In the early days of the policy this may have had some success, but by the middle of 1956 it was becoming clear that the investment goods industries were unable to absorb the manpower released. This was probably mainly because there were other impediments to the rate of expansion of these industries ; mere man-power could not enable them to overcome these. It is also possible that pockets of slackness were beginning to develop in places. The recently issued quarterly national income statistics show that the output of the investment goods industries in the second and third quarters of 1956 was 11 per cent down on the two preceding quarters. This may have been partly due to seasonal factors. But it is to be noted that

M

if we make this same comparison in 1955, the drop was only
2 per cent. We are now long past the phase when any further
help can be given to the investment goods industries by the
release of man-power from the consumer goods industries, and
it is wasteful to have so much short time in the latter.

We may judge from reports and from the evidence of the
important figures for machine-tool orders, that ordering on
investment account is now at an unhealthily low level, likely to
give rise to serious slackness in the investment goods sector
within twelve months. It is important that there should be a
revival.

It is high time that something was done about this. Interest
rates, long and short term, should be reduced to low levels and
all the nonsense of bank directives for the restriction of advances
terminated. It is absurd to place obstacles in the way of plans
for expansion, when we need more expansion. But things have
now gone so far that it is not likely that the mere removal of
credit restrictions will alone suffice. We shall need to take
positive steps to re-stimulate consumption, so as to provide
some incentive for an increase of orders on investment account.
We ought also to have blueprints ready for sundry capital
development projects in the Commonwealth, so that work for
them can begin to be put in hand during the coming year.

What is holding the authorities back ? No doubt over-
cautious advisers have some influence ; but in this matter of
shaping policy to correct the trade cycle it is just as dangerous
to err on the side of excessive restriction as it is to err on the
side of too little restriction. However, the main substantial
reason appears to be that the authorities are still nervous about
the external balance of payments. Yet this is inherently un-
reasonable. The balance of payments is not too unhealthy.
Indeed it is a very remarkable thing that we are now told that
in the year ending next June we shall have a favourable balance.
This is in spite of the heavy losses of earnings of our oil companies, which make so important a contribution to the overall
balance. We should regard this state of affairs as eminently
satisfactory. It would not be incorrect policy to draw upon
reserves to cover a bad patch due to such an event as the Suez
crisis ; we are surely entitled to assume that this is quite an
exceptional phenomenon — not the sort of thing we have to

budget for as a part of our regular programme of events. The losses of gold last year were not symptoms of an adverse balance, but were mainly a capital payment and entailed a reduction of our gold liabilities to holders of sterling outside the sterling area.

The authorities may plead that our reserves are still too low, and that they want to get a better balance of payments simply in order to build them up. This is certainly a proper objective of policy ; but it should be kept in its due place. It would be altogether wrong to hold the great productive system of this country on slack work merely with a view to compressing imports, and that again merely with a view to building up a gold reserve. One should think of the vast size of the losses due to this slack work.

The whole national income, which is now called by the familiar name of the 'GNP', would not have risen in full proportion to manufacturing output, if that had gone at full steam ahead. If manufacturing output had risen in 1956 and were to rise in 1957 by 5 per cent each, it would be a fairly conservative estimate to put down the rise in GNP at 3 per cent in each year. The mere failure to get this rise would mean a loss of over £1,400 million. This is a tremendous loss of wealth. If there is a positive recession of output, the figure for our loss has to be increased correspondingly. And if we do not adopt measures to re-stimulate activity very quickly, the slackness may well carry over into 1958.

It is quite out of proportion to incur such vast losses merely in order to add to our gold reserve. Indeed it should never be an accepted principle for this country to depress activity solely with the view to depressing the quantity of materials we import. That is a thoroughly unsound policy ; but it is to be feared that it may lie at the root of present hesitations about ending the restrictive measures.

We should be budgeting for a considerable increase in imported materials in 1957. This may involve postponing any sizeable increase in our reserves. In computing these we should always work upon the net figure, that is subtracting sight liabilities outside the sterling area. But we should even be prepared to see a small temporary dip in the net figure, as we take the shock of the aftermath of the Suez crisis.

We hope and pray that the forthcoming seasonal round of wage increases will not be so great this year as it has been in the last two years. But it is *not* a helpful way of meeting the strain which may result from excessive wage increases to have our productive machine running below capacity. On the contrary, the best way to temper the inflationary tendency of an increase in *demand* due to higher wages is to produce the fullest possible flood of goods. And on the *cost* side, it is easier to absorb increases when one is working to full capacity. Slack working is detrimental, not only because it reduces the capital wealth of the country below the level that it might achieve, not only because it needlessly deprives consumers of enjoyment, but also because it makes the problems raised by higher costs more difficult to cope with.

19

The Two Types of Inflation — 1 [1]

THERE are two distinct kinds of inflation. Confusion between the two not only leads to misguided policy, but also to undue despondency at home and a loss of confidence abroad. In fact, our economy, on both internal and external accounts, has never been so healthy as it is now. It is through bad presentation that sterling is being sold.

One kind of inflation is that due to the excess of the overall demand for goods and services over the power of the economy to supply them. This may be popularly worded by the expression 'too much money chasing too few goods'. The excess is sometimes called 'the inflationary gap'. We shall refer to it as *demand*-induced inflation. We had that kind of inflation rather severely in 1954, 1955, and the first quarter of 1956. It is now over.

The other sort of inflation is *cost*-induced inflation. This happens when money wages rise more on average than output per person. This kind of inflation is with us now. It takes time for excessive wage increases to work through the system. Thus the 'price freeze' in certain sectors last year may cause an upwrad movement of prices this year, quite apart from that caused

[1] *The Financial Times*, 17th July 1957.

by further wage increases. The consequent rise in prices may set up a spiralling between wages and prices. It is to be feared that this may continue mildly in Britain for a while ; we have no reason to suppose that the spiralling here will be serious or as large as it is now in the United States.

Although cost-induced inflation is at present in everyone's mind, I will deal with demand-induced inflation first, leaving cost-induced inflation for my article to-morrow.

Demand is now running below our supply potential, and our economy, as a consequence, is not now working to full capacity. There are still indeed some bottle-necks, but we must guide policy by the overall position, not by the worst bottle-necks. In 1954 and 1955 demand was unduly high. Not that there was too much production — to say that would be absurd. But *orders* for production were excessive, because they gave rise to delivery delays, inefficiencies, and a failure to meet export opportunities.

A curb was desirable and (belatedly) imposed. This curb was bound to cause not only a fall in orders, but also, owing to the necessity to shift and reabsorb labour, some fall in production itself. The Americans have the happy phrase, 'a rolling readjustment'. But our recession has now lasted too long to be so named.

Industrial production was at its peak in the last quarter of 1955, when the index, even after being reduced by a 'seasonal correction', stood at 139·6. In no quarter since then has the seasonally-corrected figure been above 137. The seasonally-corrected index of manufacturing production then stood at 145. In the first quarter of 1956 it stood at 141·3, but in no quarter since then has it stood above 140. This is a big drop. This drop, however, is not nearly so important as our failure to get a normal increase of production, which betokens widespread under-employment in our factories. Between 1948 and 1955 industrial production per person employed rose on average 3·2 per cent per annum and manufacturing production 3·3 per cent per annum.

This increase in productivity ought to be continued, and the ground lost in 1956 to be caught up. Indeed, the increase ought to be considerably accelerated, since the amount of industrial investment that has been coming into commission recently and currently has been far more than in the earlier years. Even if no acceleration occurs, the index of industrial production *ought*, by simple continuation of the previous trend of output per person, to stand at 150 in 1958 and that of manufacturing production at 157. They stood at 137 and 140 in the first four months of 1957.

In the modern world we must focus our thoughts upon rates of increase. Our competitors certainly do. Witness the report by the German research institutes, supported by industrialists, quoted in *The Financial Times* of 10th July. The Americans watch rates of increase also. The Russians base their planning on rates of increase, and they have become more sophisticated than they were some years ago in avoiding impracticable targets. In such a world as this we cannot possibly afford to sit back and allow stagnation to occur for two or three years in the (probably vain) hope that it will be helpful in checking the cost-price inflation. Such an attitude is totally out of date.

Consumer demand has shown a welcome increase this year, but by itself is not likely to take our manufactures index any substantial part of the way from 140 towards what should be our minimum target level of 157 for 1958. The expanded programmes of the nationalized industries are unlikely to offset the decline of investment orders by private enterprise. If we do not attain this target in 1958, our policy must be set down as a failure ; our competitors will do better.

We now have a credit squeeze of unprecedented severity. At first (in 1955) it was rather mild. The most fundamental figure in this connection is the quantity of cash available to the clearing banks, upon which they build their superstructure of credit. Between the second half of 1954 and the second half of 1955 the monthly average (omitting December) was reduced from £531 million to £523 million. But in the first five months of 1957 it was only £505 million, at which it was less than the £510 million (again omitting December) available as long ago as 1951.

Credit squeezes should be short and sharp. This one has been long drawn out and progressive. An expanding economy needs an increase of cash. If we supposed that the modest production targets named above for 1958 were achieved and that the total flow of goods and services ('gross domestic product') rose by only two-thirds as much, we should have to finance a flow of goods and services some 10 per cent more in volume than those of 1954. Furthermore, there has since 1954 been a rise of prices (cost of living 12 per cent up) which, having regard to what has already happened to wages, no one thinks can be reversed in full.

It is unlikely that the production targets of 1958, and these should be at the very centre of our policy, can be achieved without some expansion in the cash basis. I do not suggest anything very large at first ; we should proceed by trial and error, but we must go forward if we are to come nearer to achieving our targets. Having written as actively against inflation since 1945 as any man, and having asked for a credit squeeze in 1954, a considerable time before others did and before it was imposed, I strongly resent being dubbed an inflationist when I propose a relaxation now.

What I am suggesting has nothing to do with inflation, but should be regarded as a partial return to normalcy. Incidentally, unless this is done, nothing can revive the gilt-edged market, the depression of which is not only costly to the taxpayer, but has a gravely injurious effect upon the standing of sterling in world markets.

But how would this proposal affect the wage-price spiral, from which we are admittedly suffering ? I shall deal with this in the next article.

20

The Two Types of Inflation — 2 [1]

THERE is no doubt that in 1955 and 1956 wage rates rose ahead of productivity. The index of rates rose by 6·7 per cent between 1954 and 1955 and by 8·2 per cent between 1955 and 1956. Between 1954 and 1955 manufacturing production per person employed in manufacture, which is what matters for our competitiveness in foreign trade, rose by 3 per cent, while the gross domestic product, per person employed altogether, which is what matters for the domestic cost of living, rose by 2 per cent.

[1] *The Financial Times*, 18th July 1957.

Clearly, if these two years represented the normal pattern of wages increases for the future, we should be in for trouble. But it would be utterly wrong to suppose that.

Things have gone slightly better so far this year. The increase of wage rates from May 1956 to May 1957 was 4·8 per cent only. It is true that in the last eighteen months production per person has declined. But it would not be sound to compare wage increases with the rise or fall of production when a 'rolling readjustment' is on. One should compare them with the *trend* of increase in production. The seven-year trend of increase in manufactured output per person prior to the credit squeeze was 3·3 per cent per annum and the trend of increase in the gross domestic product was 2·5 per cent per annum.

If we hold that, with the increased investment of recent years, manufacturing output per person should — the 'rolling readjustment' apart — now be rising at somewhat more than the 3·3 per cent of earlier years, the recent 4·8 per cent increase in wage rates has been only fractionally excessive. Greatly exaggerated ideas have been current about this.

Of course there are troubles still to come. Not only may there be belated wage increases in 1957, but also we have not yet seen through, in the field of prices, the effects of the large increases of 1955 and 1956. We had the 'freeze' in administered prices in certain sectors last year. With unfreezing and other delayed adjustments, we may have to face a further seeping upwards in the prices of end-products.

One must not forget that our competitors too have their troubles. U.S. hourly earnings rose by 5 per cent in the last year. Their seven-year trend-increase in manufacturing output per person appears to have been exactly the same as ours, namely, 3·3 per cent.

But what of the future ? Are we, perhaps along with other countries, to have a slow, seeping inflation ? One must take a broader look. First it must not be forgotten that in the post-war decade there were other forces sending prices up here — the world-wide post-war inflation, including the inflation of dollar prices, the devaluation of sterling, and the further inflation of dollar prices following the Korean outbreak.

All these things were bound to send British prices up, and our wage increases were to a large extent an adjustment to that.

The investment boom of 1954–56, with its acute labour shortages and firms bidding for labour by offers far above Trade
Union rates, was not helpful.   But, it will be claimed, this does
not account for the continuing upward pressure now.

One central and all-important fact lies beyond all this.
Consider the following figures carefully.   Between 1948 and
1955 the gross domestic product per person in the working
population went up 18 per cent, consumer expenditure per
person (at constant prices) went up 10 per cent, and average
weekly wage earnings divided by the index of the cost of living
went up 21 per cent.   On that showing the wage-earners do
not seem to have done badly ; they were in a position to raise
their consumption by considerably more than the national
average and by fractionally more than the gross domestic
product.

But next consider this figure.   The index of basic wage
rates divided by the cost-of-living index went up only 4 per
cent.   This meant that the average man — an abstract concept,
admittedly, since different industries have fared differently —
who earned no more than the basic rate, was not able to enjoy his
proportionate share in the national rise in consumption.

It must be remembered that the trade-union spokesman is
concerned not with firms that pay higher wages, with bonuses
or with the effect of overtime pay, but with the standard basic
rate.   The low level of those rates in real terms has been the
fundamental cause of what seems to so many an unconscionably-
protracted pressure of demands for higher money wages.

And what has been the cause of this low level ?   Owing to
the claims of defence, investment, and exports, there just have
not been enough consumer goods not only to meet the demands
for goods of those who earn bonuses, etc., but also to provide
the plain basic wage-earner with a proportionately higher standard of living.   The position has improved for him since 1955,
but not by enough to produce a cessation of the pressure.

And what is the remedy ?   To produce more goods.   A
credit squeeze that holds activity below our supply potential is
utterly out of place in this situation.   Of course, investment and
exports must continue to have their shares of rising output ;
but their *fractions* of the cake need not increase so much as in
the last decade.

Once that happens, and the ordinary basic wage-earner feels intuitively that he is getting his proportionate share in the rising national output, the wage problem, which has been such a worry, is likely to die a natural death, anyhow in its more acute form.

We need not fear that an increase of output now will inflame the upward tendency of prices. I do not believe that most firms have been raising prices because they think that the market will bear them, but rather under the dire necessity of rising costs. A larger turnover should even have the opposite effect, by enabling the firms to get a better spread of overhead costs.

What we now need is a new policy, not guided by an abstract and confused doctrine of inflation, but gripping the situation as it actually is, and based on the idea of expansion. We must continue to give first place to investment. As earliest advocate of the credit squeeze, I pronounce it obsolete now. At least let us ease it off gradually by trial and error, until we see orders and manufacture rising sufficiently to reach the index point of 157 by mid-1958, itself a minimum target. Looking further ahead, we should hope to see gross fixed capital formation at £5,000 million (1957 prices) in 1965.

Let us release the capacity of the consumer goods industries, so as to give them the best possible chance of 'absorbing' wage and fuel-price increases by spreading their overhead costs. Let us seek to meet the workers' desire for a better living standard, not by more money, but promoting the flow of cheap consumer goods. The effort to hold 'administered' prices down should be continued, and the cost of living should be prevented from rising, by the reduction of indirect taxation.

Then we should tell the woebegone foreign bankers outside the sterling area, that, if they sell sterling, we shall pay them in gold, pound for pound. Gold is not of great value to us by comparison with the aims of policy discussed in these articles. We can remember that, if we lose the gold, we simultaneously discharge what are in effect gold liabilities. It will all come back to us in due course — and more than all.

In any case it is a mistake to suppose that a policy of expansion would have so bad an effect on confidence as exaggerated statements about our difficulties.

CHAPTER IX

THE GILT-EDGED MARKET

21

The Gilt-edged Surplus [1]

THE best schoolboy howler I ever had to correct referred to 'guilt-edged securities'. They have been suffering some punishment lately. There are two quite distinct problems — the long term and the short term. The former arises out of very far-reaching changes in the balance of supply and demand. For centuries the British Government never had to borrow net in peace-time. But owing to the nationalization of certain industries it now has to find finance for about half the industrial investment of the country ; and it has to do so on a gilt-edged basis. It makes little difference whether the nationalized industries issue their own stock or the Chancellor, as recently, finds the capital from the Exchequer 'below the line'. The Government now has to be a net borrower from the market, year by year, upon a large scale.

It is true that quite a substantial part of the new money required by the nationalized industries has been found by taxation. But this is not a system that is likely to continue. To cover 'below-the-line' items out of taxation is a good method of curbing inflationary pressure. It was adopted by Sir Stafford Cripps in the late 'forties and has been adopted by the Conservative Government during the recent investment boom. There have been recurrent causes of inflationary pressure since the war, arising out of an excess of aggregate demand for goods over the economy's potential for supplying them. But this is most unlikely to be the normal situation. In the ordinary run of years in future we may expect a prosperous

[1] *The Director*, August 1957.

economy to make quite enough savings, personal and corporate, to finance the capital requirements, not only of private enterprise, but also, as always before the war, for the capital requirements of those industries that have since been nationalized. If in a normal year the Government insisted on finding the finance for genuinely capital expenditures out of taxation, the economy would be subject to deflationary pressure of an acute kind. In the long run it will have to find most of this capital by borrowing.

That is one side of the picture. On the other side, we have a very widespread movement, by many different types of bodies with large capital funds, out of gilt-edged securities into equities. It is usually said that the cause of this change of viewpoint by the bidders for securities is the recent experience of inflation and the fear that it will be continued into the future. But it is not quite clear that this is, in fact, the main reason. This movement began in a big way before the war, and inflation was altogether absent between 1920 and 1939. On average, prices fell considerably in that period, and were falling in most individual years. Yet insurance companies and pension funds were shifting, and humbler bodies, such as colleges, had made a beginning. It has recently been stated that the post-war shift of funds of the insurance companies was basically a reconstitution of their pre-war position. During the war they patriotically and properly used all their new capital to buy government securities, and this left them at the end of the war with an unduly large amount of these securities in their portfolio. What applies to them may have applied to other capital funds also.

One reason for the change may be the altered composition of the body of investors as a whole. More net investment is done by large corporations (the insurance companies, for example) which can spread their risks. Formerly, a higher proportion consisted of private individuals of moderate capital who went for Consols, lacking enough capital to get a good spread. There has also been, over a number of decades, an increased proportion of firmly-established large-scale corporations, the securities of which are regarded as not really very risky. Thus we need not attribute this shift of emphasis wholly or even mainly to the fear of inflation, though that too has undoubtedly played its part.

The net result of this great increase in the supply of gilt-edged securities and this great reduction in the demand for them is disastrous from the point of view of 'government credit', and it is bad also for sterling — just at a time when sterling is far more vulnerable than it was in the old days, though not as poorly situated as our pessimists make out. It is to be feared that this position will continue unless the Government can find some miraculous way of removing the nationalized industries from the gilt-edged market. What one really ought to do is to start issuing electricity shares, etc., with some equity in them, but that would be politically very difficult. If the present position continues, we ought to expect that a curve showing the yield of equities — as published, for instance, by *The Financial Times* — will cross the yield of gilt-edged securities and then stay indefinitely below it.

All this is not the reason for the recent poor showing of the gilt-edged market. That is simply due to the credit squeeze. Were it not for this squeeze, the values *both* of gilt-edged securities and of ordinary shares would rise far above their present levels. In the normal course of events the business public requires a certain amount of cash in hand for normal transactions, and it usually prefers to have a certain proportion in cash by way of reserve. This means that, as the volume of business goes up, *i.e.* as the actual quantity of goods and services that are exchanged against money goes up, the quantity of cash that is required increases. When we look at our own history, or that of perfectly respectable foreign countries, we find that the quantity of cash available is usually increased in proportion to the growth of trade. For this purpose we should look at the quantity of cash (notes in hand and balances at the Bank of England) available for the clearing banks to build their superstructure of credit upon. Clearing banks have consistently maintained a fixed ratio — fractionally over 8 per cent of cash to total liabilities in recent years.

A credit squeeze in the strictest and most proper sense consists of a reduction in this cash. It was most important to carry out such a reduction in 1954 and 1955 to curb excessive demand which was causing inflationary pressure. At first the credit squeeze seemed rather small in relation to the magnitude of the pressure ; it was difficult to have a large squeeze, so long

as the banks had to find enough funds to take up, or to enable
the Discount market to take up, the large quantity of Treasury
Bills put out for tender each week. This obstacle has become
less difficult, especially recently. The Bank of England has
maintained and increased the squeeze. But it is not in line
with past practice to have a squeeze continue for nearly so long
as this one. It almost looks as if the authorities, vexed at the
early obstacles and pleased at being able to overcome them
eventually, have persisted in their squeeze, long after it had
ceased to be required.

The amount of cash available for us to conduct our affairs
is now below its level seven years ago.[1] But meanwhile, the
output of goods has gone up quite considerably, and might
have gone up more in recent months, but for the squeeze.
Furthermore, there have since 1951 been considerable increases
in wages, and, although we may not like these, we have to
adapt ourselves to their consequences. The authorities are
presumably not intending to maintain this squeeze, until the
trade unions offer large wage reductions ! Consequently a
considerably greater amount of cash is needed to-day than
in 1951 to circulate a larger flow of goods at an inevitably somewhat enhanced price level. The gross domestic
product now stands at about 42 per cent above its value in
1951.

The high interest rates now prevailing are the direct consequence of the restriction of cash to its level in 1951, while the
money value of the goods that have to be circulated is so much
higher. This fully accounts for the recent condition of the
gilt-edged market and the inability of the authorities to do any
effective funding. Their success at the beginning of the year
was due solely to the anticipation of some easement. The
shortage of cash makes it necessary to liquidate other assets and
the market remains a buyers' market.

It is a fallacy to suppose that the high interest rates have
anything to do with an alleged shortage of savings in relation
to investment needs. The very few extra personal savings we

---

[1] The text suggests that the reference is to 1951, and that 'seven'
should accordingly be amended to 'six'. The average cash basis in the first
half of 1957 was below the average of 1951 as a whole and equal to the
average in the first half of 1951.

may get in consequence of high interest are more than offset by the reduction in company profits and savings caused by the undue prolongation of the squeeze. At the same time the squeeze is curbing investment, so that the recently heightened desire to save is frustrated.

CHAPTER X

THE BOGUS CRISIS (1957)

Before presenting some contemporary articles written later in 1957, it may be well to recapitulate certain features of that year.

It will be recalled that the demand for consumer durables showed a welcome upturn at this time. Despite this, 1957 should be regarded as representing the early stages of a cyclical downturn. Three aspects of 1957 have to be considered, namely, the state of demand, the wages question, and the sterling question.

1. It was held by some that the inflationary pressure, which had been present in 1954 and very evident in 1955, was still continuing, and even increasing. This was totally untrue, and the following facts may be cited.

i. *Factory Building Starts.*—These began falling in the last quarter of 1955 and had been falling ever since. They continued to fall throughout 1957. In the last quarter of 1956 they fell below completions. In the second quarter of 1957 starts were 18 per cent below completions and in the third quarter of 1957 they were 27 per cent below completions. (All expressed in square feet.)

ii. *Machine Tool Orders.*—These began falling in the second month of 1956 and had been falling ever since. They continued falling throughout 1957. In the third quarter of 1956 they fell below deliveries. In the second quarter of 1957 they were 20 per cent below deliveries and in the third quarter of 1957 they were 22 per cent below deliveries.

iii. *Orders in Electrical and Engineering Goods Industries.*[1]— For these orders the Board of Trade has given annual figures only, and the index number method of presentation obscures the information that we require for our purpose. It can be seen, however, that orders fell below deliveries in 1956 and fell further below deliveries in 1957.

[1] *Board of Trade Journal*, 8th May 1959.

iv. *Investment by Manufacturing Industry.*—Despite the fact
that a backlog was still being worked off, investment by manufacturing industry was no higher in the second quarter of 1957
than it had been in the first quarter, and began falling in the
third quarter, according to the seasonally adjusted figures provided by the National Institute for Economic Research.[1] It
was destined to fall 16 per cent below the peak, before beginning
to revive in the second quarter of 1959 under the influence of
the re-expansionist measures taken in 1958.

v. *Industrial Investment.*—Owing to the working-off of the
backlog, this continued to advance in 1957, but at a slower pace
than before. It reached its peak in the first quarter of 1958.
It would certainly not have turned down then had orders in the
second and third quarters of 1957 been excessive.

vi. *Consumption.*—This was growing, but only at a moderate
rate. The seasonally-adjusted figure for the second quarter of
1957 was only 2·4 per cent above the average of 1956, and the
third-quarter figure was only 2 per cent above the 1956
average. And it must be noted in this connection that consumption in 1956 was heavily depressed, being only 0·9 per
cent above 1955.

vii. *Unfilled Vacancies.*—Attention was drawn at the time
to the fact that during the four summer months of 1957 unfilled
vacancies were slightly above the number of unemployed.
This was due (i) to seasonal influence, (ii) to the increase in the
demand for consumer durables already noted, and (iii) to the
maintenance of activity in the investment goods industries,
owing to orders placed in earlier years. It should be noted that
the seasonally-corrected figures provided by the *Economic
Review* (Table 3) show the number of unemployed as greater
than the number of unfilled vacancies in every separate quarter
during 1957.

viii. *Basic Material Prices.*—These were falling at a substantial rate throughout the year. This was no doubt partly
due to foreign influence, but would have been affected by any
inflationary pressure in Britain. The pattern in other countries
in 1957 was not dissimilar to that in ours, viz., the emergence
of a depression.

ix. *The Budget.*—In each quarter of 1957 the Budget

[1] *Economic Review*, November 1959, Table 7.

N

surplus was greater or the deficit less than in the corresponding quarter in the preceding year.

x. *External Balance.*—The balance of trade was almost the
same in the first half of 1957 as it was in the first half of 1956
and much better than in the first half of 1955 ; the balance of
payments was also almost the same, if we included 'other (net)'
which showed a decline of £50 million, doubtless owing to
Suez. Even so it was much better than in 1955. Compared
with the first half of 1956 the volume of exports for the first
half of 1957 had risen more than the volume of imports.

These data seem fairly comprehensive. I conclude that
there was no inflationary pressure on the demand side and,
further, that demand had already, before September 1957,
fallen to a level which was likely to lead to undue slackness in
the following year as in fact it did.

2. There is no doubt that wages were continuing to increase
at a rate that was unsatisfactory. In consequence of this, the
price level of finished goods was still moving upwards. I
believe that some of the price increases then occurring represented the delayed adjustment to cost increases in earlier years.

It was certainly incumbent on the authorities to do what
they could by exhortation or other *appropriate* measures to
cause greater restraint in wage demands. I did not take the
situation too tragically at the time. For eighteen years circumstances had been such as to make large wage demands natural,
and in most cases justifiable. Between 1939 and 1948 we had a
steep rise in import prices owing to the world-wide rise in dollar
prices, and between 1949 and 1951 owing to the devaluation
of sterling. In these years an upward movement of wages in
excess of productivity was absolutely essential in order to get
the necessary domestic readjustment. This readjustment was
by no means complete in 1951 and the excess to date in the
rise of the cost of living over the rise in wages certainly justified
further increases. Between 1939 and 1951 and again in 1954
and 1955 there had been a strong demand inflation which
naturally generates excessive wage demands. The year 1957
was the first in which it could be said that the wage demands
were neither justified by a rise in the cost of living due to other
causes nor the natural consequences of a demand-inflation.
The fact of the matter was that, after seventeen years, large

annual wage demands had become a habit; it was certainly expedient to break this habit. But one should not argue from the experience of a single year that excessive wage demands were likely to be made during an indefinite future.

The granting of excessive wages was undesirable from the point of view of maintaining the commodity value of the currency, an objective of the very first importance. It is impossible to over-stress this. On the other hand, a totally false impression got abroad in 1957, namely that wage increases here were so great that they would give rise to the need for a devaluation of sterling. That was absolutely untrue, since the wage increases proceeding in our competitor countries were equally great.

It may have been justifiable to caution trades union leaders by saying that 'if this sort of thing goes on year after year, and is not paralleled by corresponding increases in our competitor countries, sterling will have to be devalued'. Or, I suppose that, in the heat of advocacy, one might feel justified in dropping the pedantic qualification, 'if wages do not increase in other countries', although currently and recently they had been thus increasing. Unfortunately, that was not the end of the matter. It seemed in 1957 to be widely believed by responsible people here, and it was certainly believed in other countries, that wages were already increasing at a much greater rate in Britain than elsewhere.

It may be useful to present the actual facts.

TABLE I

PERCENTAGE INCREASE IN 1957 OVER 1956

Germany			United States			United Kingdom		
Hourly Wage-Rates	Weekly Wage-Rates	Retail Prices	Hourly Wage-Rates	Weekly Wage-Rates	Consumer Prices	Index of Wage-Rates	Average Earnings	Retail Prices
+ 9·0	+ 5·1	+ 2·8	+ 4·5	+ 3·1	+ 3·4	+ 4·8	+ 4·6	+ 3·7

There is nothing here to suggest that a devaluation of sterling would be required. If one compares with the United States, one may find an ever so fractionally greater increase here. The export figures that we now know certainly do not suggest that we were pricing ourselves out of the market as against the Americans at that time.

It may be interesting to add that the rate of increase of wages, although still excessive, was already beginning gradually to ease off. In the year ending July 1957 the index of wage-rates rose by 4·7 per cent ; in the year ending July 1956 it rose by 8·1 per cent, and in that ending July 1955 by 7·8 per cent.

3. The sterling crisis that came on in August and September was real enough. This was due mainly to a perfectly specific cause, namely the opinion that the German mark would shortly be valued upwards. At that time I remained convinced by the German arguments that such a revaluation would be inexpedient. Our authorities, on the other hand, seemed to allow it to be supposed that they favoured it. The natural and inevitable consequence of this was a drain on our gold reserves. For the most part this operated through the 'leads and lags' of trade, affecting both our balance and (in an opposite sense) the German balance but, to a minor extent, through outright speculation.

The question of the dollar was also involved. Everyone in Europe knew that the Germans had at that time a watertight case against an upward valuation of the D. mark against the dollar, and would in no case consent to that. Therefore, when the British seemed to favour an upward valuation of the D. mark, it was assumed that they were favouring a devaluation of sterling against the dollar. All this remains a mystery and I doubt whether it will ever be unravelled. Did those among our authorities who appeared to favour an upward valuation of the D. mark (a) not know (what everyone else knew) about the German watertight case against an upward valuation of the D. mark against the dollar, (b) seriously contemplate the devaluation of sterling against the dollar, or (c) not know about the 'rule of three' ?

The drain on sterling was the natural and inevitable consequence of the foregoing. If we really thought that an upward valuation of the D. mark were a good thing, we should have faced a loss of gold with equanimity until the matter was settled, whether at the IMF meeting in Washington at the end of September or at the projected meeting of OEEC Ministers in Paris during October. There was no point whatever in trying to stem a movement of gold, *due to this cause*, by a 7 per cent Bank Rate, since a 7 per cent Bank Rate was obviously insufficient to prevent it. What finally terminated the drain was not 7 per cent, but the declaration by all parties concerned at the IMF meeting, that the D. mark would not be valued upward, and the cancellation of the Paris meeting previously billed to consider this matter. Still less did it make sense to adopt internal measures of restriction as a means of dealing with an exchange crisis due to such a cause.

It must be admitted, however, that there were also other minor causes of the drain. There was a widespread belief that Britain was in fact the victim of 'inflation'. Eminent persons have stated that, on their travels in the United States and Canada in the summer of 1957, they were impressed by how grave a view American and Canadian bankers and financiers took about the inflationary position in Britain. What on earth did they suppose that these Americans and Canadians knew about our position ? The appropriate action for these itinerants would have been to furnish their American and Canadian interlocutors with the facts listed in paragraphs (i) to (x) above, and with the wage and price relations shown in the Table ; or, if those particular facts were not then available, there were plenty of others of similar character, with which they could have been briefed.

It is possible, of course, that the distinguished foreigners would not have been convinced by the facts and figures. This is not probable, since the Americans pay more attention to figures than we do. But even if they had not been convinced, that was not a reason for panic measures. If to the drain which was the inevitable and proper consequence of the discussions about the D. mark, had to be added an extra drain due to ignorant chatter in the Western Hemisphere, our right course of action was simply to sit it through. We had at the time enough gold for that purpose.

I was deeply worried through all that period, not by the 7 per cent which, although foolish, did not matter very much. I was told on the Continent that as an expression of firm resolution, it laid us open to the charge 'Thou dost protest too much'. I had more serious worries. For a number of years after the war, large adjustments had to take place and controls

were necessary. Now for the first time we were setting ourselves the task of keeping a free economy in balance without the
aid of detailed controls. Fine management would be required.
I had been watching the situation month by month with
meticulous care, and by mid-1957 it seemed evident that we
were in the early downward phase of a cyclical depression. I
believe that no serious economic historian will now challenge
this view. But this did not seem to be the view held by the
authorities. I had the feeling at the time that the British still
had a certain contempt for facts and figures. That struck me
as a hopeless attitude in our modern scientific age. How
would an engineer get on who paid no attention to the relevant
figures ? If the findings of history, or of theory, weak vessel as
that is, had any lesson, it was surely a most dangerous act to
give a strong downward push to an economy that was already on
the downward slope.

The measures taken did a certain amount of harm. There
was a needless prolongation of our 'pause' and indeed a
recession in 1958, which was bad, not only for our own welfare,
but also for that of the developing countries, and incidentally,
it now seems, for the United States itself. A tiresome by-
product has been the untimely emergence of trade union
demands for a shorter working week, the natural reaction to a
prolonged period of undue slackness in the factories.

But the consequences were not as bad as I feared. The
economy was still helped in the autumn of 1957 by the revival
in the demand for consumer durables, which has already been
noted, and by the fact that there was still some backlog of
orders on investment account to sustain it.

More important was the fact that the bark of the authorities
in the autumn of 1957 was much worse than their bite. The
element of bogosity in 1957 belonged not only to the crisis
itself, but also, to some extent, to the measures taken to cure it.

Of cardinal importance was the paradoxical fact, which has
not been widely commented on, that, despite all the sound and
fury, the quantity of money was substantially increased in the
autumn of 1957 for the first time since the spring of 1955.
As, in my judgement, the quantity of money has a more powerful influence on the economy than the interest rate structure,
the easement in the former may well have served to mitigate

the effect of the rise of the latter. The upward movement in interest rates and yields in the absence of monetary stringency was doubtless the psychological effect of the announcement of a crisis ; at a slightly later date the high short-term rate was sustained by the more plentiful offerings of bills.

But I believe that the matter went deeper than this. In 1955 the majority of people in business knew from their personal experience that there was inflation ; they experienced delayed deliveries and there was a shortage of labour and steel. It is true that in the early months of 1955 they were sceptical about the two increases in the Bank Rate ; but by the autumn of that year they perceived that the Government really meant its restraining policy seriously. And thus these business people began to review their projects of expansion with a more jaundiced eye, and cut down their orders accordingly. But in 1957 experience was running the other way ; most people did not have personal experience of inflationary pressure, since there *was* no overall inflationary pressure. On this second occasion many must have felt, despite the newspaper headlines, that there was something phoney about the whole business. There is a canny element in the British, even in the English, character. This sceptical attitude mitigated, although it did not quite eliminate, the evil effects of the restrictive measures — and how serious really were the restrictive measures in 1957, *e.g.* in the nationalized industries ? Thus, once again Nature took a hand, policy failing, to relieve the situation.

All the same the situation did deteriorate. Luckily, before many months had passed in 1958, the authorities experienced a great change of heart. It is not widely appreciated what a prodigious campaign of re-expansionist policy the Government undertook in 1958. It had to work harder in this direction than it would have had to, but for the needless and untimely restrictive measures of 1957 — just as it had to work harder in 1955 to restrain inflation than it would have had to, if it had taken action at the proper time, namely in the autumn of 1954.

I call attention to the next following article, which was written with a sense of responsibility in the middle of the crisis in which gold was draining away. I made the prediction that the situation would remain uneasy — as it did — until the meeting of the International Monetary Fund. I draw attention also to my praise of the 'commendable coolness' of the British authorities! [1]

22

Memorandum on the Current Economic Situation, 2nd September 1957 [2]

THE FRENCH FRANC

It is now more than five years since the need of a further devaluation of the French franc, after the two devaluations of 1949, came up for active discussion. Experts were saying, at that time, that France would not be able to resist one for more than a few months longer. Yet, as things have turned out, she has resisted it for more than five years.

In that period her economy has made vast strides forward. In the last four years her industrial production has, contrary to general belief, risen as much as that in Germany, although she did not have the advantage that Germany has had of a large increase in her working population. Investment has been running at a good level ; but consumers also have had their fair share of the rise in output. Exports have risen, although not quite in line, but at least at a rate that merits comparison with other countries. These, however, have had to be supported by subsidies of various kinds.

From the point of view of money value, her regime has been somewhat artificial. Wages, including family-allowances and other social benefits, have risen strongly all through, much more so than here. Special measures have had to be taken to prevent rises in costs being reflected in the cost of living, and thus avoid an even more severe spiral. None the less she has been a high-cost-of-living country.

The basic reason for her maintaining this artificial system for so long, is that her people are psychologically allergic to devaluation. So the experience of 1949 and also, to some extent, her inter-war experience suggest. The point is that her business people, right down to the shopkeeper, are apt to take

[1] Page 197.
[2] Memorandum submitted for private circulation to a firm of stock-brokers.

note of a devaluation and mark their prices up right away in precise proportion. Wage-earners do not lag behind. The consequence of this is that if the devaluation is carried out with a view to making the external trade balance more favourable, or to get her internal price level into better line with the price levels in other countries, its good effects are immediately frustrated. Prices and wages being moved up at once, everything is where it was before, except that the value of the currency has been depreciated. This seems to make it pointless to have a devaluation at all. One gets all the evils of a currency debasement and no advantages. The French, in this regard, may be contrasted with the British ; many producers and traders treated the sterling devaluation of 1949 as none of their business and went on quoting the same prices as before. Prices in Britain rose by a very slow process, as higher import prices worked their way into the cost of living. It may be argued that we have not even yet quite come to the end of the long-drawn-out effects of the 1949 devaluation in respect of the slow seeping upwards of our internal prices. Some might suppose that it all comes to the same in the end, and that the French are sensible to get the inflation over quickly. So French private traders might argue. But, of course, this is not so ; *in the interval*, while the whole slow process of adjustment is being carried out, the external trades get the benefit of low internal costs and have a chance of winning new positions in foreign markets and consolidating them.

Certain new factors have come into operation to make the French artificial system tenable no longer. The industrial boom, through which France, along with other countries, has been proceeding during the last three years, has greatly expanded her import requirements. Investment and consumption have risen in line with expanding production, and the import content of investment and consumption requirements has risen also. Exports have not done badly, but not sufficiently well, and the French balance was precarious before the boom started. It is not absolutely clear that devaluation is the right remedy for this situation. It is not as though French exports have shown any tendency to decline. It might just not be possible to make them expand at a greater rate, even if the advantages of devaluation were going to be valuable. She was already employing a system of subsidies. Other things being equal, it might have been better to struggle on with the artificial system.

And then another factor came into operation — the project for the European Common Market. Although France surrounded her adhesion to it with many reservations, it really did not seem feasible for her to become an integral part of the Common Market with a monetary structure which was so artificial and out of line with other Common Market countries.

And then came a third factor. The Common Market having been ratified, and even before that when ratification began to seem probable, everyone felt that, as a logical corollary, France would have to make some monetary adjustments ; in fine, at long last devaluation seemed inevitable. This caused a general 'bearing' of the franc, which in fact made it inevitable.

All the same, the French authorities have been at great pains not to make this a normal kind of devaluation. They have been desperately keen to prevent it setting up an internal spiral of wages and prices, such as, as already noted, occurred in 1949. One very real contribution to this is the exemption of all necessary imports from the 20 per cent tax. This is in effect a multiple currency arrangement. But there has also been a psychological aspect. By stating that this was not a real devaluation, but a complex system of taxes and subsidies, it was hoped to prevent traders automatically marking up their prices.

It was, accordingly, by no means helpful when the British market, followed by other foreign exchange markets, immediately quoted the franc as though there had been an ordinary devaluation. Foreign opinion tends to ignore such psychological niceties as I have mentioned. There has been a crude attitude for many years about French devaluation, which tended to argue that it was just pig-headedness that prevented the French from embarking on it, and paid no regard to the fact that there was a very real problem. If we had closer international consultation and co-operation, it is unlikely that the various European authorities would have allowed their exchange markets to mark the franc down in this way.

As a further safeguard against internal inflation, the French have imposed a price freeze. Whether this will succeed must remain, for the time, in doubt. Uncertainty whether the French have found a real solution will continue to affect other European currencies.

THE GERMAN MARK

Corresponding to the 'bearing' of the franc, there has been a 'bulling' of the mark, and a widespread opinion that it ought to be valued upwards. This cannot yet be regarded as certainly correct.

For some years Germany has had favourable balances of external payments on current account. These have increased markedly in the last eighteen months. This strong position has led to 'leads and lags' in trade payments favourable to her and to speculative movements, which have caused the inflow of funds into Germany considerably to exceed the external favourable balance. During 1957 the Bank Deutscher Länder has conducted open market operations on a large scale, to offset the increase in liquidity due to the inflow of foreign funds. At the same time, high interest rates have prevailed.

Foreign opinion has been critical of this. The *Economist* newspaper carried an article (24th August) commending a study by a German, Dr. Hahn, advocating an easy money policy, which would cause internal prices in Germany to rise to the international level. It may well be, however, that the German authorities are in the right on this issue and Dr. Hahn in the wrong.

The Germans have their own internal problem of inflation, and a good deal of past experience of its evils. Wage increases have been very large there recently and it is feared that another big round is shortly coming along. The length of the working day is in the process of being reduced. They do not wish to see a vicious circle of rising prices and wages gather momentum. In this respect there is a striking analogy between the German position now and that of the United States after the first war. The latter had acquired a very large gold reserve, and persons outside tendered advice that they should increase their internal money supply accordingly, so as to cause internal prices to rise. But the American authorities were apprehensive of a new bout of inflation and did not do so. Instead they adopted a system of internal credit policy designed to hold internal price levels stable, as near as might be. It is likely that the Germans now will follow the same idea. They have got themselves into a position of strength, and will not see why they should be forced into an inflationary system to suit the needs of other people.

The current position in Germany seems to be one of what is now coming to be called 'sideway' movement. The investment boom is now flattening out. For some time the increase in consumption has been stronger than that in investment. In 1957 there appears to have been a further shift away from manufactured consumer goods and towards the service trades. This corresponds to what is now happening in the United States, and to a lesser degree in Britain also. The correspondence between the trade cycle patterns in different countries is striking.

It may well be that Germany will soon come to the position in which it is felt that some re-stimulation of the economy is needed, but this is not likely to be drastic, and cannot be relied upon to be the main solution of the external balance of payments problem.

This brings us back to the question of an upward valuation of the mark. The question is to be considered whether the German favourable balance is really markedly excessive. It cannot be held to have been so until 1956, and it is dangerous to attempt anything so drastic as a currency revaluation on one year's experience. Her favourable balance on current account in 1956 amounted to £468 million ; this must be reduced to £343 million, when allowance is made for 'indemnification' payments. In the first half of 1957 her favourable balance has been running at the annual rate of £622 million, or £478 million after allowing for indemnification payment. It is not absolutely clear that this is very excessive ; it is the kind of external balance that Britain aims at having. Of course, for Britain, it is claimed that she has great external responsibilities (in regard to overseas investment, etc.) for which she needs such a balance. It may be that a true answer is for Germany to take on similar responsibilities. Furthermore, it is not absolutely certain that the upward valuation of the mark would cause a reduction in the favourable German balance. Germany is producing goods which the rest of the world, and particularly the rest of Europe, needs, and her customers might be willing to pay higher prices for them.

None the less, it must be admitted that there is a prima facie case for an upward valuation.

But here there is a snag. Germany does not enjoy a favourable balance with the dollar area. In 1956 her deficit with that area on trade account was £230 million. Accordingly, she would much object to the idea that the mark should be valued upward against the dollar; and so there have been discussions in Germany on the lines that the existing dollar valuation of the mark should be retained and that there should be an upward valuation of both against other currencies. This proposal at once put sterling under pressure. There is some logic in the German case; that has been clearly seen, and accordingly the opinion was formed in many quarters that Britain might have to be accommodating and allow the devaluation of sterling against the dollar and the mark. Britain will by no means agree to this, but it took time for that to be made plain, and in the interval sterling was sold on a large scale.

STERLING

And so it has happened that the final surrender of France to the logic of developing events has put sterling under pressure. This has subsequently eased off. After a couple of weeks' turmoil, it has become plain to foreign opinion that Britain will by no means consent to a devaluation of sterling against the dollar to suit German interests.

There is, unfortunately, an alternative proposal that may still cause weakness. There is no doubt that the intra-European currency problem is not solved, and it has been suggested that the solution might be found by allowing the European currencies to float freely against each other. If they did this, that would also mean movement against the dollar — since at the stage we have now reached there would be violent objections to having 'disorderly cross rates'. If sterling was party to such an arrangement, this would mean abandoning the existing par of sterling with the dollar, or allowing wider margins. Against this too the British set their face. But there may still be a residue of doubt about whether Britain may not be induced to make some concession, for instance, at the meeting of the International Monetary Fund towards the end of September. It is to be hoped that no concession will be made, but it is impossible to be absolutely certain, since the British may be reluctant to seem to sabotage all methods proposed for sorting out the quite genuine currency difficulties of continental Europe.

The British are now happily clear that the pound is not over-valued against the dollar. Her balance of payments is sound, and remained so despite the impact of Suez. By any test got by comparing the internal price and wages levels of Britain and the United States, the pound at $2·80 would appear to be under-valued, rather than the other way round.

Difficulties arise from time to time in the foreign exchange market and gold is lost, owing to the vast sterling liabilities outstanding from the war which, although greatly reduced since then in relation to foreigners' need to hold sterling, are still great enough to make Britain's position uncomfortable. Selling is apt to break out on any adverse turn of events, even though this may be in truth unimportant. The issue between a fixed rate and floating rates has been much talked over during recent years. The opinion has now been reached that if one is to have periodic difficulties owing to the lack of confidence among foreign holders of sterling, it is likely to be less costly in gold to maintain a fixed rate than to support a freely-floating rate. The British would not wish to have, or consent to allow, large oscillations in sterling in consequence of every chance rumour ; accordingly, she would use her Exchange Equalization Fund to protect the floating rate from such disturbances, just as she did between 1931 and 1939. This support would be likely to cost her more gold than the support of a fixed rate in similar circumstances. And since her gold reserve is narrow, this must be a decisive consideration.

Foreign opinion, which continues to be bearish about British prospects, holds that, if the rate is allowed to float, it will probably float downwards. Accordingly, so long as there is any doubt at all about what the British attitude may be at the International Monetary Fund meeting — and it is impossible to get rid of doubt altogether — the foreign exchange position may remain uneasy.

The authorities have behaved with commendable coolness during August. A loss of gold is likely to be recorded, and as usual a corresponding discharge of gold liabilities will not be shown in the published figures, so that here again we shall have a shock to confidence. There has been no change in Bank Rate ; the moderate upward movement in the Bill Rate has been a small price to pay in a period of alarums and excursions.

During the autumn the authorities will have to return to the fundamental question of whether an easing of credit is now due. Controversy will, no doubt, continue between those who do, and those who do not, regard a credit squeeze, pushed to the point of causing slackness in the economy, as the right anti-dote to a cost-push inflation. In practice, the exigencies of Government finance during the autumn are likely to tilt the Government to the side of allowing some credit easement, whatever view they take on the wider issue.[1]

WAGE EARNINGS

The half-yearly survey of the Ministry of Labour on earn-ings, relating to April 1957, has now been released. Comment has been unduly pessimistic and such phrases as 'rapid rise' have been (wrongly) used.

(A table showing the relation of wage-rates to earnings is omitted.)

These figures need close scrutiny. If wage earnings rise more than the average of wage-rates, this may be taken to indicate a 'demand-pull'. Ever since the war, wage earnings have been tending to rise more than in proportion to the average of wage-rates, and in some years much more ; there have been two exceptions only, one was in 1952, a year of recognized depression, and the other in the period since October 1955.

The figures for the last eighteen months may be a little confusing. At first glance they suggest that earnings had lagged behind in the six months between October 1955 and April 1956, but resumed a very slight lead between April 1956 and October 1956, and had then run level. This is probably not correct, and is due to the particular dates on which a census

[1 This happened.]

was taken. It so happens that most of the major increases in rates in 1956 took place prior to April, while in 1957 some of them were deferred until after April. The increases in wage-rates go in jumps while the increases in earnings probably proceed more steadily. If one smooths out the increases in wage-rates, it appears that the lead of earnings over rates continued, although very slightly indeed, from October 1955 to April 1956 (by a small fraction of 1 per cent) and that since April 1956 earnings have continuously lagged behind wage-rates. This suggests that a demand-pull ceased to be a force making for inflation early in 1956.

PRODUCTION

There has been a moderate revival in production in the course of this year. The July figure for the index of industrial production is quoted as 140/141. This is satisfactory as far as it goes, but it does not go far enough. One cannot expect the industrial production to rise at the rate at which it had been proceeding prior to 1955 (about $6\frac{1}{2}$ per cent a year) because in that period additional man-power was being pulled into employment, and particularly into the industries covered by the index, and one cannot expect that to continue.

The previous increase in the production index may be deflated for the increase in the numbers employed in these industries, and the result is an increase of about 3·1 per cent per person per annum. Had this increase continued in the last two years, the seasonally-corrected index for July 1957 should be about 145. But owing to the abnormally high rate of completion of new factories and industrial equipment during those last two years, one ought to expect the increase in output per person to have been greater than it was in the preceding seven years. The economy was put under great pressure and a crisis in the external balance precipitated, in order that we might produce an abnormally high level of industrial equipment in 1954 and the following years. It would be rather disappointing if all this effort and all this pressure served to give us no larger an increase in output per person than we had in the earlier years.

The recent revival has taken place largely at the consumer

end.   While it is arguable that the stress on the need for more investment has been over-done at certain times in the past, and that a readjustment in favour of consumption is quite healthy — and may indeed help us with the wage-push inflation problem — it is rather curious to continue in operation artificial obstructions to investment — credit squeeze, directives on bank advances and to the Capital Issues Committee — in these circumstances.

————

I was about to leave London for a very brief holiday when the Bank Rate was raised to 7 per cent on 19th September 1957. I had to compose the two comments that follow that afternoon.

It will be observed that the one intended for publication deals more leniently with the 7 per cent.   I was absolutely convinced at the time that the authorities would not for a moment contemplate the devaluation of sterling.   The 7 per cent, ill-judged although I deemed it, seemed at least to confirm this ; it struck me as very important to underline this point in public. Compared with the ghastly idea of a devaluation, such misjudgements as were made at that time were indeed trivial.

23

Memorandum on the Current Economic Situation, 20th September 1957 [1]

BANK RATE

THE reasons for the recent pressure on sterling were explained in the last memorandum.   The final collapse of the French franc, after it had been expected for so long, flashed a query into the sky about all other currencies not outstandingly strong. The special position of the German mark was a cause more real and important.   There has been a widespread wish, especially in relation to the European Common Market, that the mark should be revalued upwards.   Some British have unwisely joined in the move for a higher mark.   The Germans

---

[1] Memorandum submitted for private circulation to a firm of stockbrokers.

O

are understandably reluctant to have the mark valued upwards
against the dollar, since they have a large dollar deficit, and,
the rest of Europe being in a somewhat parlous condition as
regards currency, the Germans cannot place absolute reliance
on a continued flow of dollars being available from that source.
But they would not object to valuing the mark upwards against
European currencies.   For them to do this, while holding the
mark stable against the dollar, would imply British acquiescence
in the devaluation of sterling against the dollar.   The awkwardness of having the German mark over-valued against continental currencies is thought to be so great — although it may
not really be so — that there is a feeling that the British cannot
well resist the appeal to comply.   This is a real dilemma.
Finally the over-emphasis of our wages problem and of 'inflation' both in headlines and ministerial statements, in a year in
which actually inflation has been more moderate than in most
years since the war and in which other countries have had wages
troubles as great as our own, has given foreigners a sense of
alarm about Britain.   Thus there is a widespread feeling, not
only that Britain may be manœuvred into devaluing as a contribution to solving the German mark tangle, but also that she
may be driven to it by her own 'inflation'.

The raising of the Bank Rate to 7 per cent is intended to be
a forthright statement that we have no intention of devaluing
notwithstanding all the foregoing.   It is not certain that, as
such, it will be successful.   Seven per cent is normally regarded,
and in fact always has been, a crisis rate.   Foreigners may infer
that the British condition may be much worse than appears on
the surface (although in fact it is much better), on the ground
that they (the British) would not take a crisis measure without
real cause.   Thus the pressure on the pound may continue.
On the other hand, there is another side to the case.   If the
British economy remains in good shape (on trade account, etc.),
foreigners may gradually be persuaded that Britain both means
not to devalue and is in a position to carry out her intention.
No sudden dramatic resurgence of sterling can be expected.
But patience may see us through the critically 'bearish' attitude
to it.

According to reports, the pressure on sterling eased off in
September compared with August.   The Bank Rate move may

mean *either* that the pressure was much greater than supposed and that the drawings on 'sterling balances' continued to be large *or* that extreme deflationists have temporarily the upper hand in our counsels and have exploited the existence of more moderate drawings to get away with their views.   The gold figures for September may give some indication which of these views is true, although it will not be a certain one because a return flow of gold in the last twelve days is, although unlikely, not impossible.

Traditionally a crisis Bank Rate has not been maintained for very long.   It can hardly be supposed that it will be this time.   If it is successful and causes a return flow of gold, that will be a signal for reducing it.   But if it is unsuccessful and the drain continues, sterling balances will before long be drawn down to the absolute bedrock of genuine requirements, which is certainly above zero, and some stability will then be reached. (We have more than enough gold to honour *all* the sterling balances outside the sterling area, so that devaluation cannot again be forced on us against our wish.)   Maintenance of the high Bank Rate will then seem pointless ; and it is very expensive both on account of our external balance and of the budget.

Meanwhile the Chancellor has come down very firmly on the side of deflation on the home front.   This is presumably intended to impress foreigners, as it may, and to have some effect on the wages front, which is unlikely.   As the ill effects of the cramping policy on industry become diffused, there will be strong pressure on the part of those who advise the Government about public opinion in favour of relief.

It is obvious that there is no prospect of a quick reversal of the policy announced on 19th September.   But there are probably already second thoughts about the wisdom of what has been done, and the logic of events is likely to cause some considerable change towards easement before the winter is out.

FOREIGN CURRENCIES

The French appear to have held the line moderately well to date.   The 'devaluation' checked the speculative movement against the franc, and has produced a visible improvement in the external balance, although, from a long-run point of view, this is not of great significance. Pressures for the marking up of prices have occurred as expected. The most severe pressure comes from the side of agriculture. Even prior to recent events, the peasants were claiming that they were not getting their fair share. The authorities are determined to hold food prices down. Certain adjustments have been made in the cases of wheat and beef, and a new plan has been put forward for having an automatic adjustment of price increases related to index numbers of farming costs. How far this will go to meet agricultural views or abate pressures, is not yet known. The wheat-beef proposals are somewhat analogous to the annual price review with which British farmers are familiar.

Despite the price freeze, a seeping up of prices has been reported. It is hoped that this is not very serious and has not reached the dimensions of the price adjustments that occurred after the devaluation of 1949. It is feared, however, that the French lack administrative machinery for enforcing the price freeze. The wages position is not, so far, too bad, and it is hoped to get a truce for six months. Really substantial budgetary economies have been proposed, and it remains to be seen how far they will be implemented, and whether parliamentary troubles will be encountered. Thus the French position remains uncertain, but events to date do not require a pessimistic view.

The victory of Adenauer is a stabilizing event of first-rate importance. The official view remains that there should not be an upward valuation of the mark. Meanwhile, prominent Germans outside official ranks, such as Herr Abs of the Sud-Deutsche Bank, and Herr Berg, president of the Federation of West German industries, have pronounced strongly against an upward revaluation of the mark. It is appreciated in Germany that these rumours are creating difficulties for the French and British. The Germans are wisely sensitive to international repercussions and wish to do their utmost to relieve existing pressures. It is reported that Herr Erhard will not go to the meeting of the International Monetary Fund. This decision, if true, is most helpful, since it serves to play down the importance of the forthcoming meeting. The implication of his not going is that important decisions, in regard to the realignment of European currencies, will not be taken there. This reduces the current sense of uncertainty.

The existing situation presents a very bad setting for any decisions having long-run effect. The flurry caused by the unfortunate French crisis makes it impossible to see things in their correct proportions.

The pound has remained under some pressure. The figure for the gold loss during August proved, as predicted in the last memorandum, to be substantial. This figure reflects purely speculative movements. As usual, it was unaccompanied by a figure showing a simultaneous discharge of gold liabilities, owing to the difficulty of obtaining up-to-date information on the latter point. There are likely to be further losses in September. It can no longer be hoped that the authorities will take these temporary movements with *sang froid*. In the decade before the war, these movements of 'hot money' were encountered on a large scale ; but in those days we did not publish a monthly gold figure, and the movements therefore attracted less contemporary attention. It is unfortunate that, in recent years, the need to have a large gold reserve has been somewhat over-stressed. When it was decided after the war not to fund the outstanding 'sterling balances' held by foreigners, it was rendered inevitable that our reserves should be vulnerable to every wind of rumour. It would have been more sensible to have recognized that our reserve, *net* of foreign liabilities, was bound to be very low and to have declared it to be the British policy, in line with our former tradition, to accept a narrow reserve. It should have been strongly stressed throughout that no significance should be attached to the rise or fall in the reserve, which is merely due to increases and declines in the foreign holdings of sterling balances.

UNITED STATES

The decline in the investment boom in the United States continues, and the economic pattern there remains similar to that of Britain about a year ago. Orders are below supply potential and backlogs are being worked off. It is reported that in the second quarter of 1957 factories delivered three billion dollars worth more goods than were ordered in that period. There has been a shift of employment out of industrial production into the servicing trades. The overall recession is, so far, slight. House building starts have improved owing to the adjustment in the provision of finance, but are well below their high level of two years ago.

'Inventories', however, have been rising rather steeply, and this would appear to portend a further cut back in orders. It is not yet clear that there are forces at work likely to make for revival or halt the slight downward tendency. Hopes are built on the strenuous efforts by the motor industry to promote larger sales; this industry is a very key factor in the American economy. State and local expenditures (on schools, etc.) are rising strongly.

Meanwhile the full dress debate in the Senate committee on inflation has proceeded. The controversy there is on precisely similar lines to that in Britain. The Federal Reserve System has continued to apply a credit squeeze as an antidote to inflation, which takes the form of rising wages and prices. Critics have pointed out that the American economy is now working decidedly below capacity and that the cost of government borrowing (4 per cent) has become needlessly high in consequence of the squeeze. Thus the issue there is similar. The restrictive policy has caused a flattening in the level of activity and orders are running below deliveries. It does not appear to have been effective in halting the wage spiral. And so the question has been asked, with some vehemence, whether it is an appropriate policy in the existing situation. It is having the same effect there as here, in making government finance difficult — although the problem is not clearly so acute for the Americans as it is for us with our nationalized industries, etc.

The Americans claim that their overseas investment has increased very rapidly indeed in 1956. Despite this there has been a slight revival of world dollar shortages. This is no doubt due to the conditions of boom that have been generally prevalent in the world and the satisfaction of marginal requirements by purchases from the United States.

WORLD TRADE

The flattening out of the boom appears to be a fairly widespread phenomenon. If conditions are not helped by American

revival we have to face the possibility that our export markets
will lack their recent buoyancy and that we shall not be able to
maintain the rate of increase in exports that has obtained in
recent years. Some may argue that this is an additional reason
for caution in regard to the re-expansion of British business,
entailing additional import requirements. There is, however,
another side to this question. British imports make a sizeable
contribution to the whole world economy, and an active policy
here could have a definite effect of the right sort on forces
making for world recession. This is not to say that the British
could expect to get back the extra spent on imports by increased
exports, pound for pound. But a rather larger view should be
taken ; a more active British policy would not only be an
advantage to Britain, but also, to the extent that it tipped the
scale against world recession, could, at this juncture, have
longer reaching consequences.

NATIONAL INCOME BLUE BOOK, 1957

The appearance of the annual Blue Book makes it possible
to take a wider survey of certain trends.

For the first time the Central Statistical Office has felt able
to bring a figure for 'capital consumption' (the American for
'depreciation') into its first table. It appears that in 1956 gross
capital formation absorbed 19·5 per cent of our national product, and that this must be reduced to 11·5 per cent for *net*
capital formation. The corresponding figures for the United
States appear to have been 15·9 and 7·6 per cent only. It must
be remembered, however, that the Americans are working to a
much higher level of national income and that a lower percentage for capital formation represents a much larger amount
of capital investment per head.

The increase in personal savings was notable. They appear
to have risen by 42 per cent in money terms. This agrees with
the flattening out in personal consumption in 1956. Company
savings, on the other hand, were, as predicted in these memoranda, slightly down in money terms (by about $3\frac{1}{2}$ per cent),
owing to the disinflationary policy.

The following table of percentages shows the redistribution
of productive effort in 1956 compared with 1955 :

PERCENTAGE OF DOMESTIC PRODUCT

	1955	1956
Consumption	51·7	50·9
Capital formation	15·2	14·9
Exports	18·3	19·0
Government	14·8	15·2
	100·0	100·0

Note.—The figure for gross capital formation is below that quoted above (19·5 per cent). The reason for this is that, by our exports we earn imports, and these imports supplement our own production and are distributed among capital formation, consumption, etc.

It is satisfactory that a higher proportion of our effort went into exports. But it is unsatisfactory that a lower proportion went into capital formation. It was understood that orders on investment account had fallen considerably and were running below our supply capacity after the first few months of 1956. But it was supposed that the working off of the backlog of orders placed in 1954 and 1955 was continuing to give as much expansion on the investment side as in the economy generally. The decline in the proportion of resources going to investment already in 1956 should be noted by the authorities.

The actual amounts of capital formation and consumption appear to have been running at an almost dead level compared with 1955.

Attention should be drawn to the important item, within capital formation, of plant and machinery. In the two years from 1953 to 1955, this item (at constant prices) rose by 21 per cent, and in 1955 stood at 16 per cent above the highest year before 1953. Between 1955 and 1956, however, it rose by 2 per cent only. Investment in new buildings and works, on the other hand, rose by 14 per cent in that year. This difference is due to the fact that there was a bigger fulfilment of orders placed before 1956 in the category of buildings and works (owing to the longer time taken for completion) than in that of plant and machinery.

Deliveries on capital account for manufacturing industries rose (at constant prices) by 14 per cent. In the four years' period from 1952 to 1956 the rate of capital formation in manufacturing industry (constant prices) rose by 33 per cent, while capital formation in mining, gas, electricity, water, and transport rose by 34 per cent. Thus each broad division got a proportionate share. But, whereas between 1952 and 1954 deliveries to manufacturing industry were stationary, deliveries to the basic industries rose by 24 per cent; but between 1954 and 1956 deliveries to manufacturing industry rose by 34 per cent, while deliveries to the basic industries rose by 8 per cent only. Thus it appears to have been the case that the nationalized industries did, in fact, stand aside a bit to make way for the big boom in private enterprise investment. This is quite satisfactory, and it would be satisfactory also if the basic industries forge ahead more rapidly in the next two years to make up for a sagging of private enterprise investment. From this point of view, the recent announcement by the Chancellor of cuts in the nationalized industries' programmes is unfortunate.

In 1956 wages appear to have constituted 40·8 per cent of total domestic income. This gives a fractional rise over their share in 1948 (40 per cent), and that, in turn, was slightly above the 1938 share of 39·2 per cent. It is worthy of note, from the point of view of getting to see the militant wage demands of recent years in proper perspective, that in 1950 and 1951, during the aftermath of the devaluation of sterling, the wage share was only 38·6 and 38·3 per cent respectively. It did not rise again to the 1938 level until 1952, nor to the 1948 level until 1955.

24

7 per Cent [1]

BANK rate has been raised by 2 per cent in order to make it abundantly clear to foreigners that we are prepared to do all that may be required to prevent another devaluation of sterling. The Government evidently regards the maintenance of the existing parity as the prime objective of policy, to be placed in front of all others. In that they are abundantly right. A devaluation of sterling in existing circumstances would probably have a bad effect on our external balance of trade and payments, it would disrupt the sterling area, and it would spell a renewed bout of inflation on the home front.

[1] *Financial Times*, 21st September 1957.

In so far as the Bank Rate move is a sign that the Government is adamantly resolved to maintain the existing parity, it is to be welcomed. First things should be put first, and it is heartening to have this evidence that the authorities are putting them first. Our satisfaction in this cardinal fact should outweigh qualms that we may have about the method chosen for impressing foreigners with our determination.

It has to be admitted that foreigners may interpret the gesture in the wrong spirit, arguing that 7 per cent savours of panic. They may infer that the situation is in fact worse than it looks — whereas in fact it is much better — and that in that case the hands of the authorities may yet be forced. Unhappily, denials of an impending devaluation were themselves devalued by the unfortunate pronouncements of Labour Ministers in the early part of 1949. There is, of course, a difference ; we are now in a position to prevent a devaluation, if we do not wish to have one ; and it can be argued that this was not so in 1949. But foreigners may not know enough to accept the validity of this distinction. Accordingly it is possible that pressure on sterling may continue for a further period, despite the Bank Rate gesture.

It may be that the time will soon come, or perhaps has now already come, when we should abandon the attempt to influence the foreign speculator by words or deeds. We should have a clear idea of what should be done, step by step, if foreign opinion continues for a sizeable time to be 'bearish' of sterling, and non-resident balances continue to be sold.

This trouble has tended to recur since the war, even at times when, as now, our current external balance has been healthy. Some of us wanted to fund the greater part of the non-resident 'sterling balances' outstanding when the war was over. By leaving them on open account we put ourselves in an exposed condition, the consequences of which are still felt. At first the balances outside the sterling area considerably exceeded our gold reserve ; but they have not done so since 1953. Our first step towards a more independent line of policy should be to regard our effective gold and dollar reserve as consisting of our actual holdings *net* of sight liabilities outside the sterling area. Accordingly, we should view with indifference any loss of gold due to a drawing down of the non-resident sterling balances, and conversely, we should adopt a blithe attitude to speculators. Let them have it their own way ; we carry on just the same.

If the greater part of the remaining balances were, in fact, drawn down — an event most unlikely to happen for more than a very brief period — we should be left with a very narrow gold reserve. We should face this possibility. Traditionally Britain always has worked on a narrow gold reserve ; the idea that we need a large one, sufficient to cover several months' imports, is entirely new-fangled ; reference is often made to the sterling area and our responsibilities to it, but these are by no means new.

There is no question of a massive drawing down of the sterling area balances. We like each member separately to feel that it can draw freely if in difficulties. Trouble only arises if the greater number begin to draw heavily at the same time ; then we organize a meeting of Finance Ministers and get a joint recognition for the need of retrenchment. We need enough gold to meet deficits by a few members, or to meet deficits by many members only for a period sufficiently long to give time for measures of retrenchment ; similarly for a possible deficit of our own.

If, in the unlikely event of a large and *sustained* drawing down of non-sterling area balances, we found that our gold reserve was inadequate for these strictly limited purposes, then we should impose restrictions on imports. When all are seeking to remove restrictions on trade, we should do this with the utmost reluctance. We should do it only when the need was clearly proved, which it certainly is not now. One must eventually cut one's coat according to one's cloth.

The essential point is that we should regard a restriction of imports as a lesser evil than a devaluation. It might be salutary for a Minister to say this at once. The crisis has arisen only because people believe that we will devalue, as a soft option. It is not enough to say, 'we shall not devalue' ; to say that we should impose import restrictions rather than devalue is stronger ; it would have all the more effect in being known to command bi-partisan support.

The main causes of the crisis — I fear that we have to give that name to 7 per cent — have been the readjustment of the French franc, although this was long foreseen, and the peculiar condition of the German mark. It is by no means certain that the German mark *ought* to be valued upwards against the dollar ; but unless it is, we cannot accept its upward valuation against sterling, since, in the absence of disorderly cross-rates, which in the stage we have now reached are surely unthinkable, this would mean a devaluation of sterling. There has been too much talk on this side, based on insufficient information and thought, to the effect that we should like an upward valuation of the mark.

Added to these causes has been the over-emphasis recently given to our domestic wages problem. It is a tiresome one, but not momentous. And wage increases have been troubling our competitors in equal degree. Alarmist statements about our domestic 'inflation' make a far greater impression in causing foreign bankers to sell sterling than ever they do in abating wage claims.

This foreign exchange crisis has supervened at a most un-fortunate moment on our domestic discussion about a demand-pull and a cost-push inflation. The arguments against holding down the production of the country below its potential by an artificial credit policy remain the same as they were before. Such small revival as we have had lately has been mainly on the consumer side.

Investment is decidedly sagging. I have never joined those who over-stressed investment, but surely a substantial recession of investment in our present condition would be rather shock-ing. During the recent boom in private investment, now over, the tempo of expansion in the nationalized industries abated ; that this adjustment occurred was satisfactory. What we now need is a revival of the nationalized industries' programmes, to fill the gap caused by the diminished tempo on the private side. One lays oneself open to criticism by naming a particular figure, but I will not hesitate to do so. I judge that the programmes of the nationalized industries ought to be stepped up in the next two years by £300 million per annum (at 1957 prices).

The wages problem will have to be thrashed out on its own ground. It is probably true to say that the upward seeping of wages and prices, which has troubled the ordinary citizen so much in recent years, was due more than anything else to the devaluation of 1949, which caused a complete divorce between

the external and the internal value of sterling. Let those who
hanker after the 'soft option' now remember that it would
infallibly cause a further inflation of the cost of living here in
the years to come.

25

Memorandum on the Current Economic Situation, 17th October 1957 [1]

WASHINGTON

THE meeting of the International Monetary Fund in Washington towards the end of September proved to be a useful one.
Doubts about the pound sterling during August caused a
focusing of attention upon the forthcoming meeting in Washington, since it was thought that the whole question of the relation
between the pound, the French franc, and the D. mark would
be thrashed out there, and possibly some decisions reached.
Dr. Erhard very helpfully announced some time before the
meeting that he did not intend to go, which made it certain that
no final decision would be reached, and even that proposals for
an adjustment of the D. mark could not be discussed with full
German authority. Thus anxieties about the meeting began to
ease off, and this was helpful to sterling.

The British Chancellor formally declared that the British
had no intention of devaluing sterling against the dollar. He
had already behind him the raising of the Bank Rate to 7 per
cent, which was taken to be a guarantee of the seriousness of
British intentions. The German representative declared that
the Germans had no intention of valuing the D. mark upwards.
What was even more important than these unilateral declarations
was the mutual recognition by the British and the Germans of
the position taken by each other. There was no question of the
British pressing upon the Germans that it would be a good
thing for them to alter the German mark. On the contrary, the
decisions of both parties were accepted by the others as final
and reasonable in the circumstances. Thus there was a joint
British and German authority behind the propositions that

---

[1] Memorandum submitted for private circulation to a firm of stock-
brokers.

neither currency would be altered. Mr. Jacobsson, Managing Director of the International Monetary Fund, made the helpful statement that in his opinion the pound is not over-valued. This consensus of view must have made an impression, and has probably had a greater effect than 7 per cent in strengthening sterling in international markets during the following weeks.

It was also declared that neither party had any intention of asking for or allowing wider margins of fluctuation. This also was helpful.

GERMANY

The affirmation that the German mark will not be revalued does not, of course, solve the problem. If the heavy drain of gold into Germany continues, some action may have to be taken. This might be constituted by the imposition of discriminatory restrictions upon imports from Germany.

It is important that the German point of view should be well understood. It has been stated that only one-third of the accruals of gold to them is due to a genuinely favourable balance on trade and capital account, and that the remainder is due to what may loosely be called speculation. It is thought, however, that only a very small part of this is due to outright speculation, viz. the purchase of German marks for subsequent resale at a profit. Much the greater part of the surplus is said to have accrued through 'leads and lags' in foreign trade. Purchasers of German goods have been paying in advance — as a precaution against upward valuation — even, in cases, by as much as a year or two. Similarly, exporters to Germany allow funds accruing to remain in German accounts, with the same object in view. This is not generally due to the high rates of interest prevailing in Germany, as the German banks are not allowed to pay interest on foreign accounts. It is basically a speculation on upward valuation.

The genuine surplus on trade and capital account, the latter being mainly governmental, is said to have been running at the annual rate of £300 million in 1957, this being somewhat lower than the surplus in 1956. From the British point of view, this would not be regarded as an excessive surplus. The position of the Germans is different, as they do not engage in overseas lending on any scale.   The surplus in the European Payments Union is bigger, but is offset by a large and growing deficit of Germany with the dollar area.   Hence the unwillingness of the Germans to value the mark upwards against the dollar.

The Germans contend that this surplus has accrued for too short a time for good judgment, that it is precarious and probably temporary only.   They point to factors that may well alter the situation — growing internal expenditures on defence and social security payments.   German expenditure on imports has almost doubled since 1953, and has risen more than twice as much as the internal demand for goods and services generally.   Imports in 1957 have been 15 per cent above those in the equivalent period in 1956.

There is anxiety about the German wages situation.   The increase in wage payments between 1953 and 1956 was 25 per cent.   This increase appears to have been about the same as the rise in British wage earnings and greater than the rise in the average of British wage rates.   It is clear that each country has special anxieties about its own wage increases, ignoring what is happening to its neighbours.   The British have been arguing that their wage increases will price them out of the markets. The Germans hold that, whether for this cause or through higher imports, they will serve, if prolonged as expected, to redress their favourable balance of trade.   It may be argued against Germans that they started from a low level.   Comparisons of absolute wage levels are exceedingly difficult.   Dr. Jacobsson ventured the statement at the IMF meeting that 'so far as comparisons of existing wages costs (including employers' contributions) are concerned, existing differences are tolerable'.

The Germans protest that they by no means welcome the inflow of funds and would most gladly take any reasonable steps to prevent it continuing.   It causes what they regard as an embarrassing amount of liquidity in the system, and it must be admitted that they have taken some measures to sterilize this money by open market operations on the part of the Bundesbank.   Since its reconstruction, it has a little more ammunition (formerly belonging to the state banks) for the purpose of open market sales.   The Bundesbank has now already exhausted much of the total amount available to it. These open market sales, which have been criticized, seem a perfectly natural, and even proper, procedure. Having twice suffered the extremes of inflation, they are somewhat shy of another outburst. They feel that they should not be expected by the rest of the world to let prices rip inside Germany, merely to accommodate the embarrassments of others due to the favourable balance. They claim that, rather than ask the Germans to inflate, other countries ought to keep their aggregate demand under better control. Incidentally, in relation to inflation, it has to be remarked that the German cost of living has risen more than the British in the last eighteen months.

As against this criticism the Germans point out that they have reduced their official rediscount rate three times recently, and it is now the lowest in Europe, except for Switzerland, Portugal, and Norway. The most recent reduction was nicely timed, not so much by concerted action, as by like minds thinking alike, to fit in with the British increase before the Washington meeting, so that both nations were able to claim that they were doing the right thing to correct their respective imbalances.

It is sometimes suggested that the Germans might solve the problem by a more vigorous policy of overseas lending, analogous to that of the British. But they do not see matters quite in that light. To the Germans, it appears that their position is still precarious and that they are suffering from a lack of internal capital. The capital market in Germany is very narrow. Gilt-edged securities have been wiped out, and most of the equity of industry is internally held. Insurance companies are bound by law to invest their funds in government securities (central or local), and to absorb new issues, *e.g.* those made by the local authorities for house building and public works. It is a remarkable fact that when the Germans removed the embargo on the export of private capital, hardly any money went out of Germany. How different the position would be if complete freedom were allowed to British companies and individuals to take as much money as they liked to America. The fact that there was no outflow at all of German capital is favourable to the German contention that very little private capital exists. Accordingly it is not unnatural that German companies of the highest repute have been offering bonds at 8 per cent ; great satisfaction has been recently expressed because it has been possible to sell these bonds at one or two points below par. When they are so frightfully short of private capital for domestic industry, and their greatest concerns rely almost exclusively on self-finance, how can it be expected, the Germans ask, that they should begin to divert funds of substantial amount overseas ?

Theoretically it may be replied that they must have sufficient funds for overseas investment, since they have *de facto* a large favourable balance on trade account. They are in fact investing a proportion of their national income, not in their own industries, but in gold. Could they not transfer this surplus, and, instead of using it to buy gold, use it for direct investment in and the development of other countries ? Their reply is that to make plans for developing foreign investment interests is a lengthy and elaborate process, which cannot be achieved in a day, and is only worth doing if there is a prospect of maintaining the developments and the contacts over a long terms of years. By contrast, they regard the gold accruals as something purely temporary, here to-day and gone to-morrow.

The conclusion appears to be as follows. There is no ready answer to the German case. More time should be allowed to see how the position develops. If the German contentions are right, their oppressively favourable balance will ease off in the next two or three years. The speculative movement must in any case come to an end, although we should not rely upon any return flow. Trade may continue for some time to be carried on upon the basis now established, viz. early payments for German exports and late payments for German imports. If the German arguments about their overall balance are not right, the question of revaluation might come up again, although the difficulty about the German dollar deficit would remain. In the end, European countries might have to think of discriminatory quantitative restrictions on imports from Germany. The Germans would not take umbrage at this.

FRANCE

Anxiety continues as to whether it will be possible to hold prices and wages down. The position has not been rendered easier by the fall of the Government. French cynics are apt to

P

take the line that a prolonged interregnum may even be a good thing. During such a time it is impossible for the Assembly to vote new expenditures. Apparently, the outgoing ministers continue to sit at their desks, and it is argued that much more good solid work is done in such times than normally, since the ministers are willing to devote all their time to dealing with business in arrears and many points that need clearing up and are not distracted by parliamentary debates.

On the other hand, the position is not quite so favourable at present, as the outgoing government was pledged to implement stringent economies, and these will presumably be deferred.

Although no spectacular price or wage increases have occurred, it is feared that there will be a seeping upwards. The economy has to absorb the higher prices of imports, except on those necessary materials which are still imported on the basis of the old franc rate. Concessions have been made to farming in regard to the prices of wine, beef, and milk products. The peasants continue to press for more.

BRITISH POLICY

What appears to have happened is that the triggering-off of a crisis by the fall of the French franc has been taken as an opportunity by deflationist elements in the government to give their own ideas a trial run. A brave front continues to be put upon the restrictive policy, which evidently has some momentum, and we are promised a schedule of cuts in expenditure on nationalized industries, public works, etc.

As against this we may be sure that the government will not push the policy to any great extreme, e.g. so as to allow an appreciable amount of unemployment to develop. The Prime Minister made this quite plain at Brighton, and other utterances were not really out of accord. Events in the next few months will show which of the two diagnoses prevalent before the August crisis was correct, and official policy will be shaped accordingly. Was the economy still booming, with inflationary pressure likely to become prominent again? Or was demand insufficient, carrying the danger of a substantial decline in activity? If the former diagnosis was correct, then it may be the case that the further restrictions will have succeeded in holding the line and no serious symptoms of depression will develop. On the other hand, the new restrictions may push the economy into a rather serious recession.

Everyone knows that the economy has, in part, been kept active by the backlog of orders placed previously. The effect of this backlog in sustaining work cannot go on for ever. Government spokesmen have not made it clear where they expect a new demand to come from. Indeed it is not clear that they have thought the matter through in terms of demand, but rather they may be concentrating their minds upon wage increases.

(The concluding sections of this report, which relate to the domestic economy, have been omitted to save space.)

26

These Directives Should Go [1]

THE Chancellor's renewed request to the banks to restrict advances is the least necessary of his new measures, and it will do harm. A reduction in the amount of money in circulation, coupled with an overdraft rate of 8 per cent, are discouragements enough. There is nothing to be said for adding to these concrete measures a generalized directive to limit credit. At best it is superfluous ; at worst it will handicap those sectors of industry which ought to be helped.

These directives are injurious to good banking, and fine expertize in banking has been, for many generations, a pride and source of strength to Britain at home and abroad. Banking has its own high skills, like any other business. The directives complicate and confuse the issue for working bankers. Banks have their own methods of dealing with customer relations and of sorting the sheep from the goats ; where an abnormally high overdraft rate is not imposed upon them, they may make differential charges according to the circumstances.

The matter is further confounded by recent instructions to refer large advances to the Capital Issues Committee. For big investment projects it is quite a normal and proper procedure

[1] *The Director*, October 1957.

to obtain big transitional finance from a bank in order to bridge a gap. The reference to the CIC involves delay. This is enhanced if there is some special point requiring explanation, even though the explanation may be a perfectly good one. Not all times are equally suitable for a new issue. Dare one whisper that the CIC does not always appreciate the timing complexities of the market for new issues, nor time its own business to suit them ? These delays may hurt the country, especially if they touch projects affecting overseas investment and our export trade. All this rigmarole reduces our competitive efficiency.

The central point is that directives to the banks are, or should be, a subsidiary weapon in the policy of credit squeeze. I am not suggesting that it was wrong to use them in 1955, and indeed recommended them myself several months before the Chancellor of the Exchequer wrote his celebrated letter to the Governor of the Bank of England in July 1955. The investment boom was gathering dangerous momentum in that year, and it was needful to use all available means of checking it. Such directives must create awkward problems for the banks, but these should be accepted and endured, if applied for a short period only. It is when prolonged that they undermine sound banking. In 1955 it proved technically impossible to impose a strong credit squeeze, such as the situation required, of an orthodox kind. The prime method of an orthodox credit squeeze is the reduction in notes and balances at the Bank of England available to the deposit banks (the 'cash basis'). The monthly average of these from August to November 1955 showed a reduction of only 2 per cent on the equivalent period of the previous year. The credit squeeze started with the raising of the Bank Rate in January and February ; it was in the period from February to May that the banks had to adjust themselves by selling short-dated gilt-edged ; in that period the cash basis was only down by $1\frac{1}{2}$ per cent on August to November 1954 and was actually up on the corresponding period of 1954. (January, June, and December are exceptional months and have been omitted from these calculations.)

When the Chancellor wrote his letter in July, it was evident that it would be technically impossible to impose a strong squeeze in the near future. The reason for this is well known.

The need for the Government to find large finance for the local authorities (especially in the early part of that year) and for the nationalized industries (especially in the later part of that year) meant that, despite all its efforts, it could not make a strong reduction in the flow of tender Treasury Bills. This meant that the Bank of England could not reduce the cash basis too much without putting the discount market into an impossible situation. That was the central point; I regard the question of the 'second line liquidity ratio' as of minor importance. If one cannot have a strong credit squeeze, one has to fall back upon the less satisfactory expedient of directives about advances, knowing that it may have the unfortunate effect in certain cases of transferring the provision of finance from the banks to other sources less well qualified to handle the business.

But since 1955 the position has been entirely transformed. The credit squeeze proper has become very strong indeed. This has made the subsidiary method of bank directives unnecessary; if unnecessary, they certainly ought not to be applied, since they are injurious. On the average of August to November 1956, the cash basis was down 3 per cent on the equivalent period two years earlier; from February to May 1957 it was down 6 per cent on the last period of 1954 and 2 per cent on the first period. But the strength of the squeeze is by no means to be measured by the actual decline in the figures. The point here is that the money value of the goods and services that bank deposits have to circulate has grown greatly in the interval. When a squeeze is first applied, its strength may be measured by the actual decline in the cash basis; but, if it is prolonged, one has to measure it by the relation of the cash basis provided to the (higher) money value of the national income, *i.e.* of the goods and services that the money has to circulate.

Between 1954 and 1956 gross domestic expenditure rose by 13 per cent. This was partly due to the growth in the flow of goods and services and partly to the rise in prices. If it is said that it is just this rise in prices that we object to, it must be replied that this is now a *fait accompli*. No one supposes that the credit squeeze, or any other disinflationary policy, is going to get an actual reduction in wage-rates; nor, clearly, could it cause the prices that we have to pay for imports to fall.

Accordingly, no one could suppose that the money value of gross domestic expenditure will fall to any extent — unless our production falls seriously, which is not desired. And so it appears that between 1954 and the early part of 1957 the fall in the cash basis relative to the total value of goods and services which our money has to circulate, was at least 17 per cent. This figure of 17 per cent measures the strength of the credit squeeze proper in the early part of 1957, and must be contrasted with 2 per cent, which measures its strength in the later part of 1955.

It might be objected that the cash basis may have been unduly swollen in 1954 itself. There is no evidence for this. The causes of the investment boom in that year were quite different. If we use the pre-war year of 1938 as a yardstick — and no one can claim that there was any inflation in 1938 — we find that gross domestic expenditure had risen from 100 to 307 by 1954 while the cash basis had risen to only 285.

Since May the cash basis has been somewhat increased. It is dangerous, however, to judge policy by the figures of only three months, owing to the multiplicity of transitional influences. The June figure is always swollen, and in August the franc crisis produced abnormalities. The Government has presumably decided to maintain reduction of the cash basis, but this does not weaken the case for abolishing the directives. They are as unnecessary now as they were before.

All this is independent of the wider issue as to whether it is right to intensify the credit squeeze at all. It cannot be denied that, despite some revival this year, the economy is still running below capacity. Furthermore, owing to the backlog, the level of activity is higher than the level of current orders, and it is to affect the latter that the restriction or relaxation of credit should be addressed. The revival in production that has occurred this summer has been on the side of consumer goods. I have never, since the war, been a fanatic in pressing the claims of investment against consumption, or believed that if we fail to raise our proportion of resources devoted to investment to the levels reported from other countries, we are necessarily doing wrong. We may not require so much investment as they. An enlarged flow of consumer goods could do more than anything else to reduce excess demand for higher money wages. But still, investment should not be neglected. It is surely rather curious to impose artificial obstacles in the way of investment at a time when investment orders are running below our capacity to meet them, and such revival of activity as is occurring rests solely on consumer demand.

CHAPTER XI

WORLD RECESSION

It was with great pleasure that I agreed in the autumn of 1957 to join with others in signing a letter to *The Times* newspaper,[1] written by Sir Donald MacDougall, which pointed out what ill-effects the continued pause and the restrictive policy in mature countries would have on the developing countries, and thereby on the whole world economy. I believe that attention was given to this letter in many countries. It was written before the Americans went over to their monetary policy of ultra ease.

I give one article only for the year 1958, but this does not imply any relaxation of my literary endeavours (see appendix for 1958)! In the early part of the year I continued to inveigh against the restrictive policy, but very soon one had the more pleasant task of applauding all that the Government was doing in the opposite direction. My main themes were the analysis of the American recession and recovery, and of the world recession and its less satisfactory recovery. One of my contentions was that the trade cycle in Europe was more important from the world point of view than that in America, and that Europe had great responsibilities in relation to the developing countries.

27

Why we should back Japan [2]

A BRIEF visit, however active, cannot achieve knowledge in depth. It may, however, enliven appreciation, and be an occasion for reviewing the economy of a country, whose progress plays a significant part in the balanced — or unbalanced — growth of the world economy.

From her own point of view, Japan needs to press on with investment at a high rate. She has been doing so. According

[1] 29th October 1957.   [2] *The Director*, August 1958.

to available statistics, production of producers' durable equipment rose from 10·2 per cent of national income before the war to 14·8 per cent in 1956, both very high figures. She needs investment, to cater for a still rapidly-increasing population, to draw the semi-employed in agriculture into industry, and to furnish those industrially-employed in small establishments and at low wages with more modern equipment.

Her population problem, though still formidable, is in principle solved. The small family is now established, and the peak of population will therefore be reached in a foreseeable time, perhaps in 1985–95, at under 110 million, compared with 90 million now. Accordingly, she can have hope and plan rationally.

Every square foot of available land in that mountainous country is intensively cultivated. With a smaller cultivated area than Britain, she employs about 16 million in agriculture and forestry against the British round million ; it is odd to think that those small islands have much more than twice as many working in agriculture as the vast area of the United States (6,200,000).

She has great industrial establishments of modern efficiency ; she is somewhat lacking in medium-sized plants, but has a great mass of small and very small units, paying very low wages and producing light goods or working on sub-contracts for the large firms. The trade unions hold sway only in the large-scale units ; a law is now under consideration for minimum wages, to needle the small units, which must play a large part for a great many years, into modernization and more efficient methods.

Owing to her narrow confines and limited resources, there is a high marginal propensity to import in relation to increasing income and investment. A steep increase in exports is accordingly required for rising investment and manufacture ; it has so far been achieved. But it is a hard struggle, what with the great Communist blocs on one side and understandable ex-war inhospitality in the free world on the other. Her planners are thinking in terms of the export of capital goods to the under-developed countries and of high-class 'Japanese' consumer goods to the rich countries ; for the latter target the small producing units have their part to play. The era for expanding common or garden textiles is realized to be over, as with Britain ; but these, along with other cheap consumer goods, will remain an important constituent of total exports for a considerable further period.

Last year (1956–57) Japan had an investment boom of colossal dimensions ; this was phased about a year after those of Britain and Germany. Having large labour resources to draw upon, Japan achieved a much greater spurt of investment than we were able to do, but, like us in 1955, she developed a great backlog of orders, and there were bottle-necks in the basic industries, including the railways. (Her trains are mainly electrified, clean, rapid, and punctual to the minute. But her roads are execrable.)

The great investment boom led to an ultra-sharp increase in imports, owing to the marginal material and fuel requirements of industry and to some stockpiling, her imports in 1957 being 57 per cent in *volume* above 1955, while exports rose only by 33 per cent. This was a heroic tempo of expansion! Accordingly, she imposed a really sharp credit squeeze by a rise in the Bank Rate and open market sales, and at the same time increased import restrictions. The exchange crisis is over for the time being.

Now another trouble looms. There is the world recession. Being much dependent on primary producer custom, she is acutely alive to this recession. Her planners have proposed an expansion in gross domestic product of 6·5 per cent per annum, which is considerably below that of recent years, but may none the less be a little optimistic. It could, however, be sabotaged by a world recession. At this moment she has the awkward problem whether or not to let the economy become unduly slack in anticipation of declining exports and in order to avoid a renewed exchange crisis. The Japanese dilemma may be regarded as a heightened version of the British — almost a caricature of it — the narrow island territory, with an urgent need for higher investment and vitally dependent on expanding export markets.

It may be useful to look at Japan in relation to the overall world picture. Of one thing we may be sure — she will have no lack of propensity to import. More materials and a balancing supply of food are urgent requirements, if she is to achieve her own aim of raising living standards. If she engages in vigorous export drives in various quarters, that will not be out of a mere love of exports for their own sake, but to give her the wherewithal to pay for needed imports.

The first tendency of the other industrial countries is to regard her as a rival, even as a dangerous one, since her wage structure may allow her to do severe price under-cutting, and, if she balances her exports by higher imports of food and materials, as she surely will, that will only go further to turn the world 'terms of trade' against the industrial exporters. It is not clear, however, that, even from the point of view of the selfish interests of the older industrial countries, this should be the last word on the matter.

More and more it becomes plain that it is incumbent on us to look at the problems of each separate country in relation to the whole world economy ; what is to be desired is balanced growth. In the post-war decade the under-developed countries of the world were confronted with a rise in the demand for primary products of abnormal steepness. They enjoyed more favourable terms of trade than obtained during the period of inter-war depression, and some had some ex-war reserves to help them with their imports. The flattening out of demand in 1957 had a bad effect on sensitive primary product prices and the prospects for the undeveloped countries has on the whole deteriorated.

We are at a turning-point now ; and diagnosis falters. Even if the recession in the United States develops no further and the European 'pause' gives place to renewed expansion, it seems unlikely that the tempo of expansion of the post-war decade can be resumed ; there is accordingly danger that the under-developed countries will continue in the doldrums. This may spell favourable terms of trade, and to that extent be an advantage, for the mature countries. But are we sure that it would be an advantage for them *on balance* to have a continuing phase of semi-stagnation overseas ? It did not seem to be so in the 'thirties. Furthermore, we have to be *political* economists, and to plan therefore for rising prosperity throughout the non-communist world.

Thus thoughts turn to financing investment in the under-developed countries and diversifying their economies by moderate industrialization. This has its place. But the best thing of all for them is that the rise in the demand for their exports should be sustained. That gives them an increasing income as of right, is preferred to growing dependence on foreign capital, and could maintain their prosperity in the *near* future ; industrialization by contrast must come very slowly.

Within this world picture, we should favour the continued expansion of Japan. If the European increase in demand is less great in the coming period, that will be because her need is to that extent satisfied ; but the increase of imports that Japan needs will continue to be very great. Thus Japan could make a substantial contribution to sustaining the growth of the under-developed countries. The corollary of this is that we should favour an expansion of Japanese exports. In an expanding world there is probably room for a rising level of exports from *all* the mature countries, reckoning in Japan as one of them.

The older industrial countries have no self-interested need to expand exports more than is required to buy their imports ; but, as we have argued, their requirement for imports may not rise quickly enough to keep primary producers reasonably prosperous.

It is difficult, yet most necessary, to look at the problems of an expanding world economy in a detached way. If one can rise to that, it is probable that one ought to regard expanding exports from Japan, not primarily from the point of view of rivalry, but as a contribution to the balanced growth of the whole non-communist world.

CHAPTER XII

PROBLEMS OF 1959

Throughout 1959 I have been much concerned by the fact that the Government, in its admirable and far-flung policy of recovery, has made so little use of the monetary weapon. This concern is related to the belief expressed in earlier articles that we should continue to refine upon our use of the monetary weapon and that this would be most potent in maintaining the balance of the economy. Although the Bank Rate was reduced from 7 to 4 per cent, the long-term rate has not fallen, and the quantity of money has been only moderately increased. If monetary policy is to be used with effect to curb inflation, as I am confident that it was in 1955, it is essential that ammunition for this purpose should be recaptured during periods of pause or recession. We have not been recapturing our ammunition in 1958–59.

I believe that this has been due to a deep-seated confusion, which, it will readily appear, has a close connection with the themes of dynamic economics. During the 1955 credit squeeze it was found very difficult to reduce the flow of tender Treasury Bills by the method of funding the National Debt. Accordingly, it seems to have been argued that it would be expedient for the authorities to proceed with funding at the earliest convenient opportunity. And this they have been doing from time to time.

This seems to imply that a credit squeeze can be better effected if the floating debt has been rendered smaller. I believe that there is very little in this. What matters on the occasion of a squeeze, is the rate at which one can get funded debt into the hands of genuine investors *during the course of the squeeze*. It is, in fine, the rate of change that matters.

It is a familiar point in dynamic theory that it is all-important to have clarity in relation to dimensions. And, of course, this is relevant in the application of dynamic theory. It is precisely on this point that there seems to have been confusion. At all times the quantity of orders placed is primarily a function of the expectation of markets, with finance acting as a restraining influence. In a period of inflationary pressure, expectations are rising at an accelerated pace and it is accordingly needful, in order to counteract that influence, to increase the strength of the restraining influence of finance. It is irrelevant what the absolute quantity of money or the absolute amount of the flow of tender Treasury Bills or the absolute amount of Debt in the hands of the genuine investors are when the need to stiffen the influence of finance begins. The all-important point is that it should be possible to reduce the quantity of money, to reduce the flow of tender Treasury Bills and to increase the amount of funded Debt in the hands of genuine investors *during the period* in which it is needed to increase the restraining power of finance. Thus in the preliminary period of pause or recession, what the authorities ought to be thinking is not — 'How can we reduce the quantity of Treasury Bills now ?' but 'How can we arrange matters so that, when the time of need comes, we can *then* reduce the flow of tender Treasury Bills quickly ?' From an ordinary common-sense point of view, but on this I must be subject to correction, it would seem that a drive to get a lot of the funded debt into the hands of genuine investors in the interim period would make it more difficult to get a lot of funded debt into the hands of genuine investors later during the credit squeeze period. It is possible that the previous stocking-up with gilt-edged securities by the genuine investors will diminish their appetite for yet more just at the time when it is expedient that they should have the largest possible appetite for more. I accordingly believe that the policy of intensive funding during the interim period is likely to make the credit squeeze policy more difficult when the time comes. We shall see what happens presently when we need a credit squeeze!

This is obviously an illustration of getting a dimension wrong.

The American deficit has naturally given anxiety during 1959.

Then towards the end of the year came the serious question of what the Germans ought to do, when their internal economy developed inflationary tendencies, while their external balance remained in large surplus. This may be regarded as illustrating a central theme of dynamic economics. The correct answer has not perhaps been formulated in theory, and in practice the problem has scarcely begun to be seriously considered. The problems of 1960 will certainly be more intellectually fascinating than those of 1959.

28

The Long-term Rate of Interest [1]

PUBLIC policy is now, wisely and correctly, directed to re-expanding the economy and to reviving the momentum of growth. On the one side, a direct stimulus to investment has been applied by the raising of ceilings in the public sector. On the other side, stress is laid on raising the level of consumption, by relaxation of hire-purchase restrictions, by allowing new forms of banking accommodation, etc. — and, in due course, it is to be hoped, by tax reductions. Meanwhile, taxpayers should, like the International Bank in relation to the proposed increase of its capital, behave proleptically, and arrange their household budgeting to-day on the assumption that some decent tax relief will shortly come to them.

Thus it is rightly desired to encourage both investment and consumption. It is to be noted that the increase of consumption, which is, of course, to be desired for its own sake, is designed to have a favourable effect on investment also. Owing to the existence of surplus capacity now, consumption will, in many lines, have to rise some distance before the industries in question will begin again to nibble at more investment with a view to increasing their capacity. Investment and consumption must have a balanced relation to one another on the path of economic growth ; otherwise, there are bound to be bad jolts and jogs in the economy.

The classic method for encouraging investment is to have a low long-term rate of interest. This weapon appears at present to be suffering from neglect. The rate on gilt-edged stock remains high by traditional British standards. Low interest

[1] *The Financial Times*, 28th January 1959.

need not be regarded as a substitute for the methods of stimulating the economy mentioned above, but as a natural and proper complement to them.

It is surprising that more stress is not laid on it, since its bias, as a stimulator, would be towards more investment. Only three or four years ago, when an investment boom of disproportionate magnitude was throwing the economy out of balance and causing inflationary pressure, there was the greatest reluctance to discourage investment, because comparisons with foreign countries and other criteria pointed to the need for a higher level of investment in Britain ; my plea for curbing investment as a necessary temporary correction at that time was considered by many as almost indecent.

But some of the arguments for high investment were valid in their own right, and are no less so to-day than then. Yet now, although investment demand has got out of balance on the *low* side, we are not resorting to the classic and most obvious method of restimulating it.

Some urge that investment is not very sensitive to the rate of interest. In that case we should surely have a low rate, since a high one is burdensome to the taxpayer, and he is already burdened enough through other claims on him. Others, taking an opposite position, urge that the high world-wide post-war demands on investment account are such as to necessitate a high interest rate and that we must settle down to that unpleasant fact if we are to avoid inflation. That argument implies that investment *is* sensitive to the interest rate, for otherwise a high rate would have little effect in checking inflation.

The fact remains that at present investment demand is too low. We need not be deterred by problematic considerations about the long-run future from trying out the classic remedy for deficient investment now, especially as this would be beneficial in other ways also. If the situation develops differently later, we can always reverse engines again. That would be in line with the principles of a 'flexible' monetary policy.

There has been some talk in recent months of reviving 'investment allowances'. These are intrinsically unsound, since they are palpably a subsidy, and one in the long run very burdensome to the taxpayer. We judge that those subsidies

that have remained with us as the aftermath of war — the hous-
ing subsidies, the food subsidies — are intrinsically unsound,
and are striving now to dispense with them.   Then we should
surely not add another subsidy, likely to mount up to a very
large sum after the passage of years.

Is it not a strange paradox that voices should be raised to
advocate a new-fangled method of encouraging investment
('allowances'), while we fail to use the traditional, ancient, well-
tried, well-authenticated, and orthodox method of doing so,
namely, by a lower long-term interest rate ?   The method of
encouraging investment by 'allowances' burdens the taxpayer ;
the method of doing so by low interest relieves him.   Does he
not need relief ?   Should we not therefore think of low interest
as our first recipe ?

The reason why we do not do so is not far to seek.   It would
not be difficult to bring the long-term rate down, but the
historic method for doing that is to increase the quantity of
bank deposits through open-market operations by the Bank of
England, and, by the most excessively muddled thinking, it is
supposed that this would be 'inflationary'.   An increase in the
quantity of bank deposits would have no more tendency to
raise prices than any other method of stimulating demand.

But we are now pursuing other methods of stimulating
demand, and with some vigour ;   it is judged, in my opinion
rightly, that in the existing environment of recession an increase
in the demand for goods and services will not cause a rise in
prices.   There is nothing in a fall in the long-term rate of
interest, effectuated by an increase in the quantity of bank
deposits, that will have a greater tendency to raise prices than
any of the other methods of stimulating demand, such as are
now being applied.

One had supposed that the fallacious form of the 'Quantity
Theory' of money which saw a direct relation between the
quantity of bank deposits and the price level had died and been
decently buried a quarter of a century ago.   It is to be noted
that the Federal Reserve System conducted open-market operations to increase the quantity of money on a bold scale last year ;
this may be regarded as having been a prime cause of the
American recovery and it has had a salutary world-wide
influence.

Q

It is difficult to measure the present deficiency of the quantity of bank deposits in Britain, owing to the well-known problem of choosing a suitable base year for comparison. If we take the ratio of the total quantity of bank deposits to the money value of the national income, as recorded by our statisticians, to have been 100 in 1938, it was 117 in 1950. This was probably inflationary. It had been reduced to 95·3 in 1953, a year of fair balance. Owing to the subsequent deflationary policy, which was needed and thoroughly justified in 1955–56, it had fallen by 1957 to 75·4. It was probably slightly lower still in 1958 and definitely sub-normal. If it were now restored to 100, or even to 95, the gilt-edged rate of interest would move easily downwards and might well regain the historic British norm of 3 per cent.

How great an effect this would have on recovery no one can state with confidence. We are encouraging consumption and we are encouraging investment in the public sector ; we should match this by trying out the time-honoured and well-seasoned method of encouraging investment in the private sector also, namely, financial ease, to be effectuated by restoring the quantity of bank deposits to a more normal level.

29

America's Payments Problem [1]

THE overall adverse balance of payments of the United States is now a major element in the world economic situation and is likely to command increasing attention. It may take some time to remedy, as did the 'dollar shortage' in the 'forties. It is incumbent on us to think of this as in part our own problem, just as the Americans had the breadth of vision to see that the world-wide dollar shortage was in part *their* problem in the earlier period, and to take it into account in shaping our policies.

If non-dollar countries do not adapt their policies to the new situation, the Americans will be forced in due course to take measures of self-protection that may have adverse effects on other countries and on the free world generally. The new

[1] *The Financial Times*, 30th July 1959.

situation does not seem to have affected American economic policy very deeply yet, except that it may be one factor causing the Federal Reserve System to be more restrictive in its monetary policy — and that itself may be unfortunate.

First, it is important to consider certain facts. The United States has had an overall deficit, namely, on current account plus transfer payments plus long-term capital movements, all through the 'fifties (except for 1957) ; in most years this overall deficit was well below the $1,000 million mark, but in 1958 it rose abruptly to $3,000 million. The change in the basic position, however, came a year, or even two years, earlier (see below).

Much has been heard about the Americans pricing themselves out of world markets ; it is not clear yet that this has been an important factor. Between 1951 and the present, the value of American exports (including 'invisibles' but omitting the despatch of military equipment) and the value of American imports (including 'invisibles' but omitting military expenditures abroad) rose together roughly in line — namely, by about a quarter each.

In 1951 the U.S. surplus on current account, thus measured, was 24 per cent of the value of her exports of goods and services, in the quinquennium 1951–55 it was 22½ per cent, while in 1958 it was 25 per cent, despite the substantial drop in her exports in that year. In the first quarter of 1959, when special factors (for example, steel) were increasing U.S. imports, the surplus was 21½ per cent. Thus it may be said that there has been a balanced growth of her imports and exports.

It is in other directions that we must look for the cause of the present imbalance. In the years 1951–55 the U.S. surplus was not quite sufficient to cover military expenditures abroad and 'transfers' of various kinds ; any investments abroad had therefore to be made at the expense of the American net reserve — thus affording a much-needed accretion to the dollar reserves of other countries.

In 1951–55 net U.S. long-term investment abroad averaged $733,000 million per annum ; it rose to $2,094,000 million in 1956, to $2,922,000 million in 1957 and to $3,131,000 million in 1958. The Americans just had not the wherewithal on external account to make these large foreign investments.

Their effect on the balance of payments in 1956 was offset by abnormally large exports, probably due to the world-wide investment boom, and in 1957 by still larger exports, due to the same cause and to the Suez affair. Thus the true position was temporarily masked. In 1958 it became visible.

In the first quarter of 1959 the net long-term investment was down to $1,400,000 million (annual rate) ; $600,000 million of this change was due to an accelerated German repayment of debt. Not much can be learnt from a single quarter ; the change appears to have been on the portfolio side, rather than in 'direct' investments abroad. It seems unlikely that a correction of the imbalance could come by an abatement of direct investments abroad, especially if, as we hope, the non-dollar world is moving out of its recession phase into one of recovery. The European Common Market appears to be a factor likely to make American direct investment increase.

The American authorities are bound, in one way or another, to seek to rectify the situation, unless the rest of the world rectifies it for them. Three lines are open to them. They can seek to influence portfolio investment by interest rate policy ; they can cut down 'transfers' ; and they can become more protectionist in their commercial policy.

From the point of view of the non-dollar world, only the first of these would be relatively innocuous. There is no contradiction in the Americans making substantial direct investments in the rest of the world, carrying their know-how and enterprise with them, while the countries of the rest of the world offset this, on balance of payments account, by buying American securities of higher yield than their own. (I am not saying that receiving countries should not watch the inflow of American direct investment rather carefully, owing to the burden that the profit thereon could impose on their balances of payments in the years to come.)

If the movement of portfolio investment is to be an important method of rectification of the American deficit, the non-dollar countries have a crucial part to play to assist it. The British authorities should take note. If interest rate differentials are to influence capital movements, it is important that this should be done by a reduction of interest rates in non-dollar countries — and many of them need such a reduction in any case on their own account — rather than by a progressive increase in American interest rates.

If the Federal Reserve authorities presently found that the level of rates needed to retain and attract portfolio or short-term capital was unconscionable from the point of view of the domestic economy, as might easily happen, then American thinking would be driven to take more seriously the other two methods of correcting their imbalance ; and that would certainly be bad for us. Thus we have yet another reason for letting interest rates come down here, by restoring the quantity of money to a more normal level.

A word may be said in passing about American transfers on the military side. The United States is at present contributing slightly more to the defence of the free world per £ of national income than we are. This difference is certainly no greater than is justified by the 'progressive taxation' principle, by which the richer man contributes something more to the community's objectives per £ of income. Equity does not require an adjustment of present burdens.

But there is no reason why there should not be an adjustment in the form of the American contribution. Subject to the technical difficulties involved in any change, NATO could ask the United States to contribute more by the direct supply of military equipment, which would be no burden to her external balance of payments (and might help to sustain her domestic recovery), and correspondingly less by ways, such as offshore procurements, which do burden her external balance. The existing arrangements were designed in part to help other NATO countries in their dollar shortages, an objective which is now obsolete.

For the main and best method, however, of curing the American imbalance, the initiative must rest, not with the Americans themselves, but with the rest of the free world. Expansion in the non-dollar world should be resumed at a greater tempo. If this happened, American exports would float upwards on the rising tide, and no more would be heard of the horrid alternatives of increasing American protectionism or reducing American aid to the free world. It need hardly be added that all discriminatory restrictions on the import of dollar goods should be removed for the time being.

30

Forward Foreign Exchange and Interest Rates [1]

THERE is at present what may be called an 'Establishment' view, or, to give it a less-dignified name, a coffee-house view, that interest rates in this country will have to remain rather high. The reasoning behind this view is obscure. The 'right' level of interest rates may be regarded as determined by the balance of savings and investment requirements. The biggest single item in the demand for new investment has historically been that required to provide the capital overhead for an increasing population ; the British population is due to be roughly stationary in the period ahead. Savings are running at a high level. We may be deceived by the abnormally high investment requirements for the refurbishment of industry during the last decade.

Attention is then drawn to the world scene. In this total scene the United States has great weight. No one can say that investment requirements there are now running at a high level relatively to U.S. savings or are likely to do so in the coming period. It is claimed that the investment requirements of the development countries — as we should now call them — are vast ; but these are ideal only, and to a great extent not backed by an effective demand for capital. These countries certainly cannot afford to borrow at a high rate of interest, and will wisely be unwilling to do so.

Britain, a mature, high saving country with a stationary population, ought to have low interest rates, and thus to put herself in the position of being able to be a lender on favourable terms to the outer Commonwealth and other parts. Why do that, it may be objected, if the return, as reflected in the interest yield, is low ? The reason is that the ramification of overseas investment is good for exports, and on the expansion of these we still vitally depend. Even where the investment seems initially injurious to exports, as in the building of factories overseas to supply goods of British make, there are indirect favourable effects ; and, if we do not build such factories, our competitors will do so.

[1] *The Director*, August 1959.

Britain has a multitude of overseas connections created by our forebears ; these should be wedded to a willingness to lend on easy terms, and an accessible capital market in London. This is the tide in our affairs, in which to utilize those connections by a fruitful flow of capital outwards ; if we do not do so now, they will soon wither away in a rapidly-changing world.

The authorities should accordingly now cause the interest rates here to fall. This could be done in a perfectly normal and regular manner. Incidentally, it is perfect nonsense from a domestic point of view to sustain high interest rates artificially, while giving investment 'allowances' — save as a purely temporary measure. The latter are supposed to encourage investment, while the former discourage it, and both are burdensome to the taxpayer.

The way in which the rate of interest can be caused to fall is by the Bank of England increasing the cash basis of the clearing banks, through open-market operations, giving them enough *both* to maintain their increase of advances to customers *and* to be buyers of government securities, and by instructing the government broker to modify his selling policy accordingly. The objection to doing this is the fear that it might be 'inflationary' ; this fear is attributable to the muddled thinking and the revival of a 'quantity theory of money' in an obsolete form, during the scare two years ago. These operations could have no direct effect on wage-bargains, which are now the primary potential cause of inflation. And if it is argued that they might have an indirect effect on wages by increasing the demand for goods, and thereby for labour, how is this argument consistent with our using numerous *other* expansive measures for increasing the demand for goods ? Why use all other methods for pushing on with recovery from the recent pause, save the well-seasoned and orthodox one of easy money ?

There may be fears that easier conditions in the long-term capital markets would pull down interest rates in the short-term market and thus jeopardize international sterling. This is a matter that needs careful watching. It should be possible to create easier money-conditions generally, while maintaining existing rates in the short-term market. The increase of funds for the clearing banks could be matched by an increased offer of Treasury Bills, even though this would go against the policy of 'funding', which is at the moment out of phase ; funding *now* is not in the least likely to make it easier to impose a credit squeeze on a future occasion.

There is another way in which international sterling could be supported during an easy-money phase. Through the mechanism of the forward market in sterling and official intervention therein, a higher rate could be offered to foreigners on Treasury Bills than can be obtained domestically. It is possible that interest rates in the United States will continue to creep up, for reasons which certainly have nothing to do with any excess of investment requirements there. The American authorities are concerned with such matters as the wage-price spiral, the trek into equities, the (moderate) boom on Wall Street, and the current phase of dollar weakness. It would be disastrous if our interest rates had to follow suit.

The question of official intervention in the forward sterling market has been bedevilled by its advocacy by enthusiasts on wrong grounds. There have been phases in the recent past when forward sterling has weakened owing to lack of confidence and the fear of a coming devaluation. It has been suggested that, if the authorities had made up their minds not to devalue, they could with a good conscience have supported the forward rate by selling gold (or dollars) forward, and thus have obviated the profit on interest arbitrage, which was causing a sale of spot sterling and a drain on their gold reserve. It is very doubtful if this would be a wise policy, since knowledge of these operations would further undermine confidence. This would increase the sale of forward sterling by outsiders, and thus raise the amount of forward gold (or dollars) which our authorities would have to sell to support the forward rate at interest parity. It is unlikely that the authorities would be willing to sell more gold (or dollars) forward than they had in hand ; but foreigners might think that they were doing so — since there is no limit to what they could sell forward. This combination might produce an impasse, which would have been avoided, had the authorities not embarked on such a policy in the first instance.

Very different is the idea of using the forward market in times when there is *no* lack of confidence in sterling, as a technical method of giving foreigners a higher rate of interest on Treasury Bills than is vouchsafed to domestic holders.

Forward sterling could be supported at a rate which would afford a moderate profit on interest arbitrage to foreign purchasers of spot sterling. Such a policy could be adopted in circumstances in which international short-term rates were edging upwards and any such increase in domestic rates was undesirable from a domestic point of view, or when it was desirable to have domestic rates edge downwards and there was no such world tendency.

This may be a situation with which we shall be confronted in the near future. Keynes, who was a very great expert in the foreign exchange market in theory and practice, was a persistent advocate of official intervention in the forward market. The project deserves consideration.

7 per cent may have increased the confidence of some foreign financiers; it shook mine. A greater shock was produced a little later by the revelations of the 'Leak Tribunal'. Not that I had supposed for a moment that the persons concerned had behaved with less than the utmost honour and propriety, and I was heartily glad that the Tribunal vindicated them. What shocked me was the revelation of the state of mind of some of them in September 1957, which seemed so utterly lacking in any grasp of the true situation.

However, one consoled oneself with the thought that any country or system has to carry some duffers in high places and that we probably had figures at the top who knew better.

But then came a third shock which was more profoundly disturbing — the Report of the Radcliffe Committee. It was more disturbing because one had expected from it the cream of high thinking, in the great tradition of such British reports. This body could not have had a more able chairman than Lord Radcliffe, whose judicial mind could be relied on to sort out and weigh the conflicting testimonies of the economists, and to make the best of the material at his disposal. He had two excellent economists to aid him. How was it possible that a document so lacking in any theoretical articulation could have been produced by this committee? Not only that; while the Report must be praised for not endorsing the foolish ideas that were so prevalent in 1957, I hope that the patient reader of these pages will agree that the knowledge that it shows of the history of the recent period is only sketchy and that, by consequence, it has altogether failed to discern the main lessons of our fascinating experience in the last ten years.

31

Is the Money Supply Important? [1]

IN a brief review, space does not allow the paying of deserved compliments to Lord Radcliffe and his colleagues on the wealth of information that they have provided, on their excellent writing, on their scholarly precision or on other allied virtues. It will not be possible to touch on many of the interesting subjects that they have discussed. For every line will be required for two or three fundamental themes. It is needful to get down to essentials.

In the tradition of British thinking on practical banking policy, from the Report of the Bullion Committee (1810) to that of the Macmillan Committee (1931), great stress has been laid on control of the quantity of money as the prime instrument available to the Bank of England for regulating credit conditions ; when it wished to damp an inflationary tendency, it could reduce the quantity of money ; and conversely. It is precisely on this point that the British have, until comparatively recent years, differentiated themselves from continental experts, who were inclined more to a *non possumus* attitude about what a central bank could do in this respect ; it was commonly believed in this country that the emphasis on the quantity of money was responsible for the good standing of sterling in the world, particularly before 1914.

Two digressions are necessary at this point. First, it has recently become customary in international publications and elsewhere to refer to the 'money supply' as meaning the sum of bank deposits (whether all deposits or current accounts only) and currency notes. The Radcliffe Committee has followed suit. It is a pity to include currency notes. In developed countries notes usually play a passive role ; they are issued, like

---

[1] Review of the Radcliffe Report, *Westminster Bank Review*, November 1959.

token coins of low denomination, to meet the requirements of
the public. Accordingly, it will be found in Britain that the
notes in circulation have risen year by year almost exactly in
proportion to the rise in the money value of the national income.
It is in the fluctuating quantity of bank deposits that the
'policy' of the authorities can be clearly seen. In 'easy money'
periods, deposits have been increased more than the national
income ; *per contra*, on occasions of a 'credit squeeze' they
have been increased less or have even been reduced. Of course,
owing to the influence of deposits on the sum of deposits and
notes, this sum moves in the same direction as deposits only.
But the inclusion of the passive element of notes blurs the
picture ; in statistics designed to give a history of monetary
policy or to estimate its effects, currency notes should be
omitted.

Secondly, it may be supposed by some that the thinking of
Keynes, which we cannot yet ignore with impunity (although
the Radcliffe Report to all intents and purposes does so),
tended to wean us away from what used to be called the 'Quantity Theory of Money'. It is necessary to draw a distinction.
Keynes challenged the older view that variations in the quantity
of money had a *direct* effect, upwards or downwards, on the
price level. It does not follow that he broke completely with
tradition and held the quantity of money (for which in his
General Theory he uses 'amount of liquidity available' as a
synonym) to be of little importance. On the contrary, the
quantity of money played a key part in his scheme of thought.
For it was an increase or decrease in the amount of money
relative to the work it had to do in circulating the national income (precisely the ratio referred to in my last paragraph), that,
according to him, had a paramount influence on the rate of
interest ; and the rate of interest influenced the amount of
investment undertaken and so could be of importance in damping a boom or curing a recession. Now this opinion about the
modus operandi of changes in the quantity of money was not one
of the points on which his thought jarred violently with the
thinking of other economists who did not subscribe to his full
doctrines or call themselves Keynesian. There were others
who held that changes in the quantity of money operated (towards inflation or deflation) mainly via the effect of those

changes in the rate of interest and in the amount of orders placed on borrowed money. Thus, whether by traditional thinking or by Keynesian thinking, the quantity of money put into circulation by the central bank was of key importance in relation to monetary policy. The question whether monetary policy can have an important influence on the course of events I leave over for the present.

On this subject the Committee writes : 'It is the liquidity of the economy, rather than "the supply of money" that the authorities should seek to affect by their use of monetary measures' (para. 10) ; 'some experts consider that the central task of the monetary authorities is to keep a tight control on the supply of money. . . . Our view is different. Though we do not regard the supply of money as an unimportant quantity, we view it as only part of a wider structure of liquidity' (paras. 388 and 389) ; 'the supply of money is not the critical factor' (para. 397).

Having thus abandoned the foundation-stone of British monetary theory, the Report offers in its place what it calls the 'whole liquidity position' (paras. 10 and 389). When making such a change in the basis of theory one would expect it to offer a definition of great precision. None such is given in the quoted paragraphs. Later, in para. 397, there is a reference to 'our review of the private sector in chapter iv, where we found that the sources of liquidity are multifarious'. This 'review' covers various lending institutions (building societies, etc.). It has always been supposed that these non-bank institutions are in essence *channels* making the savings of one set of people available for use by another. If one is asked to regard these institutions as able to increase 'the whole liquidity position', one is entitled to ask for a very precise account of how they manage to do this.

We have seen that in Keynes the 'quantity of money' and the 'amount of liquidity available' are regarded as interchangeable expressions. This may be subject to minor modifications. For instance, Keynes himself suggested in one place that one should add to the quantity of deposits the 'unused overdraft facilities outstanding'. These unused facilities, to the extent that they are real, presumably move up and down concurrently with the banks' willingness to lend, so that, in increasing or decreasing the money supply, they would simultaneously alter this other medium of liquidity in the same direction. What *other* assets had the Committee in mind which are so important that they justify the contrast it draws between the supply of money (said not to be critical) and the whole liquidity position? Treasury Bills? These may indeed be used as means of discharging a liability. But are they so used to a really significant extent in the commercial community as whole? What are the instruments that these other alleged non-bank 'sources' of liquidity create as means of payment?

Banks, within the context of the banking system as a whole, are in a different position from other financial institutions. 'Loans create deposits.' If the banks, in consequence of an enlargement of their 'cash basis' by the central bank, become willing to lend more in the aggregate, they automatically create means of payment for their borrowers in the form of deposits, which can be drawn on by cheque and can continue to circulate thereafter from hand to hand within the country.

It need not be affirmed that there are no other media of payment whatever. Suffice it to say that, in an economy of the British type, bank deposits are the preponderating medium of payment and therefore of liquidity. In so far as the 'whole liquidity position' is of real importance — but some passages in the Report imply scepticism about this — the belittling references to the significance of the quantity of money must be wrong.

It is difficult to avoid the impression that the Report is confused as between a source of liquidity and a source of lending. One of the methods of non-bank lending that are discussed in chapter iv is trade credit, which is of great importance. The suggestion is made in para. 300 that on the occasion of a restriction of bank lending, the amount of trade credit might be increased in substitution. On this the Report observes, 'no doubt the lengthening of trade credit would make the giver of additional credit rather less liquid, so that the restriction of bank credit would be bound to bring some pressure on business liquidity'. This is to admit that trade credit is not an independent 'source' of liquidity, capable of adding to 'total liquidity'; no more, I submit, are building societies, investment trusts, etc. In fact, the 'total liquidity position' will have been reduced by the bank restriction. If some trading firms are willing to render themselves less liquid *pro tem.*, out of compassion for their trading partners, that eases the position of those partners for the time being, but does not restore the 'total liquidity position' to where it was before the banking restriction. Furthermore, those who have rendered themselves less liquid will wish to restore their own liquidity position sooner or later, and any action taken by them will tend to diffuse the overall liquidity shortage created by the banking restriction.

It was observed on the occasion of the credit squeeze of 1955 that some who were denied overdraft facilities borrowed elsewhere. That could have happened even if there had been no net increase in non-bank lending, since those denied overdrafts might have had business to do that appeared to non-bank lenders to deserve prior attention. But there is another important point to be observed in relation to that episode. Owing to certain difficulties (for which see below), the total liquidity position (by which I mean simply the quantity of bank deposits) was *not* reduced in full proportion to the reduction in bank advances. I hope that the periods March–May 1955 and March–May 1956 (both averages), which avoid end- and mid-year abnormalities, may be taken as fair for this comparison. Bank advances were reduced by 7·6 per cent, but bank deposits by 4·1 per cent only. In other words bank advances were reduced substantially more than the whole liquidity position. One would expect the consequence of this to be that lending by way of bank advances fell more than the *total* quantity of lending. There is nothing here to suggest that a reduction in the quantity of money lacks effect; the trouble was that the reduction in the quantity of money was relatively weak, and less than the reduction in bank advances. So naturally the reduction in the amount of lending by others was also less!

The old orthodoxy was that when banks increase liquidity in the economy by increasing their own assets, whether through advances, investments, or the short-term market, total lending in the economy will be increased by a larger absolute amount than the original increase in bank assets — up to the point where the consequent increase in the value of business turn-over in the economy is sufficient to generate sufficient extra *require-*

ments for liquidity to absorb the extra liquidity initially created by the banks. Thus the more bank lending, the more non-bank lending in total is there likely to be ; and conversely. This old orthodoxy is confirmed by the quoted conclusions of two unpublished studies referred to in para. 311. It is quite unaccountable how the Committee can suppose that the results of these studies point in 'opposite directions'.

Now let us suppose, for argument, that there are other important outside 'sources' of liquidity. How can the authorities induce these independent sources to decrease (or to increase) the total of liquidity ? By operating, we are told, upon the rate of interest. But how can the authorities do that, except by operating on the quantity of money ? We are not told, and yet the quantity of money is said not to be critical.

This point requires strict analysis. The Committee may have been impressed by the fact — if fact it be — that the Bank of England can alter (say, raise) the interest rate in the discount market without reducing, or without reducing in any appreciable degree, the availability of funds to that market. If this is the case, two conditions must be fulfilled, namely (i) the supply of paper of the kind discounted in that market must be inelastic to interest rate changes (and this is clearly true of Treasury Bills) ; and (ii) outside (non-bank) bidding for such paper must be inelastic to the rate of interest. Now if these inelasticities were absolute, the discount market would be completely insulated, and a rise in its discount rate would have no effect on interest rates outside the market, since it would leave the supply and demand of funds in all other markets unchanged. It must be admitted, however, that the discount rate change might have a psychological effect on other rates, by changing expectations, as indeed the Report indicates ; but this could not be relied on as a regular and invariable reaction.

If a rise in the discount rate influences other rates by attracting outside funds into the paper which is the medium of the discount market, and thus altering the balance of supply and demand of funds outside, then the clearing banks and/or discount houses will have money burning their pockets — clearly an unstable position — *unless the Bank of England takes action to reduce the quantity of money*. Thus, ephemeral and unreliable effects apart, it is the power of the Bank to reduce the quantity of money that gives the authorities what power they have to enforce and maintain a change in general interest rates.

Now we come to a most perplexing point. On the one hand, the Committee holds that the 'supply of money is not the critical factor', that 'the structure of interest rates is the centre-piece of the monetary mechanism' and that control of the supply of money is only incidental to interest rate policy (para. 397). Yet in various passages there is scepticism about the effect on the economy of interest rate changes, except perhaps in the long run — but for correcting the trade cycle prompt action and quick effects are all-important. But the Committee does recognize (para. 460) that bank restriction created a 'diffused difficulty of borrowing' (an expression which they are good enough to quote from me), which tended to reduce spending or at least to strangle expansionist projects at birth. But what *causes* the 'diffused difficulty of borrowing'? I submit that it is the reduction in the money supply. On the one hand, they say that the key instrument in monetary policy is the interest rate structure and that regulation of the money supply is subordinate to that, but, when it comes down to brass tacks (and short-run effects), they seem to hold that the 'diffused difficulty of borrowing' is more important than the interest rate structure. If this latter point is correct, then the reduction in the money supply is not secondary to interest rate-policy, but more 'critical' than interest rate policy, since it is the reduction in money supply that causes the diffused difficulty of borrowing.

At the very centre of this whole confusion in the Report is the failure to perceive the relation between changes in the money supply and changes in the 'diffused' ease or difficulty in borrowing. This brings us back to the alleged contrast between the money supply and the whole liquidity position. We are bound to reiterate the complaint that no precise account is given of the Committee's notion of the 'whole liquidity position' such as to justify this contrast. What can the authorities do to reduce the 'whole liquidity position' save precisely reducing the money supply? Whether or not this has a strong effect on interest rates and whether or not interest rate changes have a strong short-term effect on the economy as a whole, what the authorities can do to produce the strong short-term effect that is needed, is to reduce the money supply — which, on any showing, must be the *main* ingredient of the 'whole liquidity position' — and thus cause a 'diffused difficulty of borrowing'. In that case, control of the money supply is, after all, the centre-piece of monetary policy.

In relation to the mechanism for controlling the money supply, the Committee appears to be more interested in the (flexible) 30 per cent rule than in the 8 per cent rule. The trouble is that the same factors that have on occasion made it difficult to use the 8 per cent leverage would have similarly obstructed the use of the 30 per cent leverage. This difficulty is the *inflexibility* of the quantity of short-term paper (Treasury Bills) that the clearing banks and discount houses are, between them, expected to carry. If the Bank used its traditional weapon of open market operations and at the same time ruthlessly closed the back door, it might put the discount market into a position in which it just could not, without courting bankruptcy, tender for the whole weekly issue of Treasury Bills — a quandary, anxieties about which the Report regards as 'outmoded' (para. 169). Since this was in 1955 an insurmountable obstacle to the use of traditional methods, the Chancellor had to make a request to the banks (via the Bank of England) to reduce their advances to customers, and, after this had been done, the 'cash basis' of the clearing banks was trimmed down *ex post*. This suggested to observers here and to foreigners that we no longer had a control of the money supply that could be used with automatic effects, but had to resort to what is sometimes called 'moral suasion'.

What is needed and will alone suffice to restore more automaticity to monetary policy is that the amount of short-term paper required to be taken up by the clearing banks and discount market should become *flexible* again, in response to discount-rate changes, as in the old days. In this connection the interest that some commercial firms showed in the holding of Treasury Bills during the high-interest period was most welcome.

The basic problem in relation to a credit squeeze is how to reduce the quantity of Treasury Bills that the banks and discount market are expected to take up. More broadly, one may say that it is a question of transferring a certain (moderate) quantity of government paper from bank to non-bank holders. The trouble has been that, owing to the large below-the-line

R

budget items, the government broker has had to keep running hard in order to stay where he was, *i.e.*, to get genuine investors to take up the new money required by the government ; he has had, on certain critical occasions, no strength left to get them also to take a still further amount in order to secure a reduction of the tender issue of Treasury Bills. Accordingly, in my judgement, the need to get the huge investments of the nationalized industries financed otherwise than by the issue of gilt-edged stock is our central problem in the field of monetary management. That the Radcliffe Committee does not so find it is the natural corollary of its playing down the importance of the quantity of money in circulation. Furthermore, it has a very perverse recommendation, which must be condemned roundly, that access of the local authorities to the Public Works Loan Board should not be restricted (para. 597). This arrangement would add to the burdens of the government broker and render him still less able than he is now to co-operate in a credit squeeze. Considering that the pushing out of local authority treasurers on to raising money by mortgages, etc., was a life-line in the fight against inflation in 1955, it is amazing that the Committee should make such a recommendation. It is to be presumed that no attention will be paid to it.

Generally speaking, the Report appears to be profoundly sceptical about the potency of monetary policy. Few will now affirm that monetary policy alone can iron out the trade cycle or deny that a 'package deal' — an odious expression, regrettably countenanced by the learned Committee — may sometimes be needed.

In my own view, the restrictive monetary policy of 1955, despite the appalling limitations to which it was subject (owing to the National Debt situation), had remarkably quick effects, as shown by the downturn in factory building starts and the first abatement in the increase of consumer expenditure which occurred as early as the autumn of that year. Accordingly, I regret that it has played so small a role in the 'package deal' of expansionist measures in the last eighteen months. Furthermore, if an undue tempo of expansion is to be checked by reducing the money supply, raising interest rates and creating a diffused difficulty of borrowing, then it is desirable that these processes should be reversed during periods of pause or recession, in order to recover ammunition. Precisely because we have not recovered the ammunition now, I believe that we shall have greater difficulty in checking the next boom that comes along. But the Report is too sceptical and, I am bound regretfully to add, too confused, for us to be able to expect any useful lead from it on the contemporary problem.

The scepticism of the Report in relation to the potency of monetary policy, and notably in relation to the effect of variations in the quantity of money, goes quite against the current trend of thinking outside Britain. Mr. Martin (Chairman of the Board of Governors of the Federal Reserve System) has claimed that easy money was the principal method — via causing an increase of spending on State and local authority outlays, on private house building and on consumer purchases on credit — through which the United States snapped out of her recent recession in so spectacular a manner. Mr. Per Jacobsson, Executive Director of the International Monetary Fund, has gone further, and claimed that the United States, by increasing the quantity of money (dollars) at that time, played a leading part in retrieving the whole world from recession. The Germans lay stress on monetary policy, and have recently made a notable contribution to world recovery by reducing their short-term interest rates to a very low level. The Japanese have recently introduced new measures relating to bank reserve requirements, designed to get for the Bank of Japan a tighter control over the quantity of money. Are monetary techniques now to sink into the background of British economic policy ?

APPENDIX

THREE main streams of writing do not enter the following list of my publications in the period 1951–1959.[1]

1. Since 1st April 1955 I have submitted, on the first day of each month, a memorandum on the current situation for private circulation by a firm of stock-brokers. Specimens of these memoranda, or parts of them, are published in this book, as numbers 22, 23, and 25.

2. From its first inception I have contributed memoranda, whether as *rapporteur* or otherwise, to the European League for Economic Co-operation. These were usually amended by the relevant committee before reaching their final form. An early one (1949) recommended the two essential features of the European Payments Union, namely that each separate country should be placed in credit or debit to the collection of OEEC countries *as a whole*, and that part payment only should be made or received in gold; this plan was successfully piloted through the Economic Committee of the Council of Europe by Sir David Eccles. The Marshall Aid authorities put forward their proposals for a European Payments Union almost immediately afterwards, and our recommendations accordingly became redundant.

3. I have reviewed most of my more distinguished economic colleagues in *The Times Literary Supplement* — anonymously.

LIST OF PUBLICATIONS (1951–1959)

BOOKS

1951	*Life of John Maynard Keynes*. Macmillan	
1952	*Economic Essays*. Macmillan	
1953	*The Dollar*. Macmillan	
1956	*The Foundations of Inductive Logic*. Macmillan	
1957	*International Economics*. 4th edition. Considerably revised. Nisbet & Co. for the Cambridge University Press; the Chicago University Press	
1958	*Policy Against Inflation*. Macmillan	
1959	*The Prof*. Macmillan	

[1] Articles marked with an asterisk are those included in the present volume.

Articles

December	*The Director*	Industry must be Equipped to Fight
December	*Bank of Tokyo Review*	Interim Policy

1954

January 2	*Time and Tide*	Review of *The Strachey Family*, by Richard Sanders
January 8	*The Liverpool Post*	A Survey of the Government's Monetary Policy
January 9 January 16	*Time and Tide*	Notes on the Way
January 27	*The Financial Times*	Sterling after Sydney
February	*The Director*	Free-er Trade and Britain's Strategy
March 15	*The Financial Times*	Productivity Budget ?
March 30	Hearings before Sub-committee of the U.S. Senate Committee on Currency and Banking 83rd Congress. Second Session	Plan for Restoration of Full Gold Convertibility of the Dollar together with a Revision of the Gold Content of the Dollar
March–April	*Société Belge d'Études et d'Expansion*	What is Convertibility ?
April	*Quarterly Journal of of Economics*	Review of *Economic Change* by Professor Kuznets
April	*The Director*	American Recession and British Business
April 2	*The Daily Telegraph*	How Britain should meet an American Recession
April 9	*The Financial Times*	A Wise Budget
April 3 April 24	*The Economist*	Horizontal Weather. (Letters on 'voluntary' depreciation allowances)
April 17	*Time and Tide*	Review of *Life of John Stuart Mill*, by M. St. John Packe
May 1	*Time and Tide*	Letter on above
May 17	*The Financial Times*	Anxieties over European Payments Union
June	*The Director*	A more Flexible Investment Allowance ?
July 1	*Bank of Tokyo Review*	Convertibility
*July 5	*The Financial Times*	Towards a New Pattern

June 12	*The Sunday Times*	Review of *Economics and Action*, by P. Mendes France
June 18	*Time and Tide*	Review of Report of Royal Commission on Taxation of Profits and Income
June 24	*The Financial Times*	Investment and Delivery
July 13	*Nihon Keizai Shimbun*	Prospects for Sterling Convertibility
July 18	*Bank of Tokyo Review*	Strengthened Sterling
*July 19	*The Financial Times*	Foreign Exchange Policy
July 28	*The Listener*	A Tunnel under Oxford ?
August	*The Director*	The Broken Promise of Nationalization
August 8	*The Oxford Mail*	Town, Gown and the Traffic Problem
August 11	*The Financial Times*	Not a Crisis
August 25	*The Times*	The Convertibility of Sterling (letter)
August 26	*The Liverpool Post*	Britain's Great Boom—Hopes and Dangers for the Years ahead
September	*Optima*	Prospects for Convertibility
September 10	*The Financial Times*	When will the Boom End ?
October	*Confluence*	Assisting Under-developed Regions
October	*The Director*	The Truth about the Crisis
October 28	*The Financial Times*	The Second Budget
October 30	*The Sunday Times*	Review of *The Great Crash*, by J. K. Galbraith
November	*The New Commonwealth*	The Credit Squeeze — and after
November	*Nihon Keizai Shimbun*	Replies to Questions
November 15	*The Cherwell* (Oxford)	Why not Tunnel ?
December	*The District Bank Review*	Current Problems and their Impact on 1956
December	*The Secretary*	The Economic Outlook
*December	*The Director*	Sterling and the Second Budget
December 2	*The Financial Times*	Continuing Boom
1956	*Handwörterbuch der Sozial - Wissenschaften*	Keynes

Winter Issue	*Freedom First*	Limits of Government Intervention in Economic Matters
January	*Bank of Tokyo Review*	World-wide Investment Boom
January	*Steel*	Expansion without Boom
January 11	*The Financial Times*	Fundamentals of Policy
January 18	*The Liverpool Post*	1955 Squeeze was not enough
February	*The Director*	How Tight is the Credit Squeeze ?
February 25	*The Financial Times*	The Chancellor's Measures
*March	*The Economic Journal*	The British Boom, 1954–55
March 28	*The Financial Times*	Pushing Consumer Durables too hard ?
April	*The Director*	Talking Ourselves into Trouble
April 21	*The Financial Times*	Budget and State Industries
May	*The New Commonwealth*	Can Sterling take the Strain ?
May 4	*The Spectator*	Review of *The Problem of Bigness*, by P. Sargant Florence
June	*The Economic Journal*	Walras : a Re-appraisal
*June	*The Director*	Tripped up by the Printing Press
June 3	*The Sunday Times*	Review of *Treasury Control*, by S. H. Beer
June 14	*The Financial Times*	Where we stand
Summer	*Progress*	The Government's Responsibility for the Nation's Economy
July	*Bank of Tokyo Review*	Continuing Boom
July	*New Commonwealth*	Britain and her Competitors
July 21	*Picture Post*	Inflation (dialogue with Mr. Graham Hutton)
July 21	*Time and Tide*	The Investment Boom
July 28	*Time and Tide*	The Wages Question
August	*The Director*	When the Boom Ends
August 25	*The Investors' Chronicle*	British Boom and Investment in the Commonwealth
Autumn	*Economics* (Journal of the Economics Association)	Future of Sterling
*September 14	*The Financial Times*	New Thinking this Autumn
September 27	*The Times*	Oxford Road Plans (letter)
*October	*The Director*	Time to Slacken the Reins

October 18	*The Times*	Christ Church Meadow (letter)
*October 30	*The Financial Times*	Should Bank Rate be Cut ?
October 30	*Sydney Morning Herald*	Britain has finally brought its Inflation under Control
Number 5	*Vie Économique et Sociale* (Antwerp)	Measures against Inflation
November	*Bankers' Magazine*	Concluding Phase of the Credit Squeeze
November	*The New Commonwealth*	World Bank and the Commonwealth
*November	Institute of Municipal Treasurers & Accountants. Joint Committee of Students' Societies	A National Wages Policy — the Problem
November 6	*The Times*	Landings in Egypt (letter)
November 6	*The Financial Times*	Borrowing (letter)
December	*The Director*	Policy for the Next Two Years
December 13	*The Financial Times*	Credit Relaxation due now

	1957	
Nos. 1-2	*Vie Économique et Sociale* (Antwerp)	Great Britain and Inflation (1954–56)
Fasc. 1	*Kyklos*	Professor Fellner on Growth and Unemployment
January	*Foreign Affairs* (New York)	Britain and the Common Market
January	*Bank of Tokyo Review*	Review of Half Year
January	*Times Review of Industry*	Time Ripe for an Easier Credit Policy
*January 10	*The Financial Times*	Warning against Delay
January 22	*The Liverpool Post*	Economic Priority Steps needed for 1957
February	*The Director*	What the Credit Squeeze won't do
February	*Bulletin of Oxford University Institute of Statistics*	The Common Market in Perspective
February 5	*The Queen*	European Common Market
February 20	*New York Times*	Monopolistic Practices Charged (letter)
March	*Nationalekonomiska Föreningen Förhandlingar* (Stockholm)	British Experience of Disinflationary Policy in 1955–56

March 1	*The Financial Times*	Future of Interest Rates
April	*The Bankers' Magazine*	Review article on *Financial Policy*, 1939–45, by R. S. Sayers
*April	*The Director*	First Signs of a Recession
April 11	*The Financial Times*	The Economy after the Budget
April 19	*World's Press News* (Westminster Chamber of Commerce)	Review of European Common Market
May	*The Bankers' Magazine*	Domestic Activity and External Balance
May 18	*Nature*	Review of *Logic and Knowledge*, by Bertrand Russell
June	*The Director*	Encouraging Selective Investment
June	*Economic Journal*	Review of *International Economic Policy*, vol. ii, by J. E. Meade
June 8	*Time and Tide*	Reversible Coat
June 15	*Time and Tide*	Riding the Cycle
June 28	*The Investors' Chronicle*	Brakes Off !
July	*Bank of Tokyo Review*	Review of Half Year
July	*National & English Review*	Gilbert Murray : A Personal Recollection
July 3	*The Oxford Mail*	Obituary Notice of Lord Cherwell
*July 7 *July 8	} *The Financial Times*	Two Types of Inflation
July 31	*The Financial Times*	Two Types of Inflation (letter)
*August	*The Director*	The Gilt-Edged Surplus
August	*Times Review of Industry*	Review article on *The World Economic Survey*, 1956, United Nations
August 16	*The Bankers' Magazine*	Demand-Induced Recession (letter)
September	*Optima*	European Common Market and the Commonwealth
*September 21	*The Financial Times*	7 per cent
September 26	*The Listener*	Review of *The World Dollar Problem*, by Sir Donald MacDougall
*October	*The Director*	These Directives should go
November 6	*The Financial Times*	Implications of the Fall in Machine Tool Orders
November 13	*The Financial Times*	The Quantity of Money (letter)

November 15	*The Financial Times*	Expansion of Production (letter)
December	*The Economic Journal*	Clive Bell on Keynes
December	*Nihon Keizai Shimbun*	Replies to Questions
December	*The Director*	The Mis-directed Squeeze
December 16	*The Western Mail*	⎫ Rates of Pay should be levelled off
December 19	*The Yorkshire Evening Press*	⎭

1958
*January	Committee for Economic Development (New York)	The Possibility of Economic Satiety — Use of Economic Growth for Improving the Quality of Education and Leisure
January	*Rivista di Politica Economica*	Recent movements of Expansion and Recession in the British Economy
January	*Bank of Tokyo Review*	Review of Half Year
January 4	*The Financial Times*	Prospect for 1958
January 21	*The Liverpool Post*	My Advice to British Government now
February	*South African Bankers' Journal*	The Role of Sterling
February	*The New Commonwealth*	Britain must Plan for Investment
February	*The Director*	Last Sterling Crisis
February 12	*The Daily Telegraph*	Speed and the Pound (letter)
March	*Books of the Month*	Review of *Prosperity through Competition*, by L. Erhard
March	*The South African Journal of Economics*	The Role of Gold To-day
March 14	*The Financial Times*	Sterling and World Recession
March 15	*The Economist*	Commodity Reserves (letter)
March 29	*The Economist*	The British Economy (letter)
March/June	*Aussenwirtschaft* (Zürich)	Co-ordination of Currency and Trade Cycle Policy in a European Community
Fasc. 2	*Kyklos*	Question for a Stabilization Policy in Primary Producing Countries
April	*The Director*	How Wise were the Three Wise Men?

May	Radcliffe Committee on the Working of the Monetary System	Evidence Submitted
May 20	*The Times*	Confidence in Sterling (letter)
June	*The Economic Journal*	Factor-Price Relations under Free Trade
	Revue Internationale de Marché Commun	Britain's Attitude to the Free Trade Area
June	*The Director*	World Recession
June 20	*The Financial Times*	What Britain can do
June 20	*The Times*	Confidence in Sterling (letter)
July	*Bank of Tokyo Review*	Period of Hesitation
July 19	*The Accountant*	The Financial Outlook
July 28	*The Financial Times*	The Commonwealth Conference
August	The International Finance Section (Princeton University)	The Pound Sterling, 1951–58
August	*Nihon Keizai Shimbun*	The Summer of 1958 (2 articles)
August	*Journal of the Advertising Association*	A New Policy for Britain
*August	*The Director*	Why we should back Japan
August 14	*The Daily Telegraph*	Brendan Bracken (letter)
August 26	*The Financial Times*	Outlook — an Alternative View
September	*The Economic Journal*	Review of *Europe and the Money Muddle*, by Professor Triffin
September	*Optima*	Why the Dollar Price of Gold must Rise
September 2	*The Financial Times*	Below the Line (letter)
September 13	*The Times*	Americans in Britain (letter)
September 22	*Business Bulletin* (Brunnings Ltd.)	Time for Expansion
October	*International Affairs* (Royal Institute for International Affairs)	World Recession and the United States
October	*The Director*	What the Cohen Report left out
	Parsons' Pleasure (Oxford)	Marx

October 1	*Nihon Keizai Shimbun*	Divergent Trends. (2 articles) (i) U.S. (ii) U.K.
October 17	*The Financial Times*	Montreal and New Delhi
November	*The New Commonwealth*	'Expansion' is the Key Word
November	*The Bankers' Magazine*	Sterling Convertibility
November 3	*Nihon Keizai Shimbun*	Outlook Uncertain
November 6	*The Oxford Magazine*	Obituary notice of Alic Halford Smith
November 21	*The Financial Times*	Has enough yet been done ?
December	*The Director*	Britain's Responsibility now
December	*Euromarket*	Europe must Act to Revive World Trade
December 1	*Nihon Keizai Shimbun*	2 Articles
December 22	*Business Bulletin* (Brunnings Ltd.)	World Trade is Bearish
December 31	*The Times*	Labour's Views on Convertibility (letter)

	1959	
January	*Bank of Tokyo Review*	World Revival still uncertain
January 1	*The Financial Times*	Britain Needs an Upsurge in Consumption in 1959
January 1	*Nihon Keizai Shimbun*	Question of Aid for Underdeveloped Countries
January 20	*The Liverpool Post*	Expansion must be the Policy
*January 28	*The Financial Times*	Long-term Rate of Interest
February	*The Director*	Case for a Budget Deficit
February 1	*Nihon Keizai Shimbun*	2 Articles
February 12	*The Listener*	A Free Pound and the Future
March	*The Economic Journal*	Review of the *History of the Dollar*, by Dr G. Nussbaum
March	*South African Journal of Economics*	Rejoinder to Mr. Katzen
March	*Irish Banking Review*	World Monetary Liquidity
March 2	*Business Bulletin* (Brunnings Ltd.)	Prospects Uncertain
March 10	*The Financial Times*	Flexible Monetary Policy needed (letter)
March 23	*The Financial Times*	The Kind of Budget I Would Like to See

September	*The Economic Journal*	Review of *Trends in International Trade* by panel of experts (Chairman : Professor Haberder), G.A.T.T.
September	*Journal of the Institute of Public Supplies*	The Trade Cycle and Public Buying Policy
September 20	*The Observer*	Why I shall Vote Conservative
September 21	*The Financial Times*	Review of *The Failure of the 'New Economics'*, by H. Hazlitt
October	*The Director*	Preparing to meet a Crisis
October	*Nihon Keizai Shimbun*	2 Articles. (i) World Economic Situation, (ii) Radcliffe Report
October 2	*The Liverpool Post* *The Birmingham Post*	An Expansionist Policy for Britain lies Ahead
October 31	*The Financial Times*	Are Yields Too High ?
*November	*The Westminster Bank Review*	Is the Money Supply Important ? (Review of the Radcliffe Report)
November 3	*The Liverpool Post* *The Birmingham Post*	Prospects for Britain's Economy
November 5	*The Listener*	Review of *The Spare Chancellor: the Life of Walter Bagehot*, by A. Buchan
November 23	*The Times*	The United States in Deficit (letter)
December	*The Director*	Making Good the U.S. Deficit
December	*Nihon Keizai Shimbun*	2 Articles. (i) Germany, (ii) The United States
December	*Bacie Journal*	Economic Impact of Changing Needs
December 1 December 8	*The Liverpool Post* *The Birmingham Post*	Now it is the Turn of the Europeans
December 15	*Nihon Keizai Shimbun*	Changing Structure of the World Economy

PRINTED BY R. & R. CLARK, LTD., EDINBURGH